Legacy of Faith
collection

T. L. Osborn

Harrison House
Tulsa, Oklahoma

Copyright 2011 Osborn Ministies International

Tulsa, OK 74112

Published by Harrison House Publishers

P.O. Box 35035

Tulsa, OK 74153

www.harrisonhouse.com

What People are Saying...

"T.L. Osborn is a legend in the faith. Not only have he and Daisy impacted millions of lives for Jesus, but they have had tremendous impact on Lisa's and my life as well."

–John Bevere

"T.L. Osborn is one of the most extraordinary pioneers of our century. His life and work of miracles has been an inspiration to me, as well as to my son, Gordon. I know that this book will build your faith as it has mine."

–M. G. "Pat" Robertson
–Chairman, The Christian Broadcasting Network, Inc.

There is no question that T. L. and Daisy Osborn have mentored me and been extremely influential in helping me to reach the world with the Word. I can never say enough or thank them enough or pray for them enough. What an opportunity and honor it's been to be part of mass miracle evangelism. No one, and I mean no one, has affected the world in our generation like the Osborn's. A recent example was their meeting in downtown Paris, with over 10,000 people. That was an impossibility that became a possibility with the Osborn's

–Dr. Marilyn Hickey
–Marilyn Hickey Ministries

Dr. T.L. Osborn is the greatest healing evangelist in the modern era. For over 50 years, he has preached face to face to more people worldwide than anyone I know. And the miracles... they just keep coming. I honor his life and his ministry.

–Richard L. Roberts

"Jesus Christ is the same yesterday, today and forever."
Hebrews 13:8

World renowned statesman, missionary evangelist, and teacher of teachers, Dr. T. L. Osborn, has been my greatest source of inspiration in ministry since the 1950's. It was not the great tent meetings that captured my heart; nor was it the massive crowds in 78 nations of the world. But as a young pastor in Pennsylvania during an Osborn meeting, I saw God use this man to put the miracle-working power of Christ on display. T.L. Osborn called a buddy of mine who had his eyes destroyed in a mining accident to the platform in front of thousands of people. He publicly asked God for a creative miracle—and my buddy walked away with two brand new eyes.

From that day forward I was passionate about pursuing God for a ministry that was bold enough to demonstrate the Gospel of Jesus Christ, pronouncing Him the same, yesterday, today and forever!

As ministers of the Gospel, both my daughter Donna and I have been deeply appreciative of the life and teaching of Dr. T.L. He is our friend. We highly recommend his LEGACY OF FAITH collection to you.

–R. W. Schambach
–Evangelist

Dr. Osborn has always been special to my family. - He is a remarkable and great man. I salute him!

–Dodie Osteen
–Co-Founder of Lakewood Church

What a powerful testimony of a man of faith and miracles. Having known T.L. and Daisy for many years, we have been personally impacted by their ministry and their love for the people of the world.

–Happy and Jeanne Caldwell
–Agape Church, Inc.

Heritage is something that is not often thought about in today's instant society. This collection of books is inspiring. The life of T.L. Osborn, as on of our founding fathers, is worthy of celebration. As servants of the Lord, our heritage is those who stood in faith before we were born and believed God to help them reach their generation. Now it is our turn to be faithful to the call of God. Take the baton from our founding fathers and reach for the legacy!

–Ron Luce
–President and Founder of Teen Mania Ministries

Conviction, compassion, caring and loving. T.L.'s desire is to see people set free, to know Christ and to walk in all that the cross purchased for them. His legacy is untold numbers in heaven. A man of humility and love. It is an honor to know him.

–Pat Harrison

Our lives have been enriched and impacted by T. L. and Daisy Osborn. They set the example for others of this generation as they preached and demonstrated the Gospel of Jesus Christ as a couple moving in faith and obedience to God.

Together they have been visionaries, as evangelists they have reached people to be saved, healed, delivered, and raised people's understanding of their value and purpose in life. Praying for people in masses to be healed of sickness and disease have resulted in spectacular miracles for God's glory and opening hearts then to be saved.

T. L. and Daisy Osborn have not only been evangelists in meetings but Jesus' witness one-on-one with individuals. Once Brother T. L. said, "You are painting a picture of Jesus to others by every word you speak and every deed you do."

In these past years, spending time with Brother T. L., I have seen a man who exemplifies the fruit of the Spirit as well as the power of the Spirit of God wherever he is. An outstanding characteristic about Brother T. L.'s life is that he wants every person to know how valuable they are and the potential that God sees in every individual to be and to do great things for God here in this world.

–Sharon Daughtery

The next generation of evangelists and Christian leaders can glean profound inspiration and wisdom from the pages of this book. May we all burn with Dr. Osborn's passion for the salvation and healing of the masses.

–Dominic Russo

T.L. brought a new level of faith, joy and identity in Christ to me and our church. His positive spirit and message changed us as it has millions around the world. He is one our greatest ambassadors for Christ. T.L. is one of our Fathers in the Lord and an example of Jesus. The Legacy of Faith will lift you and empower you for the great life that T.L. has spread around the world.

–Casey Treat

T. L. Osborn has been used by God to lift the esteem of Nations and remove the shackles of Colonial oppression through the liberating message He and Daisy decreed as an Emancipation Proclamation, the Gospel of the Kingdom. This book convicts you to examine your walk and calling and challenge you to reach further, believe greater and to love deeper the world that you've been privileged by God to reach. T. L. has impacted more nations and transformed more cultures in giving more dignity to an unreached world than anyone I know. For this we give God the glory for using such a man and making available to us such a book.

–Patricia Bailey Jones

Dr. TL Osborn is a 20th century apostle to the nations. His life and legacy are true examples of the Great Commision in action! From the African bush to the Pacific Islands, I have met thousands of pastors and leaders who were first introduced to Jesus through the ministry of Drs. TL and Daisy Osborn. Dr. Osborn is a friend, hero, and mentor to millions of people in this generation!

–Pastor Caleb Wehrli
–Founder of Inspire International
–Missions Pastor at Victory Christian Center Tulsa

Contents

Part 4: *Tragedy, Trauma, Triumph*

Part 5: *Five Teachings by T. L. Osborn*

Introduction

The Legacy series offers a lifetime of priceless insight into some of the world's most influential Christian leaders of the last century. This volume is laden with a wealth of knowledge from a lifetime of mission and evangelistic experience from one of the world's most important Christian leaders, Evangelist T. L. Osborn. Containing the rewarding and often difficult lessons of a life devoted to the message of the Gospel in an emerging generation, these lessons, if taken to heart, can help propel the Church to greater spiritual heights while fulfilling the Great Commission. The hope is that all will find this series to be an unprecedented inspiration for those who are devoted to the full Gospel of God's faithfulness and devotion to a broken world.

Since the time of the Church's first expression of the Gospel message, there have been various seasons that featured different aspects of God's redemptive plan. These movements, or revivals, have often been accompanied by signs of the miraculous healing power of the Gospel. They include the ministry of the apostles, the church fathers and early missionaries in Europe, the doctors of the Reformation, the Holiness of the eighteenth century evangelists such as John Wesley and George Whitfield, and the

Azusa street revival and subsequent Pentecostal shifts. Finally these movements are represented in the mergence of the healing and charismatic renewals of the later part of the twentieth century. All of these different developments were critical in laying the foundation that led to the birthing of the spiritual revolution that the global Christian community is experiencing today. While each move has respectfully been unique in its rich insight, wisdom, and proclamation of the full gospel of Jesus Christ, they have all been indispensable to the health and prosperity of today's church. 1 Corinthians 10:11 says: *"Now these things which happened to our ancestors are illustrations of the way in which God works, and they are written for our benefit, who are the heirs of the ages which have gone before us (or in whose lives the climax of the ages has been reached)."* Evangelist T. L. Osborn said, *"The church was established for the people then, but God re-establishes Himself for every new generation. He is as real today as He ever was."*

In each movement, God has always had pioneers who paved the way for the moving of His Spirit. These pioneers broke ground, challenged, confronted, incited, excited, and evoked God's people to growth and participation in how the Spirit was moving. They were radical, daring and willing to blaze a new path for God's absolute truth. They were passionate to the core and dedicated to the end–*they were a force to be reckoned with.*

These spiritual giants have been an unlikely group of men and women who have found themselves thrust into the spotlight and even world prominence. These men and women were bold and daring. They were pioneers who forged ahead even when they were discouraged by their peers and they traveled roads that few, if any, had traveled before. T.L. Osborn was no exception.

Evangelist Osborn has been a pioneer in many respects, including mass miracle evangelism and his establishment of networks of local ministers who would evangelize their own countrymen. Even today, he is known as a missionary, a statesman and an evangelist to the world. He was on the cutting edge of world missions, and proved more than capable of directing affairs when it came to the business of "taking the gospel to the world". As Moses led the way through the wilderness, pioneered a trail, and led the people of God, T. L. Osborn has equipped today's generation to bring in an unprecedented harvest of souls. While not discrediting the contribution of others, it can be said without reservation that, T.L. Osborn is in a league all his own.

T.L. Osborn has been one of the most influential evangelists of the twentieth century and he ranks among the top echelon of evangelistic leaders such as Billy Graham and Oral Roberts.

Throughout the ministry of T.L. Osborn:

- *He has preached in nearly one hundred nations in national crusades and seminars. His gospel-oriented literature and films have been translated into 132 languages.*

- *He was a modern pioneer of public healing evangelism in foreign nations including parts of Africa, the Middle East, India, and East Asia.*

- *Always the innovator, he pioneered praying for the sick en masse, which did away with the often long healing lines common to his contemporaries and miracles remain the hallmark of Osborn Ministries International.*

- *While drawing enormous crowds overseas, he pioneered a system of evangelism that positioned and equipped native ministers to reach their own people. This resulted in the establishment of more than 150,000 new, self-supporting churches and the financial enablement of over 30,000 national preachers to labor as full-time missionaries.*

- *He has very likely preached the gospel to more people face-to-face than any other man in history, with his face-to-face ministries among the masses having become the benchmark for dynamic and effective evangelism.*

- *Approximately seventy, of his eighty-some years, have been spent touching millions in nearly one hundred nations in national crusades and seminars and through tools of evangelism such as gospel literature (translated into 132 languages), docu-miracle films, and mobile evangelism units equipped with Osborn multimedia gospel tools.*

- *He and his wife, Daisy, conducted the first mass miracle crusades since the first century church. They were the first to erect a big platform in parks or on fields or other terrains in non-Christian nations, preach the gospel publicly, and pray for God's miraculous confirmation that Jesus Christ is the same today as He was in Bible days.*

- *He and Daisy pioneered numerous techniques for foreign evangelism. His style has been unprecedented.*

- *It is said that the Osborn family has witnessed more physical healing miracles than any family that has ever lived.*

- *He and Daisy Osborn were the first to do video productions, like their docu-miracle films/videos that combined missionary preaching with miracles, among non-Christian nations.*

Part One

The Early Years

Chapter 1

Movements of God

Prior to the evangelistic explosion of the 1950's and the revolutionary changes in the operation that accompanied it, the state of Christian missions work was connected with and severely damaged by the political imperialism of many western nations. The British Empire that ruled nearly half of the world for hundreds of years and that had only began to relinquish its reign in the aftermath of the two world wars, drove much of its cultural imperialism in the terms of Christian missions.[1] Driven by political and economic factors and masked with a fusion of enlightenment philosophy and Christian theological jargon, the type of "ministry" that took place during these years was largely an imposition of cultural values upon native peoples that left resentful feelings towards anything western or Christian.[2] This was largely what the ministers and missionaries of not only the early Pentecostal movement, but also the later faith healing evangelism movement of the 1950's, encountered and ultimately had to overcome.

The Voice of Healing Revival of the late 1940's and 1950's, was a movement that left a distinct impression upon the nation's collective memory and the American psyche. A type of revival that had not truly been seen before by the popular culture, it demonstrated flexibility, vibrancy and a passion that had largely been ignored in the traditional denominations for the better part of a century. Led by Traditional Pentecostals such as A. A. Allen, Jack Coe, William Branham, Oral Roberts, and Gordon Lindsey, the Voice of Healing affiliation of evangelists and its magazine publication became the most important vehicle for an up and coming young minister.[3] Especially one with faith in God's healing power and an emphasis on missions.

T.L. Osborn has ridden more than one of the various movements associated with the charismatic/Pentecostal experience since his entrance into ministry over seventy years ago. The Voice of Healing revival was only the first of these, one in which he was a pioneer and a pillar of strength and stability. Gordon Lindsey had a rather peculiar and novel idea for the Voice of Healing and for its time, a loose affiliation of individuals functioning primarily as independent ministries. This independence had a number of effects some positive, others not. For instance, the individuality of the various ministries allowed for the minister to remain connected and busy but still provided flexibility if he needed to travel or change direction rather sharply.[4] The negative effects though, were demonstrated by the various moral and doctrinal failures of some ministers including William Branham, A. A. Allen and Jack Coe.

There was also a pattern for ministry in that day that promoted mental, emotional and physical fatigue. Many of the leaders who are remembered from that era were dedicated to difficult work. Sometimes they spent long hours in the center of the platforms of the big tents praying, clapping, shouting and pleading. Branham was a broken man after a little more than a year; and A. A. Allen tottered constantly on the brink of psychological collapse.[5]

As the Voice of Healing began to lose momentum in the late 1950's, "T. L. Osborn had a strong foundation upon which to build when financial hard times came in the late 1950's and early 1960's." Osborn's work continued to flourish during the lean years of the early sixties and he "faced the future in the 1970's with more certainty than any other old deliverance evangelist." Truly, "Osborn's success was lasting, and the growth of his ministry was steady."[6]

Soon another revival began that would revitalize many of the healing ministries left over from the Voice of Healing era, the Charismatic renewal. This renewal had various segments or camps within itself: the denominational charismatics, the Jesus people and the non-denominational ministers, some sympathetic to the faith movement, others not. Evangelist T. L. Osborn's ministry could not be solely identified with any of these internal groups, since there were people from all of these camps who were supporters of his work. He was observed to "not make a clear transition to neopentecostalism,"[7] which was one of the terms by which the renewal was referred. "He remained, more than Oral Roberts, Gordon Lindsay or other ministers, in touch with the young evangelists he oversaw, who were still conducting campaigns."[8]

Simultaneously, the Word of Faith Movement was emerging, which encountered significant resistance and negative attention from the media, as well as the denominational church world. Some of these ministers did not handle these onslaughts well, which resulted in parts of the movement retreating into isolation while other ministers became even more public. T.L. managed to avoid the competitiveness of the ministry of his day, including the controversial denominational battles, as he consistantly turned his attention to overseas campaigns. "He also was untouched by the growing competition among the healing revivalists in the United States" and he "thus avoided the clashes between the evangelists and the Pentecostal churches in the 1950's. Osborn worked for peace." He was in numerous ways "less controversial than any other man."[9]

Osborn Ministries International's financial aid to foreign missions did not favor certain denominations and did not have any intention to compete with the various denominations on the mission field. More than 150,000 new, self-supporting churches have been established globally through the Osborn's ministry; however, none of them bear the Osborn name. They are named after their respective denomination or group. As a result, T.L. avoided the denominational assaults that were aimed at the healing and deliverance ministers of his day.

Mass miracle evangelism has been the single focus of the Osborn's ministry for over sixty years. In every crusade they conducted, the results have been the same, regardless of the religion, history, tradition, or philosophy of the particular host nation. Thousands of followers of non-Christian religions have abandoned their superstitions and become believers of the Gospel. Tens of thousands of new churches have been established as a result of their face-to-face evangelism ministry.

During their first few years, T. L. and Daisy were widely criticized for their presentation of the gospel, especially with the miraculous as evidence. It was revolutionary, and many leaders labeled their actions as sacrilege. In Costa Rica, the crowd was so large that they had to rent the massive Bull Arena, which attracted national publicity and bigger crowds, but it also opened the door to opposition. Media reports represented the Osborns as charlatans and deceivers, and also urged the faithful not to attend or bring any sick people to their meetings because they would be tricked or manipulated. When T. L. arrived at the national arena, the police had already locked the gates. At least ten thousand people had gotten inside and were seated, before the gates were locked. The chief of the National Guard dispatched a messenger to announce that the event was forbidden. Thirty official agents were on hand to prevent the public from entering. The pressing crowd in the street became so agitated that the law enforcement agents were forced to open the gates. The people poured into the stadium like a human river, ignoring the guards and filling every empty seat.

Opposition continued and the main newspaper headlined an article on the Osborns, *"Forbidden to Bring Sick People to the Osborn Meetings."* This article contained demeaning and defaming misrepresentations, but in spite of this, the stadium was filled to capacity during each event. According to the Osborn ministry, over two thousand people accepted Christ in each service. Now, over half a century later, mass healing evangelism has become the norm around the world, not only among Pentecostals but among multiple denominations. LaDonna, T.L. and Daisy's daughter, made an observation in regard to the role of miracles in her father's ministry:

This was a significant time in Church history as the truths of divine healing were being restored to the Church. During this 'healing revival' that swept across the United

States, there were those evangelists who were beginning to understand the redemptive truth that physical healing is included in Christ's atoning work, just as spiritual healing was provided by his suffering, death, burial and resurrection. The emphasis on the teaching concerning physical healing drew people's attention to this wonderful provision of Christ and to this miraculous work of His Spirit. My parents saw Christ's healing power as the answer to effective evangelism among people of other faiths. The healing ministry of Christ, continued through His people today, is the ongoing proof and demonstration of the resurrection life of Jesus Christ. This was the message of the Early Church. When people see the miracles, they believe in the Man Jesus.

All of this is the backdrop of T. L. Osborn's early years of ministry. The focus of his ministry was overseas and the hallmark of his ministry was miracles. Missions and mass evangelism to those in unreached parts of the world gave T. L. a special place within each movement and among his peers. It allowed him to stay above the fray, saving him from generalized criticisms that were expressed toward evangelists of his genre. In many ways, T. L. became a standout known for his work independent of others.[10]

T. L., at points, received criticisms due to independent ministry that was not under any particular denomination. Those who favored denominationalism over independent ministries commonly attacked every evangelist who took the same approach. In comparison to the amount of criticism his peers received, T.L.'s critics were minimal. This, again, was because of his work in helping large groups of people overseas.[11]

Throughout his ministry, T.L. slowly moved toward being identified as a neo-Pentecostal. Rather than joining an established Pentecostal denomination, neo-Pentecostals take an independent stance for the sake of being more ecumenical.[12] T.L.'s ecumenical approach to ministry and missions diversified his appeal and brought a large number of supporters from many different Christian backgrounds pouring into his ministry and missionary efforts.

A large part of T.L.'s success in financing in missionary efforts was his relentless conviction to giving every dollar that was donated straight towards helping and reaching those in need.[13] Even as late as the 1970s, T. L. Osborn Ministries' financial needs were provided for exceptionally.[14] It was T.L.'s ability to be fiscally responsible with donations, coupled with his philosophy of transparency on how donations were affecting the mission fields around the world, that legitimized him as an evangelist of integrity. This, wedded with his passion for foreign missions and his ability to define relevant evangelism, put him in an early position to allocate Christian support to people in need.

As cultural and global challenges changed, so did Osborn's ability to adapt to them. Osborn, for a time, decided to focus his attention on youth in America. The 1960s was a decade defined by reinvention and exploration. Young people in particular were going through social and ideological changes, leading to youth revivals across the country. T.L. attempted to bridge the gap between youth in contemporary society and their parents who remained disturbed about the whole situation. He began to preach a gospel that was relevant and hip. T.L. started teaching his sermons in more appropriate vernacular that would be more relatable to young people. "He urged his old-time followers 'Think younger in your faith.'"[15] He continued to reach out by changing his style of dress and hair. He captured the attention of many young people in the United States by showing them a gospel that was relevant and approachable. With a new audience listening to T.L., foreign missions and the importance of it, was communicated to a new demographic of Christians, which would have long lasting effects on the culture of American missions.[16]

By the early 1970's, T.L. Osborn integrated aspects of the prosperity gospel into his teaching and his global missions programs. As early as the mid 50's, there was conversation in the broader Pentecostal community about prosperity gospel in relation to specifically African mission. Donald McGavran, a well-known missiologist, in his work *Understanding Church Growth,* wrote about the concept of 'redemption and lift.' He argues that the majority of church growth in relation to the prosperity gospel has been among poor people. A result of this phenomenon has been entire classes of poor people becoming relatively prosperous after their conversion experience. After becoming Christian, many changed their lifestyles and became more productive members of society. In general they became more hardworking, and had a higher emphasis on community and responsibility. Historian Vinson Synan comments on possible positive effects of this historical and current situation by saying "As materialistic as the prosperity message can sound, it is also challenging huge numbers of the world's poorest people to aspire to better things. It might well be called a theology of hope."[18]

Africa's move to becoming the epicenter for the proclamation of the prosperity message came through teachers from the United States. Following the success of Oral Roberts TV ministries, many evangelists who taught the prosperity message followed suite.[19] As television became the medium of communicating the prosperity message, it was preached to larger audiences than ever. The movement, though, also became immediately vulnerable to criticism and abuse. There were some radical evangelists who "made a mockery of prosperity teachings with their strident and shameless appeals for large donations and their outrageous lifestyles."[20] This type of behavior was not a reflection of whole movement, or even the majority, yet abuses brought critics to point out the high emphasis on money and materialism.[21] This was coupled with a notable amount of 'denominational discrimination,' as demonstrated by the Assemblies of God's series of white paper publications aimed at condemning the Word of Faith throughout the seventies and early eighties. T.L., however, did not receive much criticism due to his efforts to financially support and fund large numbers of overseas missions. Even in the face of his critics, T.L. was able to receive ample amounts of respect for acquiring financial gifts to be given to "impoverished mission programs."[22]

T. L. leaves a legacy defined by sacrifice and a genuine passion for reaching all people with the Gospel message. He rose to the challenges of his generation and the generation after him. He was able to respond to some of largest challenges of the twentieth century by showing up at crucial times in such places as Vietnam.[23] In the 1960s when the Western world was changing, he opened dialogue with new forms of culture, successfully relating to young Americans in their own language. He worked towards reforming ideological prejudices that hindered successful attempts at ministry in mission. His effort went to make the evangelistic efforts overseas into a truly national experience, instead of an American program. This was an important contribution to spreading the gospel message globally, and its success was one of his proudest achievements. [24]

Chapter 2

Born in a Blaze

Tommy Lee Osborn, aka T.L. Osborn, was born to Charles and Mary Osborn in 1923. He was one of thirteen children. He was the seventh son of a seventh son. T.L. was raised on a small farm near the Pocassett Township area of Oklahoma, where his family struggled through the Depression years of economic crisis. According to his daughter, LaDonna, "He came from nothing...*poor, poor, poor.*"

When T.L. was twelve years old, his older brother, Lonnie, got converted at an old fashioned Oklahoma brush arbor meeting. The changes that T.L. saw in his brother got his attention. He decided to attend a revival meeting in an old church down by the railroad tracks in Mannford, Oklahoma, with Lonnie. T. L. shared that he was dressed in his best country overalls and since he could play the piano, he played at the meeting. When the lady evangelist made the call for sinners to be saved, T. L. received Jesus Christ as his Savior. From then on, he loved going to that little church. Often the work on the farm kept him in the field so late that he couldn't attend the meetings, leaving him sometimes weeping from disappointment.

T. L. said that he began discovering the truly *good life* when he was converted. His objectives and motives were changed immediately when he got converted. He now wanted what God wanted, and he wanted it for the reason God wanted it. Those principles were his anchor through adolescence. They guided his marriage, were the foundation of his home, and the guidelines for raising his children.

T.L. shares, "I started doing whatever I could to witness to unconverted people in my area. From that day, *I wanted to be a soulwinner;* I wanted to share with people what Jesus Christ meant to me."

He began to print Bible verses with a toy press that he received as a Christmas present. He refers to these verses on scraps of paper, today as "the good life concepts." These became his first tracts and he distributed them among the town's people, a population of less than 300. He never dreamed that within a few years he would be publishing gospel literature in 132 languages at a rate of more than a ton per working day!

In the mid 1930's, when he was still barely a teen and while "digging cockle burrs out of the corn rows" on his parents' farm, T. L. met Oral Roberts. Oral was pastoring a small church in Sand Springs, Oklahoma. Even though Oral was six years older than T.L., they became friends. Soon T. L. started helping him with evangelistic work in Sand Springs, ministering in street meetings. Oral was the preacher, and T. L. took care of most everything else, which included playing the accordion. Roberts was a frequent Sunday visitor to the Osborn farm to have some fried chicken at their family dinner.

T. L. soon lost contact with Oral, but later was reconnected when they moved to Tulsa where Roberts' ministry headquarters were be located. T. L. began to attend his tent meetings. While Roberts' ministry was concentrated in the United States with Oral Roberts University and television outreach, T. L. would veer away from television. Later T.L. was labeled as the minister who preached to more people face-to-face than anyone else in history. His ministry reached millions internationally in almost one hundred nations, over a span of a half century's time, drawing crowds from 20,000 to over 300,000 in a single meeting.

When Oral Roberts went home to be with the Lord in December of 2009, T. L. was quoted as saying this of his mentor, "He took me in and received me. He took the time to encourage us." T.L. also noted that his ministry was one of the many ministries that was inspired by Oral Roberts.

At the age of thirteen, T. L. was teaching Bible lessons to a class of fifteen to twenty-year olds. The subject was the *good life* he had found. God called T. L. to preach in 1937 when he was fourteen. While bringing the milk cows from the woods to the barn, he shared that he began to weep without knowing why. He knelt by a large sandstone boulder to pray and had a pivotal spiritual experience. His heart was filled with the desire to become a preacher of the gospel. At fifteen, he started preaching and often fasted two or three days at a time, because he wanted God to use him in His work.

When the young preacher was still fifteen, his father permitted him to travel with a respected evangelist, E. M. Dillard. T. L. provided music with his accordion and was also responsible for handling the youth services in the evenings of the revival meetings. Every Friday evening, Rev. Dillard insisted that T.L. preach, so little by little, he found the words to express his feelings about Christ and His gospel. For two and a half years, T. L. accompanied Rev. Dillard through Arkansas and Oklahoma. They also went to California when T.L. was 17 years old. This is where he met his future wife, Daisy Marie Washburn.

Chapter 3

They Are Inseparable— Always Have Been

T. L. had spotted the sixteen-year-old girl when she entered the little church at Almo, California, where he and E. M. Dillard had been invited by a friend to conduct a series of special meetings. Daisy was "blond, beautiful, serene, energetic, and smart." T. L. related that it was his "music, testimony, and commitment to gospel ministry" that made an impression on her.

Daisy lived on a fruit farm in Los Banos, which was located twenty miles to the west of Almo. She, just like T.L., also came from a large family, and was the tenth of eleven children. Her family was also *"poor, poor, poor"*- just like T.L.'s. When Daisy and her ten siblings would pick fruit, they would ride on the back of a trailer. That's the way they lived. They were very poor and had *nothing*. If you had a cow to give the older one, you had nothing left over for the rest.

Daisy came from a family that was essentially pagan, while T.L. came from a Baptist family that had a fear of God about them. Her family was so irreligious that when T.L.'s family would say that they were as poor as Job's turkey, Daisy said that she didn't even know that Job had a turkey!

From the moment T.L. was introduced to Daisy and they shook hands, T. L. confided, "It was love at first sight for both of us." He knew that *this* was the lady—no doubt about it—with whom he yearned to share his life." Shortly thereafter, T. L. proposed and Daisy accepted his impulsive proposal. She risked letting herself fall in love with this itinerant, young preacher, despite the ridicule and negative predictions of her high school peers.

T. L. and Daisy's courtship was through correspondence. He didn't have any money for telephone calls, so they wrote letters. One year later, on April 5, 1942, when T. L. was eighteen and Daisy was seventeen, they got married. T. L. borrowed a suit from his brother-in-law and budgeted his precious few dollars to include a white carnation corsage for Daisy and a boutonniere for himself. To make ends meet, he managed to get a ride from Oklahoma to California with a couple who were driving west, but they stopped a hundred miles short of Los Banos, and he had to hitch hike the final lap of his journey.

The day after the wedding, the couple began their trip back to Sand Springs, Oklahoma, where T. L. had a job. They arrived with fifty-two cents. T. L. had measured his few dollars very carefully. He was burning to get back into the ministry of evangelism. He traded his only possessions, a cow and a calf at his father's farm, for a 1930 "Model A" Ford coupe that needed overhauling. With twenty dollars from his brother Lonnie, and with Daisy working with him through the heat of the day, actually guiding him in making the necessary repairs, T.L. overhauled the engine. He said, "I could work on a mule, but I knew nothing about an automobile." Daisy, on the other hand, had grown up with two nephews who were exceptional mechanics and they taught her a lot about engines.

T. L. and Daisy wanted to go to California, but they didn't have any money. Daisy convinced her brother, Bud, to loan them thirty-five dollars so they could make the trip. T. L. was concerned that the old car might not perform, but Daisy said, "If it stops, we'll find a way to fix it." T. L. knew that they would not have enough money to stay in motels. Daisy said, "We can sleep in the car." *And they did.*

Once in California, they sold the car for needed cash and began their preaching career in Campbell, at a church whose pastor had invited them to conduct a revival. They spent two years in California. Both of them had musical talent, so they played, sang, and preached in many of the little churches in the agricultural San Joaquin Valley.

When T. L. was nineteen, he and Daisy had their first child. On March 25, 1943, their daughter, Marie LaVonne, was born in Bakersfield County Hospital. She only lived seven days and T.L. and Daisy were deeply grieved.

In the spring of 1944, T. L. and Daisy drove to Portland, Oregon, to conduct gospel meetings in an old tabernacle-barn that was built and used by the early Methodists. The meetings were successful; and, as a result, they pioneered Montavilla Tabernacle and became its pastors. When the challenge was first presented to them to establish a new church in Portland, T. L. didn't feel qualified. Daisy voiced, "It's an opportunity. Let's do it. We can learn." *And they did.*

While in Portland, their son, Tommy Lee, Jr., was born on January 20, 1945.

Chapter 4

Failure in India

As newlyweds at very young ages, T. L. and Daisy had set out in a soulwinning ministry. The superintendent of the denomination to which they belonged was a man who had gone to India as a missionary. Whenever this man preached, he preached about India and about missions until, as T. L. shared, "he literally branded India on our spirits." The couple had just become pastors for the first time, when a missionary from India appealed to them to become missionaries. "Clearly, we were facing the call of India's millions," T. L. recalled.

The couple decided that they were more needed in India to tell the people about Christ, than they were needed in their own country. They asked themselves the following question: *"If ten persons were lifting a log, and nine of them were on the small end, and only one was on the big end, which end should we help lift?"* As young missionaries, T. L. and Daisy's goal was clear: *they desired to share Christ where the need was greatest and the workers were fewest.* It was logical to them that they should help out where there was the greatest need and the fewest people available to meet the need. T. L. was concerned about the risks that would be involved but, Daisy asserted, "Other couples have done it. We will succeed. We'll learn the language. We'll work together. Let's go!" *And they did.*

Three weeks after the birth of their son, they resigned as pastors of their growing church and began nine months of ministry across several states in preparation for their five-year mission to India. They invested everything they owned to go to the other side of the world to win souls. They soon discovered that they could not convince the Hindus or the Muslims that Jesus Christ is the Son of God, that He has risen from the dead and that He is alive today as the world's only Savior.

Initially, both T.L. and Daisy were shocked when they discovered that the Muslims believed in the same God as they did. The Muslims called God, *Allah*, and we call Him *God*. T.L. thought "Allah" was a heathen god, but later learned that it was the Arabic word for God. They also thought that the Muslim people worshipped dead gods, but learned that they worshipped the God of Abraham, the same God the Jews worshipped and whom we worship today. The Muslims also prayed five times a day and loved to talk to God.

The young missionaries were amazed when they discovered that the Muslims believed that Jesus was a good man. They were amazed at how they loved to come for hours, and sometimes all afternoon, and study with them the teachings of Jesus, because they had great admiration for Him *as a prophet and teacher.* They were also amazed at how the Muslims even respected Him *as a miracle worker.*

The Osborns made many friends, including Muslim merchants. T. L. was shocked when, on many occasions, his Muslim friends would shake his hand and say, "Good morning, *Brother* Osborn." Sometimes, they would even add, *"Praise God."*

The Muslims, however, did not accept Jesus *as the Son of God, raised from the dead,* and *the Savior of the world.* T. L. and Daisy knew that if they did not believe these facts about Jesus, there was no way that they could be converted, because the Bible says, *"If you confess with your mouth the Lord Jesus, and believe in your heart that God has raised Him from the dead, you shall be saved"* (Romans 10:9). T. L. and Daisy did not know what to do.

T. L. shared:

> *The Hindus were also wonderful people and were kind to us. They were our friends and they were lovely people, but we could not prove to them that Jesus is alive. We suddenly realized that we faced the same problem, or the same issue, that the Early Church had confronted after the resurrection of Jesus Christ. He was risen, but the people did not believe He was risen. We were in the same situation, among the same kind of people. That was the real issue.*

T. L. and Daisy preached, studied the language, entertained visitors, and spent long hours in religious discourses, but they could never convince the Muslim people that Jesus was the Son of God. T. L. spoke of a group of Muslims who came one afternoon:

> *We were having such a great visit. And they said, "All right, Mr. and Mrs. Osborn, prove to us that Jesus is the Son of God and that He is risen from the dead."*
>
> *I said, "Sure, I can do that." And I reached for my Bible and I started opening the pages, saying, "Look at these Bible verses. Listen to what they say."*

But they interrupted me: "Wait, Mr. Osborn. What is that book that you are reading from?"

"The Bible, God's holy Word!" I replied.

"Oh, no," they retorted, "that is not God's Word. This is God's Word!" And they reached for their black book, the Koran.

"No! That is not God's Word. This is God's Word!" I insisted, holding out my Bible.

Who was right? Which holy book contained God's message? The Bible or the Koran? How could we know? What was the proof? Both were beautiful books. Both were bound in black leather with golden titles embossed on their covers. One of them was called the Bible, and the other was called the Koran. According to the Muslims, the Koran was the Word of God that came through the prophet Mohammed. The Hindu people also had their own book, called the Sacred Vedas. But which was God's Word? The Bible said that Jesus is the Son of God, who was risen from the dead, whereas the Koran and Sacred Vedas, denied both of these truths.

T. L. and Daisy were unable to forget the shock of that moment, when they could not *prove* which was God's Word. Since they were unable to convince the Muslims and Hindus of the fundamentals on which their faith was based, they did not know how to minister to them. These people already had a religion, and T. L. and Daisy had no proof that theirs was any better. So they decided that they weren't doing India any good, since they could not prove anything. They were in a crisis.

At age twenty-one and twenty, respectively, T. L. and Daisy had become missionaries in India, but without success. They tried to be effective, but when challenged by Hindus and Muslims to show the power of their God, they could not. In addition to this, they endured a long siege of sickness, during which their son, Tommy Lee, Jr., almost died of cholera and amoebic dysentery. T. L. also lingered near death for six weeks with typhoid fever.

In the fall of 1946, weary, bewildered, and broken in spirit, the missionary couple returned to the United States. T. L. recounted, "We decided to go home. We felt that it would be better to go back to America where most of the people already believed the Bible (or at least claimed to believe what the Bible says about Christ). So we returned home with unbelievable turmoil over our lack of success in India."

Daisy chronicled the frustration and shame the two endured in coming home before their term had ended, in one of hers and T. L.'s books, *The Gospel According to T. L. and Daisy*. "In those days you did not go to a foreign country and preach for a few months and come back. People just did not do that in those days. When you went, you were gone for five, seven or even ten years. We had gone to stay for five years. To come home ahead of our time really meant disgrace. But we were determined to find the solution to our dilemma."

As Daisy had voiced, "We had seen the masses. We had seen the need. We had seen the people who knew nothing of the gospel. We had been no match for the ancient religions of that historic nation. *But that began our search.*"

As they were coming home from India, a thriving church in McMinnville, Oregon, elected them as their pastor. This was a great encouragement to them. "I always marvel at that epoch of our lives," T. L. recounted. "How merciful God was to us! Those wonderful people in that beautiful church elected us as their pastor." Then on March 13, 1947, T. L. and Daisy's daughter, LaDonna Carol, was born.

Although the Osborns were comfortable in a lovely parsonage, there was discontent in their hearts, as they searched for God's answer to reaching the unreached. They fasted and prayed many days together, asking God to show them how they could convince non-Christian nations about the gospel of Jesus Christ. They knew that miracles were the answer to effective gospel ministry in non-Christian nations, but they lacked knowledge in that area.

Part Two

Positioning for Worldwide Ministry

Chapter 5

The Four Visions of Jesus

T.L. and Daisy's daughter, LaDonna, disclosed, "It was the vision of Jesus alive–though that may sound cliché today–that made the difference...*and I would suggest that it continues to make the difference.*" It was this vision and then three others of a different sort that followed, that majorly shifted both T. L.'s and Daisy's view of who God was, who they were in God, and how ministry was to be carried out.

First of all, T. L. saw Jesus alive and real when He walked into his bedroom. Then he and Daisy saw Jesus alive *in another person,* then *in the Scripture* and eventually *in themselves.* T.L. goes into more detail of these accounts in his book entitled, *Biblical Healing.* Altogether, these "visions" provided a pattern for what the process should be for any child of God. First you *start with Jesus.* Then you see how He works as He reveals Himself *through an actual human being.* Then you go to the Word and find how this is the essence of what *the Scripture* is all about. And then *you* believe it and *do it.* Then this cycle continues. *"And there is nothing else. There's no new message,"* LaDonna concluded.

T. L. and Daisy continued to search for, and were determined to find, the answer to the dilemma they faced in India. They read biographies of men and women who had been used of God. They studied their Bibles. They read sermons. They went to hear evangelists, preachers and teachers. They had even made plans to attend an annual convention that was only fifty miles from their church, where Dr. Charles S. Price was ministering. The renowned Dr. Price was a contemporary of Aimee Semple McPherson, a famous female evangelist. She was a pioneer in the use of modern media in the 1920's and 1930's, preacher of divine healing and founder of the International Church of the Foursquare Gospel. Dr. Price was known for his miracle ministry across the nation. The Osborns had never met Dr. Price, but had taken a large collection of his monthly magazine, *Golden Grain*, with them to India and had read scores of his sermons and reports of his crusades. While anticipating that event, they were informed that Dr. Price had died.

T. L. shared these reflections:

> *With his demise, our world of hopes collapsed. I went to the church, laid on my face and wept and prayed for hours. It seemed as though I could not contain my grief.*

> *The faith heroes and heroines of previous years began to pass before my mind like a panorama. I thought of Smith Wigglesworth, Aimee McPherson, Maria Woodworth-Etter, E. W. Kenyon, Dr. Price, and others; not one of whom we had met or heard preach.*

> *They were gone forever. The world would never again feel the impact of their miracle ministries. We would only talk of them and hear of their faith exploits.*

As I wept, I wondered why this should affect me like it did. I had not met these people. I had only heard about their ministries.

I said, "Lord, those great heroes of faith are gone now and millions are still dying. Multitudes are still sick and suffering. To whom will they now go for help? Who will stir our large cities and fill our large auditoriums with the magnetic power of God, healing the sick and casting out devils? What will this world do now?"

God responded to T. L.'s spiritual search, though not immediately. Within a few months, he received four visions that totally changed both his and Daisy's lives. They attended the camp meeting at Brooks, Oregon, where Rev. Hattie Hammond was chosen to minister in the place of Dr. Price. It was 1947, and Rev. Hammond's topic for her message was "Seeing Jesus." The Lord spoke to T. L. and Daisy through Hattie Hammond when she said, *"If you ever see Jesus, you will never be the same again."* Driving home that night, T. L. told Daisy, "Maybe that is what we need. Maybe if we could see Jesus, our lives would be changed. Perhaps that would be the key." The following morning, T. L. had a vision of Jesus that changed his life.

The First Vision–Jesus ALIVE

T. L. and Daisy had gone home and prayed late that night before going to bed. And, in T. L.'s own words:

The next morning at six o'clock, I was awakened by a vision of Jesus Christ as He walked into our room. I saw Him like I see anyone. No tongue can describe His splendor and beauty. No language can express the magnificence and power of His person.

I lay there as one that was dead, unable to move a finger or a toe, awestruck by His presence. Water poured from my eyes, though I was not conscious of weeping, so mighty was His presence.

Of all I had heard and read about Him, the half had not been told me. His hands were beautiful; they seemed to vibrate with creativity. His eyes were as streams of love pouring into my innermost being. His feet, standing amidst clouds of transparent glory, seemed to be as pillars of justice and integrity. His robe was white as the light. His presence, enhanced with love and power, drew me to Him.

After perhaps thirty minutes, I was able to get to the floor where I crawled into my little study room and lay on my face until the afternoon. When I came out of that room, I was a new man. Jesus had become the Master of my life. I knew the truth: He is alive!

He is more than a dead religion!

My life was changed. I would never be the same. Old traditional values began to fade and I felt a new and increasing sense of reverence and serenity. Everything was different. I wanted to please Him. That is all that has mattered since that unforgettable morning. The first vital vision had been revealed. I had seen Jesus IN A VISION.

Daisy had gotten up early to feed the babies and give them a bath. She had been busy all morning. Then she had to get the children lunch and get them ready for their afternoon naps. She remembered that at about that time, T. L. came out of their bedroom. "And when I looked at him, I knew I had a new husband. Something had happened. He was changed."

T. L. had become a successful denominational man, but he remarked:

> *It had affected me. Though I had seen the need of the people in India, I suppose that, having failed as a missionary—or at least it seemed to us that we had failed—I suppose that as a husband and as a leader of the home, I was grasping for success. I responded to the denominational attention that was given to me.*

> *I became almost possessed by a drive to go to the top in that field. I wanted the favor of my superiors. My world was my organization. I felt I had failed as a missionary, so success in my church organization helped my self-image. I was active in official functions. I loved it! I had an almost unnatural esteem for our district and national officials. They were my leaders, my ideals and almost my lords.*

> *But when I walked out of that room, I was delivered from that obsession to become something that was not what God wanted for me. Jesus had become Lord of my life.*

> *From that morning, nothing else mattered. It no longer mattered what my church officials thought about me. I do not mean that I disrespected them. I just mean that Jesus Christ had become my Lord.*

He was real. He loved me. He came to me. I was important
to Him. God had a plan for my life. God had created me. God
believed in me. I saw myself in a different light.

Something had happened to me. Everything had changed. I
had a new perspective on life. I knew God loved me. He sent
Jesus to me. Jesus was real to me. He was alive and He cared
about me. He had come to our home. He had appeared to me.

The Second Vision—Jesus IN A PERSON

In September of 1947, T. L. and Daisy resigned the church in McMinnville. They returned to Portland, where they had been urged to resume the pastorate of Montavilla Tabernacle, the church that they had established before going to India. They expected to invest their lives in Portland; but it was only to be a short step in God's design for their future global ministry.

As a successful denominational man, T. L. had become the presbyter of a large district, the Secretary-Treasurer of his church in four states. He was also a pastor, along with Daisy, of the headquarters church for their district. They were also in the process of hosting a very important conference.

"Then," according to T. L., "the most marvelous thing happened." During the same week this very important conference convened, "A very wonderful, humble man of God came to our area, whose ministry was known across the nation." It was in November of 1947, not too long after T. L. had received his first vision of Jesus *alive* and *real*, that William Branham was brought to a great auditorium in Portland by Gordon Lindsay. He was invited by the ministerial association to conduct a city-wide healing campaign. It was said that God performed great miracles when this man prayed for the people.

T. L. and Daisy yearned to attend those meetings and witness the miraculous. Daisy reasoned with her husband, "We went to India and were unable to convince them about Jesus Christ. We needed miracles. We came home, but the *world* is still in our hearts. We can always have conferences, but this is our opportunity to *see miracles*. I think we must go."

After T.L.'s first vision in which Jesus walked into his room, he was no longer obsessed and possessed by a drive to go to the top in his denomination, or to have the favor of his superiors. Now he faced a different dilemma. As Daisy pointed out, "That was our real test of loyalty. Up until then, T. L. was so loyal to our denomination that he never would have left the convention that we were in the midst of to go to another meeting." She also interjected, "when that happened in T. L.'s life, he did not lose respect for our denominational officials, but instead he gained a new respect for himself as an individual. He could see himself as someone important in God's plan." This became the passion of T. L. and Daisy's lives: *to help people realize that each person is unique and valuable to God, has an important role to play in God's plan, and has a divine destiny to fulfill.*

T. L. could not initially bring himself to abandon his conference. His situation was awkward, because he and Daisy were pastors of the headquarters church and were responsible for hosting the people attending the convention. This convention was held during the same week that William Branham came to their city for the great miracle meeting. T. L. concluded, "Since I was not only the official host to the convention, but also a member of the official board, one of the presbyters and the Secretary-Treasurer of the district; I saw no way to go to that miracle meeting. It would be disloyal."

T. L. had seen the Lord, Jesus had become his Lord, and he longed to see miracles, but he couldn't just walk out on his own convention. Daisy knew that she had to go see what God was doing.

Daisy, along with a ninety-year-old friend, went first. She saw the miracles and came back to tell T. L. about them. She recounted each miracle that she had witnessed. T. L. wept. This was what he and Daisy had longed for. He had opted for a conference that was not solving his and Daisy's dilemma. Daisy had opted for the solution to their lives and ministry. The two talked late that night, and T. L. knew he *had* to go see the wonders of God. "We could have conventions anytime, but an opportunity to see miracles might not come again. I decided that, whether my organization understood or not, *I had to go.*"

It had been the first time in her life that Daisy had ever seen miracles, even though she had accepted Jesus at the age of twelve. Now she was a grown woman, a wife, a mother, and a missionary in India, but she had still never seen an *instant* miracle. Every Friday night in their meetings, wherever they ministered, T. L. and Daisy prayed for the sick. T. L. shared, that they *"methodically prayed for the sick—it was almost a ritual."* They did not see much happen. There were few, if any results, but they still prayed. They had never seen deaf ears come open, blind people receive their sight, or cripples get up and walk. This is what they longed to see.

T. L. made an announcement to his convention that he had to go see the man of God and the miracles. He told those who were in attendance that he did not want to be disloyal or misunderstood, but that in India he had failed as a missionary because his good sermons were not enough to prove to non-Christians that the gospel is true. He told them that he needed miracles and had prayed for the answer. He told them that the Lord had appeared to him and he knew that He was alive and now he had a chance to see His miracles in action, *so he must go.*

T. L. handed over the church to the officials, gave them the funds, checkbook and every facility he had, and excused himself. He went to hear the man of God and to see the miracles! He saw them, and that occasion proved to be the catalyst that changed his outlook and revolutionized his ministry.

God had spoken to T. L. through Hattie Hammond, *"If you ever see Jesus, you will never be the same again."* He had seen Him in that vision. Jesus was so merciful that He actually stood before him. What a change that wrought in T. L. Jesus became Lord of his life. T. L. had seen the Lord. He knew He was alive. He knew the Bible was real. He knew that Jesus had become Lord of his life and now he had a purpose for living. He had a destiny. He had a goal. Then he pointed out, what had impressed him more than anything at Branham's healing crusade, was that, "Everybody else was talking about the man's gift of healing, but what attracted me was *how he preached about Jesus."*

At that meeting, T. L. and Daisy were getting a chance to see Jesus together, as He demonstrated Himself in miracles. They were seeing His power in action through an ordinary person. That was their second vision—they saw Jesus *in a person.*

T. L. shared, "That is really what Christianity is. It is Jesus working through people–using our hands, our lips, our ears, our eyes, our tongues. He speaks through us and loves through us."

Just as the people in Bible days saw God through Jesus, today people see Jesus Christ through us. This is the greatest revelation of true Christianity according to T. L. and Daisy. This is what they saw in William Branham. It was not the gift of healing that impressed them, but instead, it was that the man exalted Jesus, and demonstrated His love in action.

As T. L. and Daisy sat in the balcony at the Branham meeting, they watched the sick form a long line, and each one came before the man of God for prayer. Remarkable miracles took place. People whose backs were curved, became straight in a moment, like the woman in the Bible. People with braces on their legs, took them off and walked away well. Rev. Branham stopped a little girl who was deaf and dumb from birth, and very kindly said to the audience, "Everyone, please bow your heads and close your eyes. This little girl is possessed of a deaf and dumb spirit. Be very reverent because this spirit will come out of her when I speak in Jesus' name!"

T. L. had never heard anyone talk like that in his life. He knew Jesus talked like that in Bible days, "But, WOW, this was for real!" he exclaimed.

Rev. Branham prayed a very simple, quiet prayer, speaking with absolute authority. He put his fingers in the girl's ears and said, "You dumb and deaf spirit, I adjure you by Jesus Christ the Son of God that you come out of the child and enter her no more." And then he was quiet. That was all he said.

Then the man of God heaved a sigh of relief and said, "The evil spirit has gone from the girl now. You can lift your heads and look. The spirit has gone out of her. She is well."

T. L. could not believe his ears. "How did Branham know she was healed? He had not examined her. He had not checked her ears."

Daisy expressed how she looked at her husband about that time, and his eyes were a mountain of tears. Although T. L. and Daisy would see that same thing happen hundreds of times in days and years to come in their own meetings, that was the first time. They were overwhelmed.

T. L. spoke of a thousand voices whirling over his head, saying, "You can do that! You can do that! You do not have the gift of healing like he had, but you can do that! You have the same Word of God that he has preached! That is what Jesus did! That is what Peter did! That is what Paul did! That proves that the Bible way works today! You can do that! That's what God wants you to do!"

T. L. knew he did not have that gift of healing, but he knew that William Branham had spoken in the name of Jesus. And that was what God's Word said that any believer could do.

Important questions to T. L. and Daisy had been:

Is Christianity provable? Is there any need for miracles today? What was the need for miracles when Jesus was here? Even people of other religions agree that Jesus did do miracles. Is it any different now?

There are the great sacred books of the Orient—Confucius' writings, Buddha's sayings, Mohammed's teachings—and, of course, the Bible.

How can we know what is truth? How do we know that the Jesus-life is supernatural—or different, for that matter, from other religions?

Hundreds of people had come forward and accepted Christ that night of Rev. Branham's meeting. *That* was what T. L. and Daisy had wanted to happen in India. They loved those people, but could not convince them to believe on and accept Jesus Christ. They knew He was real, but they had to surrender their goals and return to the United States where they thought most everybody already believed in Him.

That yearning on the inside for the solution to their dilemma was an agony of an almost unbearable sort. T. L. and Daisy Osborn had been determined to find God's way to convince the non-Christian world about Jesus Christ. God, in His faithfulness, was now delivering the answer they had so intensely sought. *"Blessed are they which do hunger and thirst after righteousness: for they shall be filled"* (Matthew 5:6 KJV).

T.L. and Daisy had dedicated their lives, when they were married, to obey Christ and to preach His gospel. They had been to India and failed, because they did not understand faith and miracles. As pastors in Portland, now they had a chance to see miracles—and *nothing would deter them from following the Lord.*

The Third Vision—Jesus IN HIS WORD

T. L. and Daisy went home revolutionized. They sat down and talked most of that night. Many days of fasting and prayer followed. They were determined to be channels through which the Lord would minister His healing love to their generation.

They sat down with their Bibles and talked about the wonders they had beheld.

They resolved to begin reading their Bibles with a new attitude. They were determined to read the New Testament, especially the Gospels and the Acts of the Apostles, as though they had never read it in their lives. They read it like it was a brand new book, "Everything Jesus said He would do, we would expect Him to do it. Everything He said for us to do in His name, we would do it." Days of intense reading of the teachings and ministry of Jesus Christ followed.

They reflected on Jesus' message when He was attending a celebration at the Temple in Jerusalem. According to John 10:24, the Jewish leaders surrounded him and asked him, *"If You are the Christ, tell us plainly."* Jesus replied, *"The proof is in the miracles I do in the name of my Father.... At God's direction I have done many miracles to help people"* (vv. 25, 32). In verses 30 to 38, Jesus talked to the Jews about His relationship with God. They were angry because He had called God His Father and, by doing so, claimed to be the Son of God. The religious leaders viewed the idea so scandalous that they tried to stone Him. That is when He told them again, and in other words, that the *proof* of His being God's Son *was in the miracles.* In verses 37 and 38, He said, *"Do not believe me unless I do the miracles of God. And if I do, then believe them even if you do not believe in me."* Just like He said in verse 25, *"The proof is in the miracles I do in the name of my Father."* And along the same line, *"A great multitude followed him, because they saw his miracles which he did on them that were diseased"* (John 6:2, emphasis added).

Everything pointed to *God's Word of promise,* and His Word was for *everyone.* T. L. did not recognize or claim that he had a gift of healing, but rather that he had the living Word of God. He knew the Healer was living in him and in the Word of God. So, while others marveled at William Branham's *healing gift,* this man's gift only pointed T. L. to God's *healing Word.*

T. L. came to the conclusion, "A gift is a sign from God. A sign must point to something. A sign does not point to itself, but to something else. A true gift from God always points to His Word and to Jesus, who is the living Word. That healing gift pointed me to God's healing Word, which are His promises. They were for us as much as for anyone else."

Whether they were studying and praying together, or T. L. was shutting himself in their basement to read and pray while Daisy took care of the children and answered the phone, they both remained committed to the same goal in experiencing a spiritual revolution. They had seen Christ. T. L. had seen Him in *a vision,* and now both he and Daisy had seen Him in *a human person.* What they had seen made the Bible a new book for them. The Bible, which had been only a little more than a religious book, was now a living, vibrant message from God.

As they searched the scriptures, they discovered the dynamic and personal promises of Christ and the commitments He made to believers. T. L. and Daisy had seen the third vital vision–they saw Jesus in His Word.

Jesus had told His followers: *"Whatever city you enter,... heal the sick there"* (Luke 10:8-9). *"He gave them power against unclean spirits, to cast them out, and to heal all manner of sicknesses and all manner of disease"* (Matthew 10:1 KJV). Jesus *"gave them power and authority over all devils, and to cure diseases"* (Luke 9:1 KJV). And now, according to T. L., because of what the Word said, "We knew that was *for us,* too."

Those followers *"departed, and went through the towns, preaching the gospel, and healing everywhere"* (Luke 9:6 KJV). And now, "That is what we would do," stated T. L.

Jesus said, *"Fear not; believe only"* (Luke 8:50 KJV). At this point T. L. knew, "We were not afraid. We did believe. We were confident. We would do what Jesus told us to do. We knew He would do what He had committed Himself to do."

The Fourth Vision–Jesus AT WORK IN US

As T. L. and Daisy read the New Testament, they were astounded to discover scripture after scripture, where Jesus gave them authority over demons and diseases and to speak in His name–*just exactly like that man of God had done in that public meeting which they attended.* Yet, in spite of what T. L. had heard, seen and learned up to this point, he still wanted the Lord to speak to him, personally, in some audible way. He learned later that when Jesus speaks through His Word - *that is His voice.*

In order to withdraw from people so that he could hear the voice of God, he announced to his church that he would not speak to anyone, by phone or in person, until he had heard from God. He shut himself in a small bedroom for three days and nights without food or a drop of water, and instructed Daisy to "take the church and pastor it. Preach or do whatever you want, but don't look for me. I don't know how long I'm going to be in this room, but I'm not coming out until I have heard from the Lord."

"That frightened me," Daisy said. "I was petrified, because I had never had the responsibility of the church and of doing all of the preaching myself."

T. L. recounted his experience those three days, as he had approached it grappling, as well, with questions about the death of so many heroes and heroines of faith and about the global need for the ministry of healing faith. As he read the first chapter of Joshua, he was impressed of the Lord:

> *My son, as I was with Dowie, Woodworth-Etter, Lake, Wigglesworth, Ritchie, McPherson, Price, and others, so will I be with you. They are dead, but now it is time for you to arise, to go and do likewise. You cast out devils. You heal the sick. You raise the dead. You cleanse the lepers. Behold, I give you power over all the power of the enemy. Do not be afraid. Be strong. Be courageous. I am with you as I was with them. No evil power shall be able to stand before you all the days of your life as you get the people to believe My Word. I used those people in their day, but this is your day. Now I desire to use you.*

T.L. recounts, "Daisy and I, both grew stronger those days. Something *had* to happen. When I went into that room and dropped on my knees and opened the Bible, in that instant, God spoke to me. But I did not know it was God. I did not recognize His voice. I stayed in that room for three days and nights, without food or water, asking the Lord to speak to me, and every time, the same message would come to me again and again—until I finally accepted it: *As I have been with others, so will I be with you. Wherever you go, I will give you the land for your possession. No* demon, no disease, or no power can stand before you all the days of your life, IF you can get the people to believe My Word."

In retrospect, T. L. shared how that was, in reality, just a repeat of the revelation he had received in that meeting when William Branham had spoken and demonstrated that wonderful gift of healing. It was, in essence, the same message those voices over his head had said: *You can do that! That is the way Jesus did it! That is what Peter and Paul did! You can do that! That proves the Bible is for today!*

Now T.L. knew that he could do that, because he saw proof through another human being that what happened in the Bible was for today. Then he and Daisy discovered all of the Scriptures where the Lord had given them power and authority over devils and diseases, to cast them out and to heal the sick. And the Lord had said to T. L., again and again, *As I have been with others, I will be with you. No demon or disease or power can stand before you, IF you can get the people to believe my Word.*

T. L. realized, "That is why God spoke and said that I could do that! No power could stand before me, IF I could get the people to believe His Word. That was the secret—to get the people to believe HIS WORD! The Holy Spirit, working in us, would help us to teach the Word and would anoint us with power to show the proof of that Word."

This is when the Osborns discovered the purpose of the Holy Spirit in their lives, "that it was not just to make us feel good or to speak in tongues or to be holy, but that the Holy Spirit was in us to help us prove to the people that Jesus is the Christ, the risen Son of God."

T. L. shared that when he came out of that room, after God had spoken to him again, he knew, "we had to DO something. God was with us, He would back up His Word. We *had* to DO something."

T.L. and Daisy began to make announcements on the radio and in the paper. They became bold enough to invite the people to come to their church and to bring the sick, diseased, crippled, blind, deaf and dumb. They assured them that God would heal them.

T. L. confided, "That would have frightened me terribly to have made an announcement like that before. But we were revolutionized! I knew Jesus was with us and that He would do what He had done in Bible days."

People came from everywhere. The church was packed to the door. T. L. taught the promises of Christ to heal, save, and deliver all who had needs. He and Daisy began to pray for the sick and to cast out devils. One after another was miraculously healed. "God confirmed with miracles His Word that we proclaimed, because we had taken Him at His Word. We acted on His Word. If God said it, then it was so. If God promised to do it, then He would do it."

The first person they prayed for was a woman who had walked with crutches for fourteen years. Surgically and medically, she was considered an impossible case. She had been injured in an accident and her hip was crushed badly. An incompetent doctor had failed to set the bones, so the hip froze in a twisted position. The right leg was stiff and atrophied in a bent position, obliging her to walk with crutches. From all appearances, the lady would never walk normally again. While T. L. and Daisy ministered to her, Daisy took her crutches and started to hand them to T. L., but then took them from her and tossed them on the floor. *She and T. L. knew God wanted this woman well!*

Then T. L. commanded her, "In the name of Jesus, walk!" Her bones cracked loud enough to be heard, and her leg was healed instantly. With her hands held high and her eyes closed, she began walking as perfectly as anyone. Her rigid hip became flexible and free. For about thirty minutes, while T. L. and Daisy were ministering to others, that woman kept her hands up while walking about and she appeared to be listening to something marvelous. Afterwards she stated, "I've been listening to the heavenly hosts singing praises to our Lord."

A girl who was born deaf and dumb was brought forward. T. L. drew her close, placed his fingers in her ears, and prayed a brief prayer: "You deaf and dumb spirit, I charge you, in the name of Jesus Christ whom God has raised from the dead according to the scriptures, to leave this girl, and to enter her no more." Then in a quiet hush that followed, he snapped his fingers behind her head and she jumped and looked. He quietly whispered words in each ear and she repeated them clearly. The evil spirit had gone. The girl was healed. It was like Bible days.

That is when T. L. and Daisy had their fourth vision: They discovered Jesus at work in them. They believed they had seen the vision that God wanted people to see when He sent Jesus. Jesus said, *"Anyone who has seen Me has seen the Father"* (John 14:9 AMP). Later He said, *"As my Father hath sent me, even so I send you"* (John 20:21 KJV). And He promised, *"Lo, I am with you"* (Matthew 28:20 KJV); *"I will dwell in them and walk in them"* (2 Corinthians 6:16 KJV).

T. L. and Daisy realized that Jesus came and showed the Father to the world, and "now we show Jesus to the world. He is at work in the believer. We are His body. He is our life. He continues His ministry in and through us." To them, this was the great revelation, "the grand discovery. We had seen the greatest vision of all—*Jesus alive and at work IN US.*" And this is the discovery that was the key that unlocked their future global ministry to millions.

T. L. and Daisy had seen Jesus alive and real, in a human being, in His Word, and now as He manifested Himself through them. They had *seen* Him. As T. L. later chronicled in one of his books, "Thank God He gave us the answer, and thank God He said through Hattie Hammond,' *'If you ever see Jesus, you will never be the same again.'* That is as true for *you* as it was for us.

"I do not mean to suggest that you must see Him physically with your eyes, like I looked on Him. Certainly that could happen to you. But I do mean to say that Jesus Christ wants to show Himself to you. As Daisy pointed out, Jesus promised to MANIFEST (show) Himself to you. Then He added: *'My Father will love him and We will come to him and will make Our home with him'* (John 14:23).

"The Bible says that Jesus showed himself alive *'by many infallible proofs'* (Acts 1:3). He has many ways to reveal Himself to you. He has done it all over the world. Why not at your house? He came to us! He will come to you!

"I can assure you of this: Even though you may not see Him with your eyes, *He will show Himself to you in a way that you will know that He is alive and that He loves you.*"

Chapter 6

T. L.'s Solution–Daisy's Problem

Seeing God move the way He had in their meetings was for T. L. and Daisy "our real discovery of Christ at work in our lives. Our search had been richly rewarded. Our crisis was over. *We had the answer.*" T. L. and Daisy finally knew how to convince non-Christians that Jesus Christ is alive and real, but what were they going to do about it?

All they could think about were those masses in India, the Muslims and Hindus, who were wonderful people, but didn't know anything about the living Christ. In fact, these people were the reason they started their search in the first place. They loved them and knew that they needed Christ, but they had not been able to prove to them that Jesus is the Son of God, and has risen from the dead. Now they could prove it! As Jesus said, *"The proof is in the miracles."* The Osborns had the answer. Now they could help India's Muslims and Hindus.

A principle that T. L. and Daisy held to was: "Every problem contains the seed of its own solution." You can reverse that and say, "Every solution brings with it the seed of a bigger problem!" They found this to be true, and to be a reality that helped them grow.

Their search had ended, the answer to their dilemma in India had arrived, but a personal problem for Daisy had just begun. She was in the security of a lovely home, which was something every woman wanted. She was happily married and had two lovely children. Her reflection of this time in her life was: "I had everything a woman could desire. And now it seemed that everything would be uprooted, *because my man had seen Jesus.* Our lives had been changed, and T.L. had been called to go to the uttermost parts of the earth. That was my problem."

The thing that impressed T. L. about Daisy at that time was the fact that she wanted the Lord to appear to her, too. That's what she wanted. That's what she needed.

He shared, "Most women would say, 'Well, whatever my husband does, I'll join him.' And to a certain extent, we understand that. But what I liked about Daisy—and I remember how it impressed me even as a young husband—she was determined that God was going to speak to her, too."

Daisy felt that Jesus was obligated to say something to her also, because, even though she was part of T. L., she was also an individual and would have to stand before God some day and answer for her own life, her own decisions, and her own attitude. In her estimation of the matter, T. L., as her husband, certainly could not answer to God for her. And Jesus *did* speak to Daisy. She *did* have her spiritual experience. That is another story, one that T. L. supported and encouraged Daisy to write; and she did. LaDonna elaborated:

> *What is important to understand at this point is that in T. L.'s and Daisy's day, ministry was more about what the man did*

while the "little" wife raised the children and stayed home. If she was a good mother and created a nice home for her minister-husband to come home to after he worked so hard for God, then she was a good wife. And if she was faithful, that was even a bonus.

But this present day is a different time. This present society is egalitarian, maintaining and defending its belief in the equality of all people, especially in political, economic, and social life. There are ministry teams today that consist of husbands and wives. There are women who have been widowed and are out there leading great organizations. There are young women in Bible schools who have calls on their lives. It's a different day!

When Daisy, with the support of her husband, saw her role to be "a *GO-along*, not a *TAG-along*, in God's #1 job," she went against the customs of that day. T. L. even went as far as to write a book in this regard, entitled, *If I Were a Woman.* In this book, T.L. answers the question: "What would I do if I were a woman?" His logic is flawless and that is what makes his understanding and teaching on this matter significant and compelling.

In approaching this subject, those in their twenties and thirties are ahead of the previous generation. They are much more egalitarian, which has much to do with their overall education. Women don't necessarily think that they have to be married to succeed in life anymore. They have dreams, and having children is not their only dream. Someone has to stand up in the church and be a voice saying, "Hey, you matter; get out there and do something!"

LaDonna continued to relate how her parents were still pioneering in this regard decades into their ministry:

You see, my mother and my father had been in ministry thirty-five years together, doing everything together. They didn't even know there were these church imposed restrictions in the U. S. regarding the woman's role in ministry until they came back into the States.

It was in the '80s and my father was invited to speak in various churches. In the '80s, Charismatic churches were mushrooming everywhere. It was the first time my father had actually preached in a church in America in thirty-five years…literally.

So here, he and my mother were going to these meetings and, for example, he might be invited before service to go back into the pre-service room, and she wouldn't be allowed in because "your wife should be with the women." It was blatant, but, of course, my mother had been too far and had seen too much. She was real spunky, so after awhile, she stopped going if she wasn't invited.

The host ministers would ask my father, "Where is your wife?"

My father would say, "Well, you didn't invite her."

My mother was a person. She knew she was a person in the eyes of God.

My father is bold in when he sees behavior that is contrary to the work of Christ. He saw a real problem concerning the role of men and women in the church. He said, "If we start shackling half the body of Christ, we're in trouble."

Of course, the Lord really visited my mother. He gave her a vision, a dream of the female body of Christ. And in that unveiling, the body of Christ was half beautiful, but paralyzed and without strength. So during the final fourteen years of my mother's life, in every crusade she and my father had, they would include special days for women.

They would both teach, because they just saw the woman issue as a point to be challenged.

The way T. L. and Daisy saw it, God gave T. L.'s wife a choice. She chose to go. Because she chose to go, their entire family was different. They grew up around the world, not in this American culture. This was the result of her choice, and her husband's undergirding of her in that choice. She was the only wife of that epoch and for decades later that even thought of such a thing. Actually it was a matter of not knowing any better. Daisy just thought that it was between her and God, *and she chose to go.*

Since their earliest ministry as healing evangelists, T. L. and Daisy have shared in teaching and praying for the sick. When their miracle evangelism crusades began to take off, T. L. remembered the traumatic experiences in India and did not want Daisy to go back overseas. He initially felt that she and their two children should stay in the States. Daisy simply said, "You go and I'll be following you with the children."

So he said, "Okay, let's go together."

So they went together. T. L. described her as never hesitating and always an encourager. Their ministry was the beginning of what became such a pioneering norm for the ministry family.

In 1947, when their daughter, LaDonna, was born, they launched their global miracle ministry. They traveled as a family from nation to nation, erecting platforms on open fields and inviting multitudes to come and receive biblical healing. LaDonna remembered that when she was only two years old, she wanted to be a preacher and to pray for people to be healed. She also remembered the following as well:

In 1954, while riding in a betja with my parents in Java, Indonesia, I was glad we were helping people to know about Jesus. Those platforms became "holy places" where wonders of God were demonstrated among the hurting peoples of the world. As a child, I sat in awe as I witnessed cripples walking, blind people receiving sight, deaf people being restored, cancers and tumors disappearing, and tormented lives being transformed by God's love and grace.

I never resented the ministry. I never felt like my father and mother were neglecting me or my brother, because we were involved. I was there, everywhere they were. I was working with them from the time I could toddle.

Some people need to hear this, because so many ask, "If I marry, what about children?" Have children! "Can I marry and still serve God?" Be married and serve God together! But there are vital principles to live by as ministry families involve the children and create a home atmosphere of stability wherever you are..

LaDonna recollects the time her parents resigned the church in Montaville when she was barely one year old. They did not have a home that she could personally remember, until she was probably twelve, thirteen, or even fourteen years old. During this time, however, she remembers that they always had a home everywhere they went. They had their schedule, their routine, their family devotions and their work. She and her brother also had their school.

That's all we knew. We thought it was normal. These are profound things for young people who are thinking about the ministry to know.

This is even more appropriate now than it was in my folks' day, because then the norm was the resident missionary model. Now the norm is mission trips. It's going, staying three months, and then coming back to itinerate, raise money, or to see family.

Today you can just get on a plane and come home for a holiday as a missionary. Think of it!

So how much more likely it is that now whole families can go and be involved in the ministry. Save those marriages! Save those children! We don't have to have a generation of these second generations who hate God. I grew up with some of these as my peers. They have become casualties of mission life. This need not be so.

Chapter 7

Thirteen Weeks in Jamaica

T. L. had seen Jesus *alive and real.* He and Daisy had seen Jesus alive *in a human being, in the Scriptures,* and *at work in them.* The latter discovery, *Jesus alive and at work IN US,* was the door-opener to their imminent worldwide ministry. Now they had the answer and knew how to convince non-Christians that Jesus Christ is alive and real. What were they going to do about it? Once more, they knew they had to DO something. They had to GO to the people of the world.

T.L. and Daisy did not have the funds to go to India – it was too far away and the trip would cost too much. They were invited to the island-nation of Jamaica in the Caribbean, which was close enough to the States so they could get enough money to go there instead. They purposed to go. They sold their furniture, mortgaged their car, and realized enough funds for the journey and a crusade. They had resigned the church in Portland. All they had left was their car, kids, and their suitcases.

It was the winter of 1919, and their destination was Jamaica. It had been a little over two years since they returned from their fateful time in India. With their new knowledge about miracles and with fresh faith, they went abroad again, but this time with great success.

For a period of thirteen weeks, thousands were healed. Over 9,000 people came forward, knelt, and prayed the salvation prayer, accepting Jesus Christ as their Savior. Over 90 people who were totally blind, received their sight instantly and hundreds of others gradually. Over 125 deaf mutes received their hearing and talked instantly. Scores of others were gradually healed. The Lord only knows how many thousands of other people were healed of other maladies as T. L. and Daisy prayed for them.

People gathered from early afternoon to get into the big auditorium. The crowds could hardly be controlled by the police. T. L. and Daisy prayed for about six hundred people in a collective prayer out in the street before going into the auditorium, since there was no hope of these people getting inside. Marvelous miracles were witnessed. T. L. and Daisy pressed their way inside, and after preaching, several hundred accepted Christ.

When the couple ministered to the sick, there were deaf mutes, paralytics, blind people, those with crossed eyes, goiters, tumors, and all sorts of diseases that were instantly healed. The Kingston, Jamaica, newspaper, *The Express*, confirmed the healing of a lad, whose hearing nerves and vocal cords had been destroyed by typhoid fever, leaving him stone deaf and mute:

Seventeen-year old Wilberforce Morris had been deaf and dumb since he recovered from a typhoid fever attack when he was nine years old. In February last year, a man told him about two American evangelists who were preaching nightly at East Street. News had spread around the city that they possessed healing powers. Hundreds flocked to their meetings.

Young Wilberforce went one night. The place was crowded with crip-ples, mutes and others suffering from nearly every form of infirmity.

He knelt at the feet of Rev. T. L. Osborn, the evangelist. He knew. He laid hands on his head and placed his fingers at his ears. He could hear nothing. Then the evangelist motioned for him to rise. He heard the sound of singing, praying, voices for the first time in eight years.

Yesterday morning he called at The Express to tell this story....

He spoke of his life as a mute. During his years of speechless silence, he communicated with others by writing on a pad he carried around....

Before his father died, he taught him to play the clarinet, so Wilber-force, despite his illness, continued to study music. He visited the Jun-ior Centre regularly and gained the interest of Mr. Robert Verity, the supervisor. He continued to read and learn. Then came the miracle at East Street.

Telling of his first reaction to his cure, Wilberforce said: "It sounded strange to me after so long. I was excited and happy. I could not speak then but my voice came the next day. I went to see a doctor soon after and he, too, thought it was a miracle."

It was exciting, his return to the world of sound…music, laughter, voices: however, this new happiness brought its attendant difficulties. He wanted a job, but couldn't find one. Wilberforce said he does not want the kind woman who has been taking care of him to go on sup-porting him now that he can hear and speak.

As a result of the newspaper headlining the Wilberforce's story, the lad got a good job, went on to study music, and became a top clarinet player and one of the excellent male voices in his choir. Hundreds believed on the Lord because of this miracle.

On one night of the meeting, after praying for the sick for nearly two hours, T. L. slipped out the back door, jumped over the wall, and started to his car. Someone grabbed him desperately. It was an elderly woman.

"Oh, please," she begged, "I am totally blind. I cannot even see the light. If you will touch my eyes, I will be healed. I know God will heal me."

In the dark, T. L. laid his hands on her eyes and said, "Woman, in the name of Jesus Christ whom God raised from the dead, I command your blind eyes to be opened. Receive your sight."

The woman nearly pushed T. L.'s hands from her eyes as she began to look up. Suddenly she exclaimed, "Oh, thank God! Yes, I can see everything–the moon, the stars, my hands. Oh, thank God. I knew He would do it."

The Osborns saw more fruit from their labors in a single night in Jamaica than they had seen in the seven years of their ministry before the Lord appeared to them. And it was the miracles that made the difference! T. L. and Daisy stood firm on the importance of miracles and for their need today. T. L. shared, "People who are being born today need miracles. They need to see Jesus the same as people who were born in Bible days. The Church was established for the people then, but God re-establishes Himself for every new generation. He is as real today as He ever was, and He wants to prove it. That is why the theme of our crusades around the world has always been *Jesus Christ the Same Yesterday and Today and Forever.* (Hebrews 13:8.)

T. L. and Daisy preached and prayed for the people, night after night, week after week, for three months. They did it the way they had seen others do it. When the time came to minister to the sick, they instructed them to form long lines and then ministered to them, one at a time. Usually there were so many, that the line was divided. It was impossible for T. L. to pray for so many people by himself, so he and Daisy would set their two children in chairs, beside one of the pastor's wives. Daisy would stand on one side of the platform and pray for a line of people while T. L. stood on the other side and prayed for the other line.

He and Daisy worked and ministered together. Hundreds of people would line up, even out to the street, waiting for them to pray for them, one by one. And so T. L. and Daisy did–they prayed for the people, hour after hour. That was the only way they knew to do. Mass healing was unknown at that time. T. L. stated, "People with crossed eyes, blind eyes, deaf ears, cripples–they were healed just the same in Daisy's line as in mine. The people did not care which one of us prayed for them."

Part Three

Pioneering Mass Miracle Evangelism

Chapter 8

A Pivotal Point

After the Jamaica crusades, T. L. and Daisy returned to America and received an urgent call from Rev. F. F. Bosworth. He asked them to come to Flint, Michigan, to continue Rev. William Branham's crusade in the large city auditorium, because Branham became exhausted and was physically unable to minister to the thousands who attended the crusade. That Flint crusade marked the real beginning of T. L. and Daisy's ministry across the United States. It was also vitally significant in equipping and turning T. L. and Daisy in the direction of mass miracle evangelism worldwide.

T. L. and Daisy's vision for a worldwide ministry of mass miracle evangelism, was birthed in Flint, Michigan. F.F. Bosworth was the instrument God chose to seed a biblical basis for that ministry in their hearts. The Voice of Healing Revival was already underway, primarily across North America, and was noted for mass evangelism taking place under gigantic gospel tents. Up to this point the normal practice of praying for the handicapped, sick, and diseased was through long prayer lines and praying for people individually. This, in part, explained why Rev. Branham had become exhausted and physically unable to minister to the thousands attending and had to send for T. L. and Daisy to take his place. This "pattern" or "model" limited what God was able to accomplish through individuals, because of their natural limitations of time and energy.

The Flint, Michigan, meetings with F.F. and Florence Bosworth, would serve as a "bridge" or "pivotal point" that would prepare T.L. and Daisy for unprecedented mass miracle evangelism in seventy-four nations of the world. This memorable event created hope and confidence in their hearts that they could effectively present Jesus Christ to masses of people. They would no longer be limited by their natural abilities, of time and energy, to lay hands on just a few individuals. They would now be able to help thousands, or scores of thousands of people, to receive salvation and miracle healing *at the same time.* Having seen the world of suffering humanity, they knew that their faith must be raised to a level beyond the limits of their own human touch.

Although F.F. Bosworth had not crusaded beyond the United States and Canada, he was keenly interested in helping all to be blessed. He was concerned about suffering people who waited in long prayer lines for someone's special prayer, when they could embrace God's healing promises as soon as they heard them and be healed.

He often discussed this with T. L. and Daisy. Rev. Bosworth talked about how two or three million Israelites marched out of Egypt to follow Moses to a new land and a new life, despite their history of four hundred years of slavery, abuse, disease, cruelty, and physical suffering. The Bible says that, *"He brought them forth...and there was not one feeble person among their tribes"*

(Psalm 105:37 KJV). Rev. Bosworth taught: "If Moses had tried to individually lay his hands on those sick people, most of them would have died before their turn would have come. Moses could never have ministered to all of them individually. The majority of them would have expired before he reached them."

Another example that Rev. Bosworth used was the time there was rebellion in the camp of Israel, and many people died of poisonous serpents' bites. The people cried to Moses, who prayed for them *all at one time*. The Lord told him to put a brazen serpent on a pole and to say: *"Everyone who is bitten, when he or she looks upon it, shall live"* (Numbers 21:8, paraphrase mine). Moses obeyed, and *"if a serpent had bitten any man, when he beheld the serpent of brass, he lived"* (Numbers 21:9). Each person did his own "looking." If everyone looked at the same time, then *all* were healed *at the same time*.

There were further scriptural examples to substantiate this teaching. David said that God forgives *all*...He heals *all*. (Psalm 103:3.) If all who are sick believe at the same time, then all may be healed at the same time.

Jesus repeatedly *"healed them all."* (Matthew 9:35; 12:15; 14:14; Mark 6:56; Luke 4:40; 6:19.) *"They brought many sick and devil possessed people to Him. He cast out the spirits with His word and healed all that were sick"* (Matthew 8:16, paraphrase mine). He did it with His Word. If all heard His Word at once and believed it, then all who were sick, were healed by that Word, at the same time.

Jesus promised: *"Everyone who asks receives"* (Matthew 7:8). If everyone asks in faith at the same time, everyone who asks can receive at the same time. There is no need for a multitude of people to form themselves into long prayer lines so that they may "ask" one at a time. Jesus said *the truth is what makes people free*"(John 8:32) and that truth is effective, as soon as any person hears and embraces it.

If a farmer plants thousands of seeds in good soil, those seeds do not need to wait for their turn to grow, one at a time. They all grow simultaneously. That is a mass miracle. Multitudes came to Peter's meeting in Jerusalem, bringing demon-possessed folk and laying sick people on beds and couches, *and they were healed, every one.* (Acts 5:16.)

For some mysterious reason, God chose Rev. Bosworth to seed T. L. and Daisy with these and many other biblical reasons for the kind of faith to help multitudes to be healed at the same time. T. L. and Daisy had no way of knowing that they would face teeming multitudes of sick people in mass crusades all over the world. God used this dear, old veteran of the healing ministry to prepare their young hearts for a greater and far more vast healing ministry than had ever been experienced in the history of humankind.

F.F. Bosworth had been teaching "Faith Meetings" in the afternoons during the Branham campaigns. At night, Rev. Branham, who was divinely gifted of God, would address the crowds. Then the sick people would be called to form a long prayer line. Rev. Branham would only have the physical strength to minister and to pray for just so many of them.

Rev. Bosworth was deeply concerned about this dilemma. He passionately emphasized to the people that when God healed anyone, it was proof that He wanted to do the same for everyone. He stressed that the people did not need to wait for Rev. Branham's touch and prayer, that whenever they saw God's healing love poured out on *one* person, they should believe that it was present for *everyone*. He urged them to act on their faith at once and do as the Israelites had done when they looked (individually) at the brazen serpent, and lived! During many conversations with Rev. Bosworth, God was preparing T. L.'s and Daisy's hearts to minister His healing and miracle love to millions of suffering people in great mass campaigns all over the world. Destiny was at work!

T.L. and Daisy had gone to Jamaica for thirteen weeks of intense ministry, preaching, praying, and laying hands on the sick individually, night after night, until they nearly dropped from exhaustion. Yet they were only able to minister to a small portion of those who came. They were human. They had limits. But God was *unlimited*. They needed to bring that fact into practical focus.

T. L. had stepped to the podium of the Civic Auditorium. Rev. F.F. Bosworth and Rev. Gordon Lindsay had introduced him and Daisy and told about their mission to Jamaica, where 125 deaf mutes and over 90 totally blind people had been healed during the meetings. The people in Flint, Michigan, had been witnessing the phenomenal and unique ministry of William Branham. The spiritual gifts of healing, the working of miracles, the word of knowledge, the discerning of spirits, and prophecy had been operating with divine precision. T. L. had never knowingly received any of those gifts.

He told the audience: "Daisy and I come to you from thirteen weeks of miracle ministry in Jamaica. Our lives were transformed in Portland, Oregon, when we witnessed the phenomenal ministry of God's servant, William Branham."

He continued: "To my knowledge, I am not aware of having received any of the gifts that you have been witnessing here. But I have received Jesus Christ who is the giver of all of those divine gifts. And I do know that He is here with us to confirm His Word with signs, miracles, and wonders." T. L. later related how he preached with trepidation, yet with confidence that God would confirm His gospel.

As T. L. preached, apart from the message he was preaching, he clearly heard the question: *How big is POSSIBLE?* He knew God was speaking to him. He had been pondering what to do at the close of his message. He had planned to pray first for the healing of the deaf or blind people, so that the audience would see proof that God was with them. He was thinking of how long it would take Daisy and him to pray for that crowd of people. *They might be there until midnight. Would the people stay? They were in America, not back in Jamaica.*

Then that question had come. God seemed to ask him: *If you pray for one person and that one is healed by a miracle, does that not prove that I have heard your prayer?*

In T. L.'s spirit, he said, *Yes, Lord!*

Then as he continued to preach, that question came again: *How big is POSSIBLE? Are not all things POSSIBLE–if you can believe?*

Again T. L. responded, *Yes, Lord! All things are possible!*

Then the Lord seemed to ask, *If you pray for one person and that one is healed, is that a miracle? How big is a MIRACLE? Suppose you pray for two persons at a time, is My power sufficient to heal two at once? How big is POSSIBLE?*

T. L. answered, *Yes, Lord! You can heal two at a time!* He was excited because he was thinking that he could pray for twice as many people in the same period of time.

Then the voice came again: *Could I heal five at a time—or ten—or a hundred? How big is POSSIBLE? How about all who are sick?*

Then T. L. thought: *If a hundred or a thousand sinners wanted to receive Christ, could not ALL who believe be saved at the same time? How big is POSSIBLE? Is God limited in healing the sick? Is not conversion a greater miracle than the healing of the physically sick?*

T. L. knew God had spoken to him. He had birthed in T. L.'s spirit, fresh faith to proclaim redemption to *all* people, knowing that *all* who would believe and who would put their faith into action could receive His blessings, *at the same time.* But T.L. needed to put that fact to a practical test.

After a great number of people had come forward to receive Christ as Savior, he led them all in a prayer to be saved, at the same time. Then they all thanked God for their salvation at the same time. Nobody questioned their being saved all at the same time. What about the sick? Would God, could God, heal all the sick, at the same time, if they all believed?

Inside, T. L. knew the answer was *yes!* But he was still cautious. He limited his healing invitation to only those who were deaf in one ear. He later realized that this was like limiting a salvation call for only those who had committed a certain sin. Regardless, fifty-three people stood, indicating that one of their ears was totally deaf. T. L. invited them forward. There they stood—fifty-three people. The next step was crucial. T. L. asked them: "If I laid my hands on each one of you and prayed individually, do you believe you would be healed?"

They all responded, "Yes!"

Then he expressed that he believed the Lord wanted to heal all of them *at once,* if they would have simple faith in His Word. He reminded them that Jesus gave us power and authority over *all* devils, to cast them out, and to cure diseases. (Mark 3:15; Luke 9:1.) So he explained that all fifty-three spirits of deafness that had impaired their hearing were subject to him as a representative of Christ. They agreed. Next, T.L. reverently asked the Lord to confirm His Word so that the people would know that He was present to fulfill His promise. Then he addressed those spirits: "You deaf spirits, I have told these people the truth; I am a servant of the most High God and a follower of Christ. You know that He has given me authority over you, so I now adjure you to leave these persons, in the name of Jesus Christ!"

After that T.L. gave thanks to the Lord for the authority He had given him and for His loving compassion. He asked Him to re-create hearing in every ear that had been deaf. Then he told each one to stop up his or her good ear. He then commanded: "Hear me with your ear that was deaf! *Listen* to my words!" Then he said, "Thank You Jesus! Thank You for healing these people! Thank You for Your presence and for Your love!"

The people before him began to break out in broad smiles, tears, or in astonishment. *They could hear.* T. L. asked them to come across the platform so he and Daisy could examine them. *Each one* (except three) could hear Daisy's small wristwatch in one ear as well as in the other. God had confirmed His gospel.

What about those three who were not healed instantly? Within the week, each returned to show that his or her hearing was perfectly restored. That was one hundred percent proof of God's Word, not only confirmed *"in the mouth of two or three witnesses"* (Matthew 18:16), but in the mouths of all fifty-three of them!

This proof that God makes no exceptions was crucial to T. L. and Daisy. If His blessings were for one, they must be for everyone, under the same circumstances. God is no respecter of persons. (Acts 10:34; Romans 2:11). If they were to preach His gospel to the multitudes abroad, they must be able to assure them that "as many as receive Him would be given power to become the children of God" (John 1:12), and that as many as touched Him would be made whole. (Mark 6:56.) This was true in Bible days, so it must be true in T. L. and Daisy's day. This pattern, of ministering healing and miracles had shifted for T. L. and Daisy, as they embraced the new concept of mass miracle evangelism, where the people no longer needed to form long lines and be prayed for individually, but could receive their healing *all at one time.*

Chapter 9

The Re-Beginning

As young missionaries in India, T. L. and Daisy had been unable to convince the Muslims and Hindus that Jesus was the only true and living God. They returned to America after what seemed like a failure to them in India. Then things started to happen: Jesus appeared to them in McMinnville, they saw miracles in the William Branham campaign in Portland, and they became convinced that the same miracles that were wrought in Bible days were for today. They also believed that only miracles would convince humanity that Jesus Christ is alive and unchanged today.

T.L. and Daisy put the truths that God had revealed to them to the test in Jamaica. In Flint, Michigan, they proved that God's "possible," was big enough to heal *all* who would only believe. It was obvious, that to be a successful witness of Christ in other countries, miracles must validate the gospel message they preached. T. L. and Daisy knew how to reach everyone en masse, who needed a miracle. They were convinced that followers of heathen gods and dead religions would believe the gospel if they could see proof that Jesus Christ is alive and real. They were also convinced that Jesus would heal them all at the same time.

Despite their remarkable experience in Flint, Michigan, T.L. and Daisy had another obstacle to overcome concerning mass miracle evangelism. If they witnessed of Christ inside church buildings, most followers of other religions would not come. So how could they minister to these people? They would have to go out where the people are, out in public places, where followers of *any* religion and worshippers of *any* gods, would feel free to attend. Then they would have to preach and demonstrate the gospel like Jesus Christ did. *"He went throughout every city and village, preaching and shewing [demonstrating] the glad tidings of the kingdom of God"* (Luke 8:1 KJV, emphasis added).

In 1949, the Osborns instituted The Voice of Faith Ministry, later re-named Osborn Foundation, then code-named OSFO International (a.k.a. OSBORN International), but known today as Osborn Ministries International. Their life passion has been to express and propagate the gospel of Jesus Christ to all people throughout the world. Their tenet was, "No one deserves to hear the gospel repeatedly until everyone has heard it once." Their motto was, "One Way–Jesus; One Job–Evangelism." Their guiding principle was, "Every Christian believer–a witness for Christ."

T. L. and Daisy set out to proclaim the gospel in non-Christian nations. Like the apostle Paul, *"We strived to preach the gospel, not where Christ was named, lest we should build upon another's foundation"* (Romans 15:20, paraphrase mine). They were persuaded that if the people could witness the power of God to heal the sick as it was manifested in Bible days, they would accept Jesus Christ and become His followers. They went from nation to nation conducting gospel crusades out in public places, so all the people of different faiths could feel welcome. They proclaimed the gospel and urged each person to make a decision for Christ. After that, they prayed for the sick. Each miracle was proof that Christ is the living Savior and that His promises are true.

T.L. and Daisy were both powerful teachers and preachers of faith, and proven in miracle evangelism overseas. They influenced hundreds of preachers to turn from dull religion to dynamic redemption with faith and power. Tens of thousands of non-Christian people were convinced of the gospel and made public decisions to accept Christ. Multitudes were added to the churches wherever their crusades were conducted.

After the summer in the United States, T. L. and Daisy went to Puerto Rico, Cuba, and Central and South America. Everywhere they went, the results were invariably the same, regardless of national heritage, religion or cultural background.

In 1950, T.L. reported over 18,000 conversions in twelve days in Puerto Rico. In January, 1951, he reported 50,000 in Camaguey, Cuba. In 1952, he was arrested in Punto Fijo, Venezuela, for witchcraft. This happened as a result of the healings that were reported to doctors and the Roman Catholic priests.

Ponce, Puerto Rico

People Healed Listening to Radio Broadcast. A radio station offered T. L. forty-five minutes free of charge to enable him to minister to the thousands of people who were unable to get to the crusade. Policemen were sent to guard the radio station from being invaded by the people during the broadcasts.

A man reported that a woman next door to him who was listening to the broadcast, was healed of paralysis. Her leg and arm had been drawn up for many years. In a moment, she was made whole and was going everywhere testifying of her healing.

A man from a city ninety miles away brought an old woman to the crusade in order to let her testify. She was healed of total blindness that day during the radio ministry. At least fifty miracles had already been reported as a result of the broadcast.

She Walked with Her Hands. It was the ninth meeting of the crusade. The greatest miracle of the night was perhaps that of a poor woman who had, for six years, walked with her hands– dragging and swinging her body between her hands on the ground, with both legs doubled to her side, totally stiff. They were rough like a board on one side. The skin was calloused like leather where she had dragged the weight of her body for six years since an operation.

She testified, "I had been believing for twenty minutes after Mr. Osborn prayed that God was healing me. I kept feeling my knees, and I suddenly noticed a slight movement of one of my knee caps. I knew God was healing me. I began to get up and was perfectly and completely healed."

She came to the platform, shouting and walking as perfectly as any person. She showed the audience how the sides of her legs were like leather, then demonstrated how she used to drag on the ground between her hands. Then she stood up, jumped, and walked about as perfect as anyone.

Raving Insane. A raving insane woman was brought to the meeting by her friends. She was suddenly and instantly healed and began begging them to let her go to the platform and testify. She gave the most amazing testimony of how she had been insane, of how horrible it was to be out of her mind, and how suddenly she knew all things clearly. She wept for joy, and so did the audience.

Destroyed Spinal Column. Juan Santos was healed the night T. L. preached on the "Healing of the Cripple" from Mark 2. Juan had been shot through the spine, resulting in the destruction of his spinal column and the nerves below the waist. It left him totally paralyzed in both legs. For sixteen years, his legs were dead, withered. They were just skin and bones and were completely stiff, drawn in a double position. One arm was partly paralyzed. The other shook constantly, so that he could hardly feed himself.

His head also shook because he had attempted suicide by hitting himself with a club, but the blow only caused the palsy. He was losing his mind. He could hardly talk because his tongue and throat were partially paralyzed. To move about, he swung his body between his hands, his withered legs dragging in the dirt between each swing. He was instantly healed.

Total Blindness. An old lady shared her testimony of what God did for her in this crusade:

> *Friends told me about a man who was performing miracles. I tried to get someone to take me to the meeting, but no one would guide me. I decided to go myself. I finally found my way there. They told me the service began at 5 P.M., so I went there at twelve noon. I listened, but was not healed that night.*

Then I tried to get home in the dark. I got lost. I took a box of matches out of my pocket and struck some and cried, "Ciego!" [Blind!] A man heard me and came to help me; but I became fearful of him, that he was leading me astray in the night, so I told him to leave me and that I would stay there by the road and sleep that night. He left me, and I was alone again. I finally found my way home at four in the morning.

The next day, I went again and got near the platform and purposed if I could touch the evangelist's trouser legs, I would be healed. I listened closely to the message; and when the prayer was offered, I believed. The people all around me were standing tightly together. I finally managed to get some space to move a bit, and I reached out my hand around the edge of the platform, trying to touch the man of God. After a long time, I was begging God to help me touch His servant; and, finally, I heard him moving near my side of the platform. I reached for him and found his legs and grabbed his trousers.

Then my eyes came open and I could see everything clearly. I shouted, "Hallelujah! Hallelujah! I can see! I can see!" It was a very great miracle. I can see you people tonight! I go about telling of God's miracle on my poor blind eyes. I am so happy and thankful to God.

T. L. emphasized, "It was not the trouser legs that healed this woman's eyes, anymore than it was the garment of Jesus that healed the woman in the Bible. It was the woman's faith."

Camaguey, Cuba

Hip Joint Created. A young girl had suffered a calcium deficiency all her life; and nearly two years before the crusade, her hip joint had begun slipping out. It continued to get worse until her hip was always out, causing her to suffer much.

Ten months before the crusade, the doctor operated and completely removed the joint of her left hip. After spending five months in bed, the doctors put her on crutches. The girl would have to walk with these for the rest of her life, because it was impossible for her to walk without them.

T. L. prayed a mass prayer for all who were crippled, commanding both them and the paralytics to walk in Jesus' name. The young girl laid her crutches aside and stepped out by faith to walk, as the evangelist commanded. She was instantly healed and could walk, as perfect as any person. She took her crutches to the platform and gave her testimony to the newspaper reporter, and then left her crutches as she walked away.

Polio Victim Healed. A young girl who had been a victim of polio, with both legs in steel braces, removed the braces and began walking back and forth on the platform, perfectly healed.

Right Leg Grew Three Inches. A man's hip was broken, resulting in his right leg being three inches shorter than his left for the past eleven years. His right leg grew out to be the same length as his left.

Punto Fijo, Venezuela

Partly Healed, then Completely Healed. An old man who had been blind for years was partly healed one night, and then God finished the job another night—his eyes were completely healed.

San Jose, Costa Rica

Tuberculosis, Paralysis, Eye Deformity. A boy who was dying of tuberculosis of the spine and could not bend his back or even move his head, was healed. Suddenly, a child who had been crippled and unable to walk, was placed on the platform and began to walk. Paralytics shouted for joy as they began hoisting their canes and crutches to demonstrate that they were healed. Some abandoned their wheelchairs. The eyes of a child that had been turned back in his head and had never been normal, were healed.

Tumor Disappears. A woman, who had a tumor so large that she looked nine-months pregnant, was healed. During the prayer, the tumor simply disappeared. Her dress became loose. Her physician was in the stadium. He was so shocked by this miracle that he came to the podium to examine the woman. He said, "If I had not been her doctor, I never would have believed that such a thing could take place."

Another woman was healed of a large goiter that prevented her from bending her head forward. During the prayer, the goiter disappeared.

Guatemala City, Guatemala

Paralyzed for Fifty-two Years. In Guatemala City, during February and March of 1953, 50,000 people were saved. Two mass meetings were held daily for at least five weeks. Maria Luisa Gutierres, who had smallpox and other serious fevers when she was a child, was present in these meetings. She was paralyzed from the waist down. For fifty-two years, she couldn't stand or walk. Her legs and hips were calloused from dragging her body on the ground with her hands. She was carried to the crusade in Guatemala City, and when the paralytics were commanded to rise and walk in Jesus' name, her son (who had never seen his mother walk), lifted her up and she was healed.

Demon-possessed. A man who had been tormented by demons for more than twenty-five years was brought to the crusade. The demons would throw him on the ground and literally pound his head and chest on the dirt. That night the demons tormented this man, and he cried out with loud voices until he greatly disturbed the meeting. People pressed around him to see him in this condition. Not at all coincidental was the fact that this night, T. L. and Daisy were preaching on demon possession, and it seemed that satan had come to challenge the truths which they were proclaiming.

T. L. told the audience to believe with him, be reverent in God's presence, ignore satan's demonstration, and give attention to the Word of God. Then he told them that satan would not be able to stand before the authority of God's Word. The audience joined him in their faith and did as he told them to do.

As T. L. was preaching about Christ's power over demons and the power of Jesus' name today, this man shouted, "I'm an enemy of Jesus! I fight with Him! He cannot overcome me!" All sorts of blasphemous words flowed from this man's heart. But when the mass prayer was prayed and the people, with one accord, joined in faith, the demons could not resist the truth. In one last desperate attempt on this man's life, the demons threw him to the ground and literally pounded his head on the earth. Then with a loud scream, they left him; and he was delivered in peace.

Just a few moments later, the man came up the steps with tears in his eyes, and gave the testimony of his deliverance. He told how the demons had tormented him, but now they had gone from him. He also testified how Jesus Christ had come into his heart, bringing him peace and satisfaction.

An elderly gentleman testified that night that when he came on the grounds and saw this completely crazy man, he had gone to the opposite side of the audience because he was afraid that some danger might result from this man in this insane condition. This gentleman wept as he expressed his gratitude to God for setting this captive free. Esteban Crispin, at one time insane and possessed of demons, is now a faithful member of a church in Guatemala.

Crazy, Blind, and Paralyzed. A beggar in Guatemala had diabetes, which resulted in total blindness. After the diabetes had destroyed his eyesight, it affected his mind and he became insane. In addition to this, one side of his body was paralyzed and he hobbled along on the streets with an old cane. He was crazy, blind, and paralyzed. He also begged for a living.

One day a man told the old beggar about the Osborn crusade, and urged him to attend. Jose Antonio Solorzano, the beggar, replied that he did not know the way to the crusade and that it was impossible for him to go.

The friend offered to carry him to the meeting, so he came and carried Jose to the crusade on his back. He set him down on the ground where he could listen to the message. That was the last time Jose ever saw his friend.

Jose listened to T. L.'s message. When the prayer was offered for healing, God, instantly and completely, healed his body, from his head to his feet. When people in the audience were asked to raise their hands if they knew him and knew that his testimony was true, many hands were raised, signifying that they not only knew him, but had given bits of money to him on the street. Before his sickness, he had been employed by the government as an architect. In less than two weeks after his healing, he had his old job back again.

Proof for the Muslims in Java, Indonesia

T. L. and Daisy headed for Java, where the population was ninety-five percent Muslim. Some of the Christians were frightened. They did not know if it was wise to go out on a public field and call thousands of Muslims together to talk to them about Jesus, pray for the sick, and expect miracles to confirm that Christ is alive. This was the first time that T.L. and Daisy preached to the Muslims with miracles in manifestation. They did not believe the Muslims were different from the Buddhists.

The first night T. L. preached in Java, he thought it would be a good idea to tell the crowd that he did not expect them to accept Jesus unless they saw proof that He was risen from the dead. He believed that people were the same then as they were in Bible days, and needed to see *proof* that Jesus is alive. Otherwise, all he had to offer was a *religion*–a ritual, a tradition, a ceremony. In Java, he asked for anyone who was deaf in one ear to come to the platform. Quite a group responded, and each one was instantly healed as he and Daisy prayed for them. The very first person to respond was a Muslim teacher, a man about sixty years old. He was born with one ear totally deaf and had never heard out of it in his entire life.

T. L. told the people that if the man's ear did not come open, they would know that he was a false teacher, and that Jesus Christ had not risen from the dead as the Bible claims. He explained that if Jesus is alive, He would make Himself known. He would do the same miracles that He had done *before* He was crucified.

There were over one hundred pastors on the platform. They said, afterwards, that they were frightened about what the multitude might do if that Muslim teacher was not healed. They viewed T. L.'s action as extreme, radical, and a dangerous challenge–even careless and near-irresponsible.

T. L. started to put his hand on the man's ear, but never touched him. The man did not even stand very close to T. L., as T. L. simply stretched his hand toward him. He did not want the people to think that there was something mystical about his touch, or that he had some strange power. T. L. wanted the Javanese to realize that Jesus Christ was there in their presence. While at other times he would touch the sick and lay hands on them, he wanted these people to understand that this was the power of the living Jesus, who, though He had been crucified, was alive again and was present in that meeting.

His and Daisy's position was simple and seemed totally logical to him, *If Jesus is alive, He will do the same things that He did before they killed Him. But if He is dead, He can do no miracle and His name has no power.*

There were two things that Daisy later shared about that instance: "One was that my husband did not touch the man, and the other was that he did not close his eyes." Usually T. L. would bow his head, close his eyes, and ask the people to do the same, but he wanted that Moslem teacher to believe that Jesus Christ is alive. He wanted everyone to witness that he was doing nothing mystical. That is why he did not ask the people to close their eyes. He wanted them to watch everything he did.

Looking at the Moslem teacher, he said, " In the name of Jesus Christ, whom God has raised from the dead according to the Scriptures–Jesus who is the Son of the Living God–I adjure the deaf spirit to leave your ear; and I command your ear to hear now, so that all here may know that the Bible is true, that Jesus is the Son of God, that His blood was shed for the remission of our sins, and that He is risen from the dead to be the Savior of the world. Amen."

T. L. later shared that he spoke with authority and that the Holy Spirit was present.

> *When I finished, you could hear a pin drop. It was an apostolic moment. Across that field was total silence. Then I pulled the man to me. I stopped up his good ear and faintly whispered in his deaf ear, and he jumped.*

> *He repeated every word. I told him, "Say what I say, and say it out loud." He agreed. Then I made him confess what the Bible says about Jesus. I said, "Jesus is the Son of God."*

> *He said, "Jesus is the Son of God."*

> *I said, "He must be risen from the dead."*

> *He repeated, "He must be risen from the dead."*

"By that time," Daisy later reported, "he [the Muslim] was weeping."

As the man broke into tears, the crowd started clapping; and I think the preachers on the platform were greatly relieved. Then I turned to the multitude to help them accept Christ, asking them, "Now, is Jesus Christ alive; or is He dead?"

Being called upon to make a decision, thousands raised their hands to accept Jesus Christ as their Lord and Savior. This was probably the greatest gospel demonstration in all of the history of Christian evangelism in Java up to that time. T. L. and Daisy stayed there for several weeks, preaching, teaching, and praying, day after day, conducting two or three meetings per day. Someone who had been unable to talk for four years was healed instantly. Someone unable to walk for fifteen months was completely healed. Someone totally deaf for many years was miraculously healed.

Dreadfully Infected, Running Sores. "Lepers are being healed, blind are seeing, and cripples are walking at the airfield!" That is what one man heard in the streets and in the marketplace, as he edged around the people so he wouldn't be noticed, *because he was a leper.* For years, he had been tortured with the shame of being unclean. His nose, ears, upper lip, and gradually his feet, hands, and arms had become dreadfully infected. Running sores covered his feet and hands. In this condition, he sought out the place where such unbelievable reports were coming from.

As he approached the grounds, he saw other lepers and all manner of sick people: some being carried, some being led, and others, as himself, staying on the edge of the multitude and all alone. The very first night he attended, he was instantly and perfectly healed. The sores dried up, all swelling and deadness left, and he was clean and whole.

In his words, "This has made me, a former Mohammedan, know that Jesus is the Son of God and that He is alive just as the Bible declares. Thank God the Osborns came to Java!"

Infected, Disfigured, and Isolated. It was the seventh meeting of the Java crusade and this is the account of one of the healings that took place:

> *Eighteen years ago, I went to the doctor for an examination. I had a white spot on my right shoulder. When the doctor saw it, he sent me to a leprosy specialist who, after taking many tests, told me that I had leprosy. Immediately, my family put me in a separate room. From then on, I could only talk to them at a distance; and I had to eat, sleep and live alone.*
>
> *During the next year, my hands became swollen. I could not shut them. Bumps began to appear all over my body, and then my face began to swell. My eyes were nearly swollen shut; and my ears were several times their normal size, and hung down at least an inch longer than usual. They were about as thick as your finger. They were terribly swollen and infected, but numb.*
>
> *During the next few years, my hands were so badly infected that I lost the first joints of my forefinger and little finger on my right hand. Then, five years ago, a big ugly sore started on my left shin near the ankle. It increased until it must have been more than twelve inches long and nearly encircled my leg. My leg was terribly swollen, and drained continually. By that time, I had bumps and sores all over my body, and the odor was stifling.*

I was persuaded to attend the Osborn Crusade, where it was said that many people were being cured. After attending for three nights and witnessing what was being done for others, I began to believe that I too, could be helped. I decided to do as the evangelist said, and I accepted Jesus Christ and purposed to follow Him.

While I was following in the prayer being led by Mr. Osborn, I suddenly felt something in my hands. I found that I could open and shut them—I had not done this for years!

Then I realized that I was being healed. In one week, I was perfectly whole. My skin was clean! The ulcer dried up. Life had returned to all of my body, and I was clean within and without!

None of us were Christians, and never planned to be Christians, but we had never seen His power to cleanse lepers before. Oh, it is wonderful! My wife and I are reunited now, and can eat at the same table and live together as husband and wife should. All of my family has accepted Christ, and we are all following Him, and shall serve Him all the days of our lives.

Bangkok, Thailand

Next, T. L. and Daisy went to Thailand, a Buddhist monarchy. It was no different among the Buddhists. In the Osborn meetings, God was the same everywhere.

Tuberculosis of the Spine. As the couple arrived at the gate for the twelfth meeting of the crusade, T. L. found his Thai interpreter talking to a woman who had been healed. For nine years, she had tuberculosis of the spine, and was bent over. She had suffered terrifying pain. She had been attending the crusade and had accepted Christ as her Savior. This morning when she got out of bed, she was completely healed.

Neighbors asked her, "What happened? What medicine did you take? Who healed you?"

She told them how she had believed in Jesus and had been healed by Him.

They said, "It is better that you remain bent down and die than to give up your Buddhist religion."

She told them, "You have your heart; I have mine. I accepted Jesus, and He healed me." All day she had testified.

He Is Not Ashamed to Come to My Hut. A leprous woman was healed. The leprosy had affected her hands until they were rigid, numb, and clenched fists. Her feet were stiff and numb, also. Ulcers had erupted on her legs and hands. She said, "I was alone. I had no job. My parents died with leprosy. No one would talk to me or come near me or visit with me. I was lonesome. But now I have a friend; I am not alone. Jesus loves me. He is not ashamed to come to my hut. He is not afraid of me. I am healed. I am clean. I will always follow Him."

Kyoto, Japan

T. L. and Daisy went to Kyoto, Japan–the seat of Shintoism, a city of magnificent temples. They had been told: "Oh, it will be different here. The people here are Shintoists." But it was exactly the same in Japan.

Deaf and Blind and Crippled and Diseased…Healed. In their first crusade in Japan, forty-four deaf mutes were healed, and the Japanese were as excited and as emotional as anyone in the Western Hemisphere.

A man who had been totally blind for twenty-one years, was instantly healed. He was led to the crusade at Kyoto. As the Osborns prayed for the blind, commanding the blind spirits to leave, he received his sight immediately. Several persons confirmed his testimony.

A man in the audience who doubted that such a miracle could be genuine, came to the platform. He shoved a calling card before the formerly blind man and demanded, "Read that!" He read the card perfectly. He asked for a Bible, and to the amazement of the audience, read it as well as anyone could, demonstrating that Christ who gave sight to the blind in Bible days still does the same today when faith is manifested.

A woman was healed of cancer and coughed it up during the meeting. A woman lying on a pallet arose and was made whole. A Japanese lad had fallen and broken both hips when he was four years old. Since then he had only been able to walk with the aid of a brace and crutches. After the healing prayer in the Osborn crusade, he was completely healed and could walk normally. A victim of polio since childhood, was miraculously healed, as well as an individual who had been paralyzed for five years.

The Hague, Holland

The Cancer Simply Vanished. T. L. and Daisy and mass miracle evangelism were not only effective in third-world countries. In

Holland, more than one hundred thousand people attended the crusade nightly–the greatest crowds in Europe's history up to that time to receive the gospel face to face.

A man who had a severe back injury, a cancer on his nose, and a double rupture was healed. The cancer simply vanished. His back was as free as a child's, and both ruptures disappeared.

Lome, Togo, West Africa

Three Days He Had Lain There. A young man had been vomiting blood as often as twenty times a day. He was dying of tuberculosis. About fifty miles into the interior, he had heard of the miracles. He had been bedfast for three years and could not walk. He had no voice. His parents were so poor that they only had enough (one pig) to pay the driver of an old market-transport truck to carry the young man to Lome to the field where "the Son of God" was doing miracles. They knew if their son was not healed, he would die. If he was healed, he could walk home.

They carried him to the old truck, paid the fare, and put him in the care of the driver who helped him during the trip. When they arrived in Lome, the truck driver carried him and laid him on the ground under a tree near the platform. He had a few precious coins to buy some rice from a woman, who occasionally went to the grounds. He laid there for three days; and during the night of the eleventh meeting of the crusade, he was healed. As he testified, his voice grew stronger. T. L. said that he was one of the happiest persons he had ever seen.

Kenya, Africa

Her Feet and Hands Were Mostly Gone from the Leprosy. Archbishop Silas Owiti from Kenya shared the following testimony:

A woman, Miriam Gare, secluded herself under a tree at the edge of the multitude to avoid being noticed, because she was not only a leper, but she was paralyzed and had to crawl on the ground. Her feet and hands were mostly gone from the leprosy.

She carried her belongings in a basket on the back of her head as she crawled. That night, the Osborns prayed only for the deaf to hear. But God's love could not be limited. He came to Miriam beneath that tree, and His great healing power made her whole.

The next morning people came shouting, "Silas, Silas, come and see!"

I rushed in my car to the Jubilee Marketplace. A big crowd surrounded this woman, who was healed of leprosy and paralysis. She was walking in the street to show the people how she was healed. She had walked until she was exhausted. I rushed into the mob and took Miriam in my arms and to my car and drove away from the crowd. She was walking herself to death. Since her miracle, Sister Miriam Gare has always attended our church and has been a great witness that Christ is unchanged today.

From Manila, Philippines, to San Fernando, Trinidad, to Kinshasa, Zaire, to Benin City, Nigeria, to Monterrey, Mexico, to Port

Moresby (Papua New Guinea), to Bogota, Columbia, to the ex-Soviet Republics...from Alaskan Eskimos to American Indians to Japanese Shintoists to Thai Buddhists to Javanese Muslims to Indian Hindus to African Animists to Western Christians...T. L. and Daisy Osborn's global ministry saga continued.

Return to India

T.L. and Daisy were preaching all over the world; but finally their special dream came true–*they returned to India.* They went back to the same city, where they had talked to those Muslims and Hindus and had not been able to prove whether the *Koran* of the Muslims or the Bible of the Christians was God's Word. This time it was different. They leased a big, open field by the huge stadium in the University City of Lucknow. They set up their platform and invited the public to come.

Daisy shared that "those people had not changed. The situation had not changed. *But WE had changed.* Our thinking had been changed. Our lives had been changed. We knew God would fulfill His Word."

Fourteen years earlier, a disillusioned and defeated twosome had returned from India to the U. S. They had said, "There is no use for us to stay here if we cannot prove to these people that Jesus is alive." Feeling ineffective as gospel ministers, not managing to prove what they preached, they had found no reason to stay in India. So they came back home to the United States. But now they were back again; and, as T. L. related, "I do not think that we had ever seen greater miracles than we saw in that crusade."

Fifty to sixty thousand people were in attendance. T. L. and Daisy proclaimed to the masses that Jesus is the Son of God, risen from the dead–and this time they knew how to prove to the people that Jesus Christ is alive. As a result, great faith was evidenced in the India crusades.

Steeped in Religion, Knowing Nothing About the Living Savior. T. L. described an old Hindu holy man who stood right in front of the platform, not three feet from him in a dirt-smeared robe. His long, squalid beard and his frizzled hair shroud desperate, inquiring eyes. Yellow paint was smeared on his forehead. Mixed mud and dust covered his face and hair. In his right hand was a large Neptune spear that he guarded as his staff.

T. L. commented, "What a joy to give out the powerful gospel message to people like this dear man, steeped in religion and knowing nothing about the living Savior."

The first to be healed was an elderly Hindu man, carrying two crutches above his head. His long hair and beard were flowing. For five years he had been crippled. Now he paraded back and forth. By that time, another older man with a large red turban came bounding across the platform, completely healed, as well.

Hip-to-Ankle Brace. Crippled by polio, Shanti Sundram could only walk with a hip-to-ankle brace and one leg was three inches shorter than the other. She was perfectly healed. A man, whose foot and leg were crippled, had walked on one side of his foot which was turned directly inward with the ankle twisted over. Both feet were healed and became perfectly straight.

Blind. Two men who were blind found their way to the crusade together. Both were healed.

Crawled in the Wood to Die. A little Hindu woman, clad in dirty cloth, testified in tears. She would praise Jesus, then place her open palms together and bow to T. L. in East Indian fashion. Then she would reverently touch T. L.'s feet and repeat, again and again, her thanks. She had been a beggar and a disease had so drained her strength that she could no longer beg, so she had crawled into the wood to die. Her children and her husband were dead. She was left alone to beg. She would say how thankful she was that she was no longer in the bushes, sick and hungry. Now Jesus was her friend, and she was healed. "Now I have strength so I can beg again. Now I am not sick and weak anymore. I can talk loud enough to ask for alms and get some coins for some rice to eat."

"Frog Man" Beggar. Crippled by polio when he was a lad, there was a man who could never move about except by scooting on his hips. He was called the "frog man" beggar because he could only walk in a squatting position, like a frog.

T. L. related, "He was instantly healed, and we almost lost control of the multitude when the people saw him walking and running like anyone else. Thousands of people knew him. Hundreds of people were miraculously healed in that powerful meeting."

The Hindu Who Saw Jesus. One night during the Lucknow, India, crusade, far to the edge of the crowd there was a young student from the university—an agnostic—who hated everything that T. L. and Daisy were saying about Jesus Christ. He was a fanatical member of the religious political party of India that had vowed to drive Christianity from its shores.

He stood with his arms defiantly folded across his chest. He later reported that as the missionaries preached about Jesus, suddenly the Lord appeared right in front of him. Jesus opened His hands where the man could see His scars, and then stretched them out toward him. Then Jesus spoke these words, *"Behold my hands! I am Jesus!"*

The student fell to the ground in the dust, weeping and crying. After regaining control of himself, he came running to the platform, grabbed the microphone with trembling hands, and appealed to the multitude: *"Accept this Jesus! What this man is telling us is true! I saw Him! I saw the scars in His hands! He is alive!"*

Thousands of people that night, believed on Jesus Christ following this. Blind people, lepers, deaf mutes, cripples, invalids carried on cots, and all kinds of sicknesses were healed.

One Hundred People Saw the Lord

All over the world and in practically every crusade that T.L. and Daisy have ever conducted, Christ Himself has been reported to appear, alive–at least once, and in some crusades, several times.

One night in Thailand as the gospel was being preached to a great crowd of Buddhists, over one hundred people saw the Lord. It began when a man looked up and saw Him above the people. The man cried out in alarm, "Who is that man in white there in the sky?" Over one hundred people declared they saw the Lord's appearance in that meeting.

The next day, T. L. and Daisy spent the entire afternoon listening to the people tell about what they saw the night before–those who had seen, "that man in white walking above the multitude." With typical village gestures, they each told their story. As the

interpreter translated their words, over one hundred village people, who had not believed in Jesus before, all confirmed the same
miraculous visitation.

Chapter 10

Ministering in America

T. L. and Daisy returned to America in the late 1970's after ministering abroad for over three decades. They believed that God led them to do two things in America: 1) share in churches, Christian conventions, campmeetings, conferences, and seminars, and 2) put into seed form what they had learned and what they had witnessed over the years, so that younger generations could run with these seeds, plant them, and reap a greater harvest of souls worldwide.

Upon their return, they observed a profusion of apostolic truth being revealed and taught to millions via national Christian networks, satellite evangelism, multiplied millions of books, audio and video cassettes, and from the pulpits of enormous faith churches that were flourishing across the nation. Year after year, many of America's principle pastors and convention leaders had urged T.L. and Daisy to share more of their faith teaching and experiences with America. They finally decided to do that, because effective evangelization of the world depends on the partnership and faith of a strong soulwinning church at home.

As T. L. and Daisy increased their ministry across the home-land, the Holy Spirit birthed in them a great passion to encourage preachers, teachers, and gospel ministers to proclaim the Good News. There had been a yearning in their spirits to allow Jesus Christ to manifest His love, compassion, and healing life in and through them, not only to the people, but to the ministers also. Jesus did not come to *condemn* the world but to *save* the world; therefore, T.L. and Daisy also encouraged these ministers not to use their positions to condemn, judge, criticize or demean others.

Faith Message Was Strong, but...

T. L. related that God showed him and Daisy that the "faith" message in America was strong, but that the infinite value of each human person must be discovered and emphasized in order for there to be greater self-esteem and self-value. In one convention after another, T.L. and Daisy felt urged by the Holy Spirit to emphasize God's esteem and value for every individual and of how much He paid for each person in order to justify and make him or her absolutely righteous—so He could have them near to Him as intimate friends and partners in His love plan for humanity.

T. L. and Daisy crisscrossed America with a passion to tell people that God was not mad at them. They stressed that He loved them, needed them, had paid for them, yearned for them, reached out for them, and offered them His best. They urged ministers and lay people to pledge never to condemn again what God had paid so much to redeem...never to negate or reduce or impoverish again what God treasured so dearly...never to accuse or judge again what God paid so much to forgive and justify...never to harm, deteriorate or destroy again what God paid so much to heal, restore, and to save…never to depreciate, discredit, or disparage again what God paid so much to dignify and to make royal… never to criticize or revile again what God esteemed to be of such infinite value.

As T.L and Daisy addressed some of the largest Christian conventions in America, they were able to lift thousands to a new level of self-esteem and self-value. Many lives were transformed and T.L. and Daisy were thankful for the opportunity to play a part in this new revelation and its implementation.

In 1978-79, T. L. was searching: "How do we help Americans?" He and Daisy knew what to do overseas, but they did not know how to reach the people in America who did not know Jesus as their Savior. In the early days of their ministry, if a minister was on radio or television, it was just radio or television, because Christian radio or television did not exist at that time. By the 1970's, however, Christian radio and television emerged. T. L., as an evangelist, was trying to figure out how they could reach the most Americans through another means other than Christian radio or television. How could they do this? The secular stations were too expensive and they did not want to be on Christian radio, because most of the listeners were already saved.

The National Enquirer, The Globe, and The Star

As T.L. began looking around for ways to reach the unsaved people in America, he came up with a great idea. For one year, they took out a full-page, weekly ad in *The National Enquirer, The Globe*, and *The Star* tabloids. These were the kinds of publications that lent themselves to coverage of sensational, and sometimes even lurid, late-breaking news, including celebrity news and the latest gossip. Each of these ads was designed for the American market that was interested in, "How do you succeed?" and "How do you have the best of life?" So T. L. and Daisy offered seven secrets.

There was a big blown-up picture of T. L. and Daisy in each ad. There were also pictures of them from Florida with their blue swimming pool and lush palm trees. Even though these ads were not in color, there was an air of opulence about them. There was T. L. with his gold chain, and Daisy in her Floridian attire, both with a champagne glass of orange juice, toasting each other, while offering seven secrets in response to the following questions, "How do you succeed?" and "How do you have the best of life?"

The subscribers had to request the seven secrets. In response, T.L. and Daisy created an 8 ½ X 11 magazine to send to them. It was like a comic book. It had a glossy-colored cover with different pictures of them on the pages inside. The camera personnel would follow T.L. and Daisy to the mall, while they went on a jog, or as they sat around the pool, and would take pictures of them. T. L. and Daisy would then come up with stories to go along with these pictures, just like in the comic books, where there were bubbles inserted in the pictures with the printed conversation that was taking place.

In these comics, T. L. and Daisy would talk about what they had seen in their crusades, like the demon-possessed man, lepers, or those who were crippled, blind, or deaf and dumb. Throughout the magazine, T. L. and Daisy would talk to each other, about the wonderful things they had seen, subtly intertwining the gospel message in it. At other times, T. L. would say things like, "My dear, I don't think it's too much to say that they (the readers) can have all they want, including prosperity." Daisy would say things like, "Honey, do you remember what David said in the Bible?"

They told their miracle stories and then showed a picture of each miracle, maybe even with a caption along the bottom. For example in one comic, T. L. and Daisy might be pictured in their jogging suits running, and the caption might read: "We're going to run to help you get life's best." Then at the end of this comic-like book, the subscribers could request the actual book that contained the full seven secrets, *The Best of Life*. This book was the best synopsis of the different aspects of God's plan for people, according to Osborn Ministries International. It was written for the unique audience of America. The overall principle of *The Best of Life* is self-value. God made you. You are valuable. Because God created you; you have self-value. You are valuable because God's plan involves you. Your heritage is to have God's best, enjoy His companionship, and to use His wealth and power for the good of yourself and others. You are created for life, love, power, prosperity, success, and dignity. The seeds of greatness are in you. God never created you as a nobody, but as a real somebody; therefore, recognize your self-value. Realize that He has planned His life's best for you as His child.

There are seven principles of success in this book: the principles of self-value, identity, desire, decision, wealth, vision, and action. At the end of each of the seven sections, there is a sixty-second secret. The idea is that there are seven secrets and you can learn these in sixty seconds for seven days. You believe these; you say these; you do these. These were the secrets of self-value that T. L. and Daisy promoted. "You can't read them and not get saved----- Seven secrets in sixty seconds a day…and in seven days your life will be transformed."

T. L. and Daisy pioneered this "self-help" idea and method that became so popular in the years ahead. Thousands upon thousands requested the 8 ½ by 11 magazine. The end result was tremendous. People realized how much God wanted to help them. There were testimonies of people who accepted Jesus, got delivered from alcohol, healed of cancer, and received a financial miracle.

The National Enquirer, The Globe, and *The Star* were instruments that helped bring this message to the American people; however, this bold, daring, even revolutionary move on T. L.'s and Daisy's part could have been called worldly, compromising and probably a few other things, by the "religious" camps. "But then, those individuals would have had to read *The Enquirer,* themselves to be able to say this, and they wouldn't want to admit that," was LaDonna's conclusion.

An associate of Osborn Ministries International shared an interesting story in regard to the church's reaction to what T. L. and Daisy had done. T. L. was at John Osteen's church, Lakewood, in Houston, Texas, for a big convention involving Network World and its connections around the globe. T. L. had a copy of *The National Enquirer* that carried his and Daisy's first ad. He explained to the church how they had run this ad in *The National Enquirer.* "And it went dead quiet, dead quiet," according to the individual sharing this story.

T. L. said to the congregation, "We wanted to reach the people who didn't go to church." As the story goes, one fellow on the front row started clapping. It was like the audience was saying,

What's he clapping for? But then the applause began to catch on... and grow; and it grew to a groundswell. "It was exciting," shared T. L.'s associate, "that God could give His people new ideas that have never been thought of before." That's what T. L. Osborn has always been about.

Chapter 11

Pioneering Tools for Evangelism

T. L. and Daisy instituted Osborn Ministries International, a world evangelism and missionary church organization, in 1949, at a time when the threat of communism was strongly impacting the people of the U. S. On June 2, 1950, a speech by a U. S. senator was aimed at explaining this threat. In that speech, communism was referred to as an "atheistic…Godless force," and the war being waged against it was described as "what may well be the final Armageddon foretold in the Bible." The church, itself, was putting communism and its threat in the context of end-time biblical prophecy. While the Pentecostal ranks were swearing against this enemy of God, T. L. was paying attention to the methods the communists were using to make their advances. They were using guerilla warfare.

Osborn Ministries International birthed the National Missionary Assistance Program in 1953. In 1954, this program began sponsoring nationals to go to their own people and called them *missionaries*. Prior to that time the term "missionary" referred to foreigners who traveled to other nations to deliver the Christian faith. *Nationals* (citizens of individual nations) had never been recognized, supported, or respected as "missionaries" to their own unreached tribes and villages. T. L.'s ministry was the first to call the *national*, a missionary to his own people. In that day, many foreign nations, especially in Africa, were under colonialism, and only the foreigner could be called a missionary. So in essence, guerilla warfare led to the beginning of *national missionaries.*

Once again, T.L. became a pioneer. This time he pioneered indigenous evangelism that positioned and equipped native ministers to reach their own people. If they would go into a completely unreached area where there was no gospel witness and establish a church, his ministry would assist them. They would help them establish a church and support them for twelve to eighteen months. A bona fide program of accountability was used. Today the same forms, principles, and accountability guidelines are applied as they were in 1954. LaDonna pointed out that some things about ministry should never change.

Out of that one program, in cooperation with the Christian partners of Osborn Ministries International, over 30,000 national preachers have received financial assistance, allowing them to labor full time as missionaries to their own and neighboring tribes and villages that had been previously untouched by the gospel. In addition, more than 150,000 new, self-supporting churches have been established globally, with as many as 400 new churches being planted a year.

T. L.'s effort to make the revival overseas into a truly native experience, instead of an American program, was an important contribution to the world pentecostal revival, and its success was one of his proudest achievements. Many of today's national church leaders began in ministry as national preachers, encouraged and sponsored by T. L. and Daisy's ministry.

David Nunn, a renowned evangelist who experienced tremendous healings and miracles and had traveled widely overseas, shared in regard to T. L. Osborn's pioneering of indigenous evangelism:

> *He's got a great concept. To me, he provides...from the mission standpoint, one of the greatest leaderships of any man to come up in the last hundred years. In challenging the old line churches to change [their] old policies that never have worked properly, [the kind of policy] that brings down the people into servitude and makes them houseboys, and to lift those men up to where they belong as children of God and proud of their national heritage with confidence in them that they've got ability and that they can carry out the work of evangelizing their own countries.*

T. L. discovered that another way that the communists made their advances was by successfully using the printed page to spread their propaganda. As a result, T. L. made further advances on the mission field for God, by way of the printed page—printing salvation tracts, books, and other materials in 132 languages. T.L. decided that they would fly over an area and rain literature on the villages. Books in new languages are still being added annually, through the partnership of Christians who have accepted Christ's evangelism mandate.

T. L. has authored over twenty major books. *Healing the Sick*, his first work and a faith-building best-seller, was written in

1950. It has penetrated the world, being used as a Bible school textbook in many nations. It is now in its enlarged 46th edition and is called, "A Living Classic" by the publisher. Over a million copies are in print and it has recently been translated into Mandarin for all of China. It has already been spread across that vast nation by underground Christian witnesses at the risk of arrest and imprisonment.

Together, T. L. and Daisy produced a 512-page classic documentary entitled, *The Gospel According to T. L. and Daisy*. It is a written and pictorial world report–containing 610 photos– that attempts to tell their story. Nothing else like it has ever been published.

Daisy has also written five major books that are unmatched among Christian publications for the female members of the body of Christ, helping them rediscover their identity, dignity, destiny, and equality in God's plan for their lives.

Tons of the Osborns' arsenal of gospel books, teaching courses, and eighteen different salvation tracts are given free to soulwinners, Bible school students, and those searching for truth who are not attending a Bible school. For many years, the soulwinning tracts were printed at the rate of more than one ton per day. Through these "paper preachers," Christ is being preached to millions in locales that often restrict public mass evangelism. The distribution of these gospel materials is one of the most valuable and long-lasting investments that has ever been made by the Osborns.

Cinematography for God–the Unbeatable Tool

In emerging nations, large businesses utilize motion films, videos and DVD's to propagate and to market their secular products among millions of people, while realizing big financial profits.

The Marxists, who were adherents of a system of economic and political thought that promoted a socialist order and a classless society, exploited cinematography as one of their most forceful influences. This technology was one of the most dynamic tools available, at that time, to persuade people in society. Hollywood has demonstrated its effectiveness for both good and evil.

A French philosopher said, "The public no longer looks to the Church for truth–they look to the world of film productions and television." He was suggesting that the church no longer could attract the attention of the new generation. Overall, the younger generation absorbs their philosophies of life through the medium of cinematography. Due to the demoralizing nature of our society, cinematography became a means of portraying violence, brutality, and social promiscuity. Instead of lamenting the demoralizing use of a potentially good technology, the stance of the Christian church should be to exploit this technology for propagating the gospel of the living Christ.

T. L. and Daisy were the first ones to install a big platform, lights, and public address system out on parks or fields or terrains in non-Christian nations, and to preach the gospel publicly, praying for God's miraculous confirmation that Jesus Christ is the same today as He was in Bible days. *And then they filmed these meetings.* They were the first to produce films reproducing an evangelism event. In their days, the only thing close to it was Billy Graham's films, but they were "re-enacted." T.L. and Daisy's video productions combined missionary preaching with miracles among non-Christian nations. Public mass evangelism meetings in non-Christian lands, accompanied by signs, miracles and wonders, had not yet been captured in the age of cinematography.

These visual tools, called docu-miracle films/videos, that were created by recording those apostolic crusades and biblical wonders *live*–were not for church entertainment. They were conceived to capture the messages and miracles of some of T. L. and Daisy's historic evangelism crusades. Ultimately, they were used to attract people to hear the gospel and see it confirmed by miracles.

Today thousands of those films/videos (as well as other video and audio materials, including Bible courses for study and for public evangelism) are circulated internationally in nearly eighty languages. Ten of T. L.'s most effective miracle crusade sermons, called "The Big Ten," are among these. Gospel workers in scores of nations used them, attracting large crowds. They have proven to be among the most effective tools for evangelism yet. They were produced for reaching the unreached, for national church growth, and for home-front witnessing among the unconverted.

The Osborn ministry's wealth of cinematography provides effective ministry tools to use in schools, colleges, universities, summer camps, vacation centers, nurses training schools, orphanages, homes for unwed mothers, alcoholic and narcotic rehabilitation institutes, government projects, military bases, and special housing projects. Hospitals, homes for the aged, sanitariums, institutions for the handicapped, shelters, prisons, juvenile detention centers, refugee camps, and scores of other places have proven to be wonderful environments for this type of evangelism. Even deaf people can watch a film. Blind people can listen to the audio recording. These docu-miracle films/videos are normally admitted on an educational basis, and the presenter is given liberty to speak before or after the film/video showing.

Mobile Evangelism Units

Osborn Ministries International has furnished scores of four-wheel drive mobile vehicles equipped with films, projectors, giant screens, generators, public-address systems, audio cassettes, and cassette players, plus hundreds of tons of literature for evangelism worldwide. These mobile vehicles are called Mobile Evangelism Units and are considered to be evangelism combines, harvesting great numbers of souls through the use of Osborn Multimedia Gospel Tools. The Osborns mentor and train believers for gospel ministry worldwide, through their Multimedia Gospel Tools, which includes anointed messages and dynamic Bible and ministry training courses.

Part Four

Tragedy,

Trauma,

Triumph

Chapter 12

Wonderful Daisy

My wonderful and loving wife

for almost fifty-four years,

My patient companion and teammate

in the Lord's work

from the date of our marriage

on April 5, 1942,

My trusted colleague and associate

in mass miracle evangelism

in seventy-four nations of the world,

My courageous and untiring co-worker

in God's No. 1 Job of ministering

love in our hurting world,

My special confidant and counselor

in every phase and outreach of

our world ministries to millions,

My most cherished and loving friend,

My intimate and faithful sweetheart, and

the one and only Special Lady in my life,

Daisy Marie Washburn Osborn.

(T. L.'s tribute to his wife–who passed away in 1995–
in his book, *Why? Tragedy, Trauma, Triumph*)

After Daisy

Daisy Marie Washburn Osborn passed away on May 27, 1995. She had endured a very tough mission in Asia, suffering a leg injury in Malaysia where she was holding a conference. Then she had to undergo a painful fourteen-hour flight to England, and traveled by car more than a hundred miles to join T. L. for a British campmeeting. She then made yet another agonizing jour-ney–one that involved a ten-hour flight to Chicago, Illinois, and another to Tulsa, Oklahoma. After a three-month recovery, she conducted a historic Pan-American Women's Conference and then another National Conference in Brasilia, Brazil. In each of these conferences, she ministered to thousands. Then she headed to Hawaii to conduct a Pacific Conference for Women–*but Daisy's lungs were in trouble.*

She kept driving herself, despite two rather recent major bouts with pneumonia, one in India and another in Columbia, which took place before all of the aforementioned ministry engage-ments. In India she had coped with stifling heat and excessive humidity, while being intermittently chilled by oscillating fans as she ministered. Then she was exposed to air conditioning that ran at its maximum in the hotel between her meetings. In Bogota,

Columbia, during her Women's Conference and their Mass Miracle Crusade, she had to cope with an untimely cold and rainy spell while ministering in an open, damp, and cold concrete coliseum at an altitude of 8,000 feet, where it was almost impossible for a non-acclimatized person to get warm. Although her lungs had filled again and she was running a high fever, she kept preaching and ministering to thousands of women, day after day.

Daisy Osborn was a woman of tremendous faith who had seen miracle after miracle, healing after healing in her own meetings—even the raising of the dead. Once she almost died of malaria in Africa, but she was healed. Another time in Asia, a deadly infection invaded her throat and lungs, leaving her fevered and delirious, but she was healed. But this time her healing did not manifest on this side of heaven.

About four days before she transcended this life, she told T. L., "Ask our friends not to hold me here any longer by their prayers. I have finished my earthly course. My seed will run with the message. Keep the television off. Turn off the telephones. I want the room quiet. I'm watching for my Jesus to come for me. He's coming very soon. I am at peace." Daisy went home four months shy of seventy-one years of age.

At the memorial service to commemorate Daisy's life and ministry, John Osteen, pastor at the time of Lakewood Church in Houston, Texas, stated, "When you talk about Daisy, you talk about T. L. When you talk about T. L. you talk about Daisy. They are inseparable—always have been." That is why T. L. Osborn's legacy cannot be shared without much of Daisy's own legacy woven intricately into its fabric. She has much to reflect, by her own life and ministry, of who he is.

But Mama Did!

They say, "Women cannot preach."

But Mama did!

They say, "Women cannot pastor."

But Mama did!

They say, "Women cannot hear from God directly."

But Mama did!

They say, "Women cannot have a husband, and children and a ministry."

But Mama did!

They say, "Mothers cannot travel with their children and give them a good education."

But Mama did!

They say, "Women cannot properly juggle marriage, motherhood and ministry."

But Mama did!

They say, "Women cannot use their own name."

But Mama did!

They say, "Wives cannot contribute equally in the ministry with their husbands."

But Mama did!

They say, "Mothers cannot have a good relationship with their daughters."

But Mama did!

They say, "Women cannot trust other women."

But Mama did!

They say, "Married women cannot have close friendships with other women."

But Mama did!

They say, "Successful women do not share their spotlight with other women."

But Mama did!

They say, "Women are emotional and cannot avoid being deceived."

But Mama did!

They say, "Women cannot proclaim the Gospel with power."

But Mama did!

They say, "Women cannot fully represent Jesus."

But Mama did!

They say, "Women in ministry cannot capture the respect of heads of state."

But Mama did!

They say, "Christian women cannot function in roles of great authority."

But Mama did!

They say, "No individual woman can influence the events of entire nations."

But Mama did!

They say, "Women cannot cast out devils."

But Mama did!

They say, "Women cannot heal the sick."

But Mama did!

They say, "Wives cannot fulfill an individual divine call to ministry."

But Mama did!

They say, "Women do not leave behind seed."

But Mama did!

In tribute to Reverend Daisy Washburn Osborn
1923-1995
By her daughter the Reverend LaDonna C. Osborn

Acquainted with Grief

T. L. decided to journal this tragedy, trauma, and its culminating, ultimate triumph in his life so that he wouldn't forget what he thought and how he felt–so he could eventually write for people, because everybody eventually will lose someone. For the young "invincible" generation that, for the most part, is unacquainted with this kind of experience and has given little to no thought about its ramifications, there's some great insight here to be passed on.

T. L. Osborn has lived long enough and endured enough of life's challenges to make a convincing contribution in how to survive life's tragedies. Of T. L. and Daisy's four children, three of them were surrendered back to God. Marie LaVonne, born in 1943, lived only a few days. The very next week, a pastor asked the couple to sing at the funeral of a baby. Though grief-stricken by their own loss, T. L. and Daisy decided that they could do it; and so they did.

Their only son, Tommy Lee Osborn, Jr., born in 1945, died at the age of thirty-four. Four days after his homegoing, Daisy and T. L.–again sustaining deep grief, exceptionally deep grief–were packing suitcases to leave for ministry across France and then on to Africa, where they witnessed enormous crusades and again found healing as they were willing to go and bring healing to others. It happened again–when their third daughter, Mary Elizabeth, was born in 1950, and only lived a few moments. Within two weeks following that tragedy, T. L. and Daisy left for the historic crusades in Cuba.

Tragedy and Trauma Must Not Triumph

In T.L.'s book, *Why? Tragedy, Trauma, Triumph,* he chose to share some significant experiences surrounding Daisy's demise. Though both the chronicling and publishing of this material were quite difficult for him, he found it needful–because tragedy and trauma are universal, and a significant part of life is learning to grow through adversity. He states that while tragedy and trauma are a part of life, they must not have the last word–*they must not triumph.*

The readers, who journey with T. L. through the odyssey of his dark night of devastation following Daisy's passing, arrive with him at the dawn of a new day, surveying with him the new vista of life that is worth living–even amidst a changed landscape. They discover with him a serene and biblical secret for overcoming tragedy and trauma, and stand with him victorious on triumph's summit, at a new beginning–blurred but not blinded, dismayed but not dissuaded, wounded but not wasted, bruised but not broken.

Tragedy is universal and strikes in many forms–flood, fire, storm, bankruptcy, divorce, disease, death, and so on. T. L.'s particular stance in regard to this is that, in the midst and in the wake of it all, there is strength to be found for tough times, ease for the pain caused by the loss, seed courage to not quit on life, the healing power of treasured memories, and God's love that enables one to transcend trauma and ultimately triumph in life. A synopsis of his very sensitive, transparent teaching–*Why? Tragedy, Trauma, Triumph*–is the subject of the remainder of this chapter.

Untapping New Resources

Writing this book was a way to heal my pain and that of others who have or will experience something of a similar nature. It was a way to clarify some answers, to help people value life—even when the scenery changes—to motivate a fresh embrace of memories with a positive perspective, inducing a re-focus on God' miracle-Love. And if that is truly what happens with this teaching, then it will be worth all the tears that I shed while putting it together.

When it comes to experiencing loss, the greatest possible trauma is to lose faith and hope. If those flames are extinguished, then one is dead although his or her heart still beats. Anguish and sorrow can be overwhelming.

Amidst that anguish and sorrow, memory plays a significant role. At each onslaught of emptiness following Daisy's death, I have learned to take command of my emotions, to analyze what and where the pain is, then to examine my feelings and to guard my mental equilibrium. I query, *Am I indulging in self-pity?*

Then, always, I return to the premise: *Distress is induced by one's own thoughts. We have the power to alter our thinking.* I do not want my memories of Daisy to dissipate. Reflection on our lives and love together is a treasury for me. But I must view my memories with a new perspective—with gratitude and not with remorse. I must embrace the facts of life and discover the beauty of my altered vista.

I have learned that I can reconcile with change. I had never before lived alone. So I had to learn to value life and to function—*without Daisy,* accepting the fact that her earthly life had ended.

Her physical presence was no longer mine to touch. Her brilliant mind, her counsel, her wisdom were no longer accessible to me. I had to reconcile with life *as it is now for me.*

Delight Rather than Distress

I had to modify my thinking and re-ponder my memories of Daisy with delight, rather than with remorse. The years we shared together were full of priceless memories that constantly rekindle courage and inspiration for me.

Putting this brave philosophy into practice has been easier said than done, but I continue doing it, because I am one of Christ's living *"witnesses"* (Acts 5:32). My life has purpose. I am part of a hurting world. God and His healing grace are reflected through me. I am vital to His love plan for people.

God Is a Good God

It was just over a year after Daisy passed, that I decided to begin this chronicling of events that led to this message. I was in the third city of the ex-Soviet Union–Novosibirsk. It was the cultural and economic capital of the vast Siberian region. I was alone in my small hotel room that measured 7 ½ by 12 feet in size, with a 4 ½ by 6 feet space for a toilet stool, a basin, and a tiny tub–with only cold water. I had a few hours before my plane left, so I put my pen in hand.

God is not the author of devastation and chaos. Humanity is God's offspring. We have an enemy whom the Bible calls satan. He is the one who *"comes to steal, to kill, and to destroy"* (John 10:10).

GOD IS A GOOD GOD. He never sends evil or calamity or disaster. These are the works of the destroyer–the brutal one. God created Adam and Eve and then *"planted a garden eastward in Eden; and there he put those whom he had formed. And out of the ground He made to grow every tree that is pleasant to the sight, and good for food…and…gold that is good, and bdellium and onyx stone [rivers and treasures of all kinds]"* (Genesis 2:8-12, paraphrase mine). He created only goodness and beauty for humankind to enjoy.

When Adam and Eve were separated from Him through disobedience, their lives became dominated by the evil one–the murderer–the destroyer. The result was: *"God saw that people's wickedness became great in the earth, and that every imagination of the thoughts of their hearts was only evil continually. And it repented the LORD that He had made them on the earth, and it grieved Him at His heart"* (Genesis 6:5-6, paraphrase mine).

But even in the agony of God's anguish over humanity's disobedience and enslavement to satan, He did not abandon them. He provided redemption through the gift of His Son who assumed our guilt and endured our judgment so that we might live. *"God so loved the world, that He gave His only begotten Son, that whosoever believed in Him should not perish, but have everlasting life. For God sent not his Son into the world to condemn the world; but that the world through Him might be SAVED"* (John 3:16-17 KJV, emphasis added).

God does not send pestilence, disease, calamity, and destruction. In the agony of confusion and loss, people look up and accuse God: "WHY have you done this thing? WHY have you allowed this dilemma, this tragedy, to occur?" But He is not the destroyer. He is the Healer, the Savior, the Provider, the Life-Giver. His will is never to send desolation and plague. He bestows cure and recovery. He is not the author of disease and death. He *"forgives all your iniquities,...heals all your diseases"* (Psalm 103:3). God is the Life-Giver. He is a GOOD God.

Satisfied with the Goodness of God

It is *the GOODNESS of God [that] leads people to repentance.* (Romans 2:4) When tragedy comes, although we may not comprehend the reasons nor the implications, we can trust him for what His Word tells us, and leave in His hands what we may not understand, being assured that *"the GOODNESS of God endureth continually"* (Psalms 52:1 KJV).

I cannot understand why my beloved Daisy was lifted from my side; but I can *abundantly utter the memory of His goodness, and I can sing of His righteousness.* (Psalms 145:7.) Even in my befuddled quandary, I can fully trust God's immeasurable GOODNESS, *knowing "that all things work together for good to them that love God, to them who are the called according to His purpose* (Romans 8:28 KJV). I am one of "the called" ones, involved in "His purpose."

Despite my personal sorrow and painful sense of loss, life must continue because people need God's help; and I, as any believer, am "chosen" as one of His communicators. My mission is to abundantly utter the memory of God's great GOODNESS, and to sing of His RIGHTEOUSNESS. (Psalms 145:7.) I am resolved that I shall be satisfied with God's GOODNESS (Jeremiah 31:14), as He has counted me worthy of this calling to fulfill all the good pleasure of His GOODNESS, and His work of faith with power. (2 Thessalonians 1:11.)

The Big Plus Side of the Balance

When the heart-wrenching *WHYS?*, swell up inside me, rather than to question Daisy's not being raised up to continue with me in life, I ponder afresh, with jubilation, the tens of thousands of people who have been raised up in our ministries. I look at the plus side of the balance that is loaded with multitudes of answered prayers, triumphs, victories, healings and miracles. The seemingly negative side of the balance that I view, with its baffling *WHYS?*, because of Daisy's demise, can be surrendered with dignity and consolation to His FAITHFULNESS.

I am sure that even this one case of apparent unanswered prayer, though painful for me now, will eventually be shown to be on God's big PLUS side of the balance. I can rest in His faithfulness.

No, I am not desolate. *"Though I walk through the valley of the shadow of death [as I have done], I will fear no evil: for You are with me; Your rod and Your staff, they comfort me"* (Psalm 23:4). *"I have walked in mine integrity: I have TRUSTED also in the LORD… I have walked in Thy truth…that I may publish with the voice of thanksgiving, and tell of all Thy wondrous works…I will walk in mine integrity…My foot standeth in an even place. In the [great] congregations [of the world], I WILL BLESS THE LORD"* (Psalm 26, emphasis added).

I will enjoy the memories and give thanks. In reconciling with reality, day by day, and hour by hour, my memory bank became my comfort zone as I learned to replay the scenes of mine and Daisy's life and ministry together with delight rather than to drown myself in despair. Our years together had been good years, marvelous times, miraculous episodes, and loving memories.

Peter said that *"the trial of your faith, [is] much more precious than gold that perisheth"* (1 Peter 1:7). Paul admonished, *"In everything give thanks"* (1 Thessalonians 5:18). He didn't say "for" everything, but "in" everything. Each morning, I awaken with gratitude for all that God IS to me. I do not calculate my loss; I contemplate so much that remains—so much that makes me see that life is truly worth living.

I Still Had Today...to Learn and to Grow

The Bible speaks of Abel's righteous witness, and how that God testified of his gifts, by which *HE BEING DEAD YET SPEAKS.* (Hebrews 11:4.) We all leave our legacy of influence after our earthly life has ended. Our thoughts, our words, and our actions become the seeds of our lives that we sow—our legacy. Daisy has left hers, and it is rich.

We leave our mark on those who follow us. We are chiseling the image of life that we believe in. We may not have tomorrow to improve that image, and yesterday has already gone. But today is ours; and with our right of choice, we can improve our legacy to others. It can be better as we continue learning. I still have today. I choose to improve on my legacy and to continue learning. Knowing that I can do this, with God's help, has given me courage to face each new day with purpose and gladness for the wonder of life.

Daisy had finished her course triumphantly and had gone on to her reward, but my mission had not ended. I knew that people could not draw strength from me if I allowed myself to vegetate in grief.

I learned to refocus the present moment—*this* hour, *this* day. I learned to avoid wasting my energy in pondering loss. The life that remained seemed more valuable than before, as Daisy's passing had caused mortality to become more graphic. Every remaining day must count for God—and for the hurting world in which I live. I cast down imaginations that were contrary to God. (2 Corinthians 10:5.) And God gave me grace, to not merely survive or continue existing, *but to grow.*

At seventy-two, I had to take a new look at life. Returning from a trip to Russia, I had looked at the beautiful lawn and gardens of roses and trees that Daisy and I had beheld together as we sat on our patio spending glorious hours eating, talking, praying, reading our Bibles or mail, discussing our problems, planning our crusades, and expressing love. Now I had to learn to love and enjoy and value my world by myself—without Daisy. I had to discover myself—without Daisy.

God's Message in the Flowers

Soon after returning from Russia, I had to travel back across the Atlantic to minister at Ulf Eckman's campmeeting in Uppsala, Sweden. Two weeks after that, I would minister at Peter Gammons' campmeeting in England, and then fly back across Scandinavia to minister for a week in Helsinki, Finland, where thousands would jam the big Ice Arena daily.

Between Sweden and England, my option was to return to Tulsa for two weeks or to stay in Europe. Since I had my laptop computer with me, I could work on projects that were urgent, so I chose to spend those two weeks in the village of Thirsk, England.

Two Weeks of Self-Discovery

I checked myself into the quaint and picturesque Golden Fleece Hotel, Market Place, Thirsk, North Yorkshire. I was able to book Room 4, where the sun shined in through a rather large window overlooking the village town square.

In the mornings and evenings, I would go out for long walks. There were many pathways and sidewalks in the residential areas. The British people love to walk. I was fascinated by their manicured cottage gardens and by the beauty of their roses and multitudes of other flowers. I was captivated by the wall-mounted flower boxes, hanging flower pots, standing boxes—every shape and style of flower container meticulously arranged in every available space around entryways and on cottage walls.

Flowers of Tulsa—in England

I reflected on my trauma following Daisy's demise in regard to our rose beds and other flowers at our home in Tulsa. We always had rose beds, which I tended with great care, because Daisy loved roses. I tried to always keep bouquets in our kitchen, living room, bedroom, and even bathroom when we were home.

I enjoyed going out in the mornings to cut roses—bringing them in, trimming the stems, and arranging them in our collection of vases. Daisy always added finishing touches and lovingly placed them about in our house. She would smell each rose that I had cut.

What Good Is a Rose–Without Love

But after Daisy died, I had walked out onto our patio, bordered by a special bed of roses, and had been emotionally stunned by the thought: *What good is a ROSE without LOVE?* That notion haunted me for weeks.

I walked among those neat little British cottages in Thirsk, England, admiring the luxuriant flower gardens and the hanging flower baskets spilling their kaleidoscopic array of opulent blossoms. I paused often and I reminisced. I wept by myself there along those pathways, remembering the times that Daisy and I had meandered by our flower gardens, drawing inspiration from the tranquil atmosphere.

Provoking Questions as I Learned About T. L.

I began to ask myself: *Why are you so attracted by the flowers and the charm of these English gardens? Pondering their splendor is bringing back a thousand memories of you and Daisy together. Is this good for you?*

I began to observe something about myself–about T. L. without Daisy. For fifteen lonely months, I had been struggling to get acquainted with ME–without Daisy. Since her demise, I had not been able to tend our roses. They made her absence too vivid, because they bespoke our love and life together. I felt that I could never grow roses or hang flowers on our patio again.

But now I was asking myself: *Who am I? Do I like flowers? Do flowers bring ME joy? Or did I just hang them there for Daisy?*

God's Grace Displayed for Me

There I was, walking among the cottages of a quaint little English village, drawing inspiration from each blossom. I suddenly realized that I was discovering something about T. L. Osborn, the man whom I did not know—*alone*. I leaned over the little fences or neat stone walls there in Thirsk to touch the blossoms. I savored the rich aroma of the roses. Their fragrance made me sense Daisy. It was like a visit with her. She seemed to be with me.

But I was making a discovery, as well, about *me*. I loved flowers. *ME!* I loved them. I drew strength and inspiration from their beauty. They were displaying the grace and beauty of God—to me. They were God's gift to me. God was reaching out to me through each blossom, reminding me:

> *I love you, T. L. My grace is abundant toward you. I am here with beauty and fragrance, with form and glory, for you. Life around you is beautiful—always.*
>
> *Don't miss it. You are learning to walk alone—without Daisy.*
>
> *I am with you. I will never leave you nor forsake you. Don't miss my presence, my glory, my loveliness, my companionship.*

I was embracing the presence of God and His love for me in a new way. I was realizing how much I loved beauty and fragrance and that it all bespoke of God's love—for me. I felt sublime waves of healing love penetrating me through these flowers. They were giving me messages of love—from God.

I Will Plant Roses Again!

I made a decision there in the village of Thirsk, England. I told myself, *Next spring, I will plant roses again. I will surround myself with flowers, and they will express the fragrance and beauty of nearly fifty-four years with my sweetheart.*

In April of 1997–two years after Daisy's demise–I planted a beautiful rose bed and hung geraniums and begonias on my patio. Their fragrance is a witness of God's unfailing presence in my life.

Liberation in Music

Daisy and I had always had a piano in our home, but I decided to buy myself a bigger, nicer one. So I went on a search and bought a nearly-new, nine-foot, Baldwin concert grand. I love to play the piano. It provides an emotional outlet, releases my tensions, and helps me when I am writing. If I find myself in a stall-out for words or thoughts, I play the piano. Everything becomes free again. There is liberation in music.

I am learning to see more and more beauty along my new journey. I expect good things–beautiful things, albeit *different* things. I have decided to adapt where necessary because my life–even alone–has value.

We Have a Choice

I am resolved that my remaining life shall be a legacy of faith for those who follow me. Others have influenced and inspired me, like Daisy has, with her sun-filled life and example. It is still my time to influence and inspire those who may need to draw strength from my example. Tragedy, trauma, and devastating and demoralizing loss occur in life. They come in many forms. But we can survive if we *will* to live. We have a choice.

No one is an island. Our lives are intertwined. We are part of each other. We mark people by our example, for better or for not-so-good. (Romans 1:14.) I am a debtor to the people in my world. We are not our own; we are bought with a price. (1 Corinthians 6:20.) We are members of Christ (1 Corinthians 6:15), and of one another. (Ephesians 4:25.) I belong to God's family and am part of His plan. I count. That gives dignity to life and nobility to living.

Yes, my choice power is my control center. After the storm has swept past, then the tragic loss is realized. But a new inventory is made. Whatever remains is appraised; and, with those precious remnants, the journey of life is resumed. It is starkly different, but it is *life*. And it must go on—the sun will rise again. No one has a license to quit on living.

At my age, I chose not to love another spouse—though I could have chosen otherwise. But, on the other hand, I knew that I must choose to LOVE again—to love people, to love a hurting world, to love the ministry, to love crusading and conducting seminars, to love teaching and preaching, and healing the sick and suffering.

Chapter 13

Most Significant Mission Yet

Following Daisy's demise, I undertook the most difficult, yet extraordinary and strategic mission I had undertaken yet. My daughter LaDonna went with me. We ministered across Eurasia in a succession of strategic Miracle Life Conferences in major cities of the ex-Soviet Union, some of which were: Bishkek, the capital of Khyrzykstan (at the foothills of the Tien Chan mountain range of west China); Novosibirsk, the business capital of remote Siberia; Perm, principal trade center of the Ural Mountains; Minsk, capital of Belarus (a country in Eastern Europe); Murmansk, the largest city north of the Arctic Circle; Alma-Ata, capital of Kazhakstan (only 150 miles from western China); Kharkov, second city of the Ukraine; Saint Petersburg and Moscow, the ancient and present capitals of Russia.

Every day we were sharing primarily with hundreds of young Russian preachers, both men and women, whose lives and minds had been subjugated by communist ideology. Marxist-Leninist indoctrination had demeaned the idea of God as being only a myth, and had demeaned religion as being an opiate–even a superstition.

Following the collapse of communism, gospel ministers had begun to share Christ's message of redemption among the ex-Soviet people. The young generation was responsive–eager to embrace the hope, faith, love, and life that the gospel gives to people.

I needed emotional healing for the painful loss of my beloved wife and for the loneliness I was suffering. LaDonna, who was close to her mother, had lost her best counselor and confidant. We believed that healing would begin in us as we brought healing to others–just as it had in times past. We both knew that sharing God's life with others would quicken His life within us.

Largest Cities of Ex-Soviet Union

June-October, 1996. LaDonna and I resolved to minister for a full week in each of the largest cities of the ex-Soviet Union. I received the $50,000 insurance money from Daisy's life insurance policy, and instead of depositing it, I sent it straight to the publishing house in Minsk, Belarus, to be applied to the publication of ten of our major books in the Russian language. For the first edition, we printed about twenty-two tons of books, and later printed another twenty tons to be given away to new believers all across the ex-Soviet Union.

Nothing had ever given me greater satisfaction, than to see thousands of ex-communists turn to the Lord Jesus Christ. In every city, the response was the same. The auditoriums were packed full, and often many were unable to gain entrance.

Following the miracle meetings in the capital city of Moscow, we went to Russia's ancient, historic capitol of Saint Petersburg. Our next crusade was in the arctic city of Murmansk. God wrought special miracles among those tough, northern people.

From there, we went to Minsk, the capital of Belarus. Then we traveled over two thousand miles east to Alma-Ata, the capital of Kazakhstan, and to Beshpek in Kirghizstan, both of which were Muslim cities on the western border of China. Then we went north into the vast Oblast of Siberia, to the great cities of Perm and Novosibirsk. Thousands of lives were changed in each of these historic events.

From Siberia, we flew a thousand miles to the south for our next crusade in the extreme eastern city of Kharkhov, Ukraine, that nation's ancient capital. Then we flew back north to Moscow. All across this vast territory, we looked into the eyes of people who had existed for over seventy years in a total spiritual void, with absolutely no knowledge of God and no freedom to worship Him or to pray to Him.

During the Kirghizstan crusade, someone presented a gift to me that was inestimable in value. Under the dictatorship of Stalin, Russian believers secretly translated parts of my book, *Healing the Sick,* and typed it on an old typewriter, making three carbon copies at a time. One of those dim and torn copies had survived. That script had been sewn together with some old oil cloth for a cover, and had been passed secretly into the hands of many people who were sick, even incurable. A dear man brought that precious document to our meeting and presented it to me publicly.

Following that meeting, a big gentleman came to tell me that he was one of the people to whom the typed script had been loaned. He had been bedfast for three years due to unsuccessful operations on his spine. As he read the manuscript in secret, he had been instantly healed. He wanted me to know what God had done for him, through the truths that we had presented in that book.

In these ex-Soviet Republics, every time we invited the un-converted to accept Christ, hundreds and hundreds of people pressed toward the platform and packed the space, praying with tears to receive Jesus as their Savior. During our ministry in Mos-cow, people converged on the meeting from 210 different cities of the ex-Soviet Union. What a joy to place our ten major books into the hands of each adult who attended these meetings. These books would be transported into hundreds of villages and towns throughout the rural areas of these great republics.

A young pastor said to me, "Five years ago we didn't know that there is a God. Now we've learned to know about Him and we've believed on Christ. We are telling others and they are being saved." Then he added with a big smile, "Now I have five churches and a Bible school. Your books have solved our problem. We are young in faith and didn't know what to teach the people, but now your books will become our Bible school courses. We thank you for coming and bringing us your books."

Four Great Cities of Poland

July-August, 1997. Crusades were held in four great cities of Poland. For a long time, Poland had been on my heart. Mis-sionary Harold Groves had managed to win the good will of the

Polish authorities and of certain Baptist and Catholic leaders, who welcomed him to their formal churches to speak and to show the docu-miracle films of our crusades that we gave him to take into Poland. For each trip that he made into Poland, we would provide a projector and more films, always telling him to leave them in the country with the preachers, so they could continue sowing the seed of the gospel.

We made this investment for many years in this great nation, so when the communist walls crumbled, I had a great desire to go to Poland myself. We took steps to translate and publish our ten major books in the Polish language. Then we organized crusades in four of the largest cities–Szczecin, Wroclaw, Katowice, and the capital city of Warsaw.

We spent a full week in each city, teaching for two hours each morning and each evening, Monday through Friday. Then on Saturday and Sunday, we conducted great public miracle rallies to demonstrate to the people what we had taught during the week. Only God knew what revolutionary changes were to follow in this nation, after these powerful weeks of strategic teaching, and the public miracle rallies, all coupled with distibution of our ten major books. I feel this was one of the most significant missions I have ever conducted.

The Polish people had been enslaved by communism. They were searching for spiritual reality in their lives. At Katowice, thousands of people were attracted by the Good News that we proclaimed on a large open-air sports field, where tens of thousands of people gathered for our public miracle rallies. The extraordinary miracles that God wrought, showed them that the Jesus of the Bible is unchanged today.

One man was astounded when his left arm, that had been paralyzed and atrophied, became normal. He raised his hand, moved his arm, clenched his fist, and wept as he told the people about the miracle he had received. The multitude applauded wildly as they saw this wonder of God. One individual after another flooded onto the platform, after we had preached and led the multitude in a prayer of accepting Jesus Christ. Then we had prayer for the sick and instructed them on how to put their faith into action.

Communist propaganda had insisted that God is a myth and that religion is an opiate, but that day on that big open field, as well as in each of the cities in Poland where we had been ministering, the beautiful Polish people were seeing for themselves that the Bible is as true today as it was in the Church's early days.

One man who had not been able to walk for years came up the steps. He had been instantly healed. He threw his canes away and showed the people what a miracle he had received, as he bent his legs, doubled his back, jumped up and down as high as he could, and then ran from one side of the platform to the other.

A dear woman was weeping uncontrollably, as she told the people that she had been suffering terrible pain in her head for seven months. The neurologist had offered her no help. That day she was made free from all pain. Another lady came forward who had not been able to raise her left arm, now she had received Jesus as her Savior and her arm was perfectly healed.

Many who were deaf were healed. Blind people recovered their sight. One woman, whose right leg was swollen and inflamed, was made perfectly whole. A young man, who had been an asthmatic since his youth, was completely healed. He had almost died several times, but could now breathe completely free.

Poland has been ravaged and pillaged by war on many occasions. Today a new future of hope and love is being formed in the lives of the people there. Despite near total annihilation more than once in its past, Poland is now on the rise; this time with faith in God.

Kiev, Ukraine

July 2000. Kiev, the capital and largest city of Ukraine, is an important industrial, scientific, educational, and cultural centre of Eastern Europe. Our crusade there was probably the most significant and historic that I had ever experienced. It was the first mass miracle evangelistic crusade that was ever allowed out on an open public terrain in the history of the ex-Soviet Union.

The multi-level, ex-communist government in Kiev argued that religion belongs inside buildings, not in the open air, so they wanted to keep our meetings indoors. I told them that we did not have a religion, but that we are bringing the living Christ to the people, and since He always ministered to the multitudes out in the open air, that's what we wanted to do in Kiev. Finally, with the help of some parliamentarians favorable to the gospel, we obtained the permits.

The crowds poured onto the enormous field. Hundreds of automobiles lined the roads and the main road was like a river of walking people that flowed from the trains, trams, and public transportation vehicles to the crusade field. The repercussions of this apostolic crusade were phenomenal. Young pastors across the ex-Soviet Union would be imitating what we were doing there.

I preached on the subject, "Something Better than Religion." I painted the vivid pictures of religions around the world, and then I contrasted what it must have been like to attend Jesus' meetings in Galilee. The people were rivetingly intrigued to hear me compare orthodox religion in the Ukraine with the beautiful, miraculous ministry of Jesus as He, out on open fields, taught the multitudes and healed their sick. I related many cases in the Bible where Jesus healed the sick, diseased, crippled, blind, and those who were insane. Following each Bible case, I related similar cases that we have witnessed in our meetings around the world. This made it possible to present the Bible record with great clarity and reality to the people. I kept reminding myself that these were people who had never in their lives known about God or the Bible.

Thousands in tears responded by accepting Jesus Christ as their Savior and Lord. Then it was easy to lead them in prayer for healing, by encouraging them to put their faith into action. Across the field, healings became obvious. Small groups here and there began to exhibit excitement and commotion in the crowd as some cripple or some sick person suddenly received his or her healing. At one point I counted thirty or forty canes, several pairs of crutches, and four wheelchairs that were raised above the heads of the people in the multitude that crowded before the platform.

We Have So Much to Share

Daisy and I had been living witnesses *together*–in seventy-four nations and for over a half century–of the power and effectiveness of preaching the gospel with signs following. Since my wife's demise, I have continued in this ministry to many additional nations. With God's help, I will carry to fruition the projects Daisy and I planned together–projects that she did not get to finish with me. We have so much to share with the coming generation so they can benefit by what we have learned.

Chapter 14

A Sustaining Ministry

T. L. Osborn and his ministry have endured over the years with great respect and integrity. *T.L. has been, in many ways, more respected by other evangelists than any other man. There was a moral seriousness about the Osborn ministry and about the Osborns themselves, which impressed their peers. While the miraculous healings that his meetings were noted for were often of near-unbelievable nature and there were those of his era who embellished their reports of success, those who did the major publicizing of this particular revival found T. L. to be a scrupulously honest reporter.* T.L. has continually been known for his strict regard for what was right, even during a time when it was not uncommon to compromise moral character for success, big offerings, notoriety or big crowds.

LaDonna expressed that her father never knew how to say, "I had a special anointing. I had a special call. I had a special touch." People come to him yet today and ask, "Would you please lay your hands on me. I just want a double portion."

He just looks at them and asks, "What do you mean—'a double portion' *of what?*"

"Well, like Elijah and Elisha."

He says, "Oh, that was Old Testament. Now what *I* have is what *you* have. I have *Jesus*. I have His Spirit. You have Him. Why would you want anything from me when you can receive it directly from Him? It's the same thing! Do you want a double portion of Elijah? *I want one portion of Jesus."*

Sacrifice and Perseverance

What T. L. and Daisy did, when it came to mass miracle evangelism in non-Christian nations, was aggressive and earth-shaking. They went into unchartered territory ministry-wise; it was unfamiliar and exposed them to the possibility of hazard and danger. Some of the crusades were held in unstable, dangerous places of anarchy that appeared totally inappropriate and inopportune, when it came to both time and place for such a crusade. Their very lives were at risk on many occasions.

With all due credit being given to God–His love, mercy, grace, strength, power, understanding, ideas, and the list goes on forever–T. L. Osborn's lasting, transcendent ministry has not been the fruit of soft-bellied, fearful, haphazard, or slothful endeavor, but rather the relentless, assiduous, and sacrificial total surrender and investment of two brave souls in the service of their Lord. There has been the boarding of planes…walking across the tarmacs and winding through the corridors of foreign airports…sustaining time and climate changes… adapting to different food and living quarters and being crudely transported across all kinds of terrain.

They suffered inconvenience, discomfort, being unfashionable, and being looked at as crazy, worldly, or even brazenly egotistical. LaDonna said that her father has been called everything from apostle, to Jesus, to the devil. He and Daisy have been acquainted with persecution and rejection. As a result, what was unfamiliar and risky for them has now become familiar and safer terrain for today's generation, as they step in and reap where the Osborns have so bravely and sacrificially sowed.

Mass Miracle Evangelism

T. L. and Daisy conducted the first mass miracle crusades since the first century Church. They were the first to erect a big platform in parks or on fields or other terrains in non-Christian nations, preach the gospel publicly, and pray for God's miraculous confirmation that Jesus Christ is the same today as He was in Bible days. There were no choirs, no chairs, no aisles, no VIP sections, and no formal preliminaries–nothing but the Bible, a sound system, some lighting, and raw, hurting humanity...nothing but that bold, simple witness and multitudes of hurting people gathering to experience the life of Jesus Christ.

Close to seventy of T.L. Osborn's eighty-some years have been spent touching millions in nearly one hundred nations in national crusades and seminars. For over sixty years, he has preached to multitudes of 20,000 to over 300,000 daily in mass gospel crusades, covering seventy-four nations. T. L. and Daisy have probably reached and led more people to Christ in non-Christian nations, than any other ministry couple to date. The Osborn family has probably also witnessed more great healing miracles than any family that has lived—"not because of any special faith," T. L. would assert, "but simply because we began this global ministry so early in life and have ministered to so many multitudes, in so many nations, for so many years."

The ministry of T.L. and Daisy has made an unprecedented impact on the world. Their style of mass evangelism had not been witnessed since the epoch of the early Church. T.L. and Daisy were the first to go onto open fields in foreign nations, in what is today called crusades, and invite everyone to come. They addressed audiences of tens of thousands throughout the dangerous years of nationalism when foreign political domination was being repulsed by the awakening third-world nations.

In addition, T. L. and Daisy announced publicly to these masses that, if Christ is alive, they, as the Bible teachers, can pray and expect Him to do the same wonders that He did before He was crucified; but, if He is only a historic, religious figure, then His name will have no power in prayer, nor will He do wonders today as He did in Bible days. They had discovered that undeniable miracles, wrought by Christ, are the proof that turns people from dead religion to the miracle life of Jesus Christ. And it has been the occurrence of miracles as proof that Jesus rose from the dead and is alive that has made for a believable gospel message and a believable ministry through this couple.

T. L. and Daisy ignited a worldwide renaissance of apostolic faith for physical miracles to confirm the gospel. These miracles—that made for mass miracle evangelism—are the hallmark of Osborn Ministries International, and have had much to do with this being a sustaining ministry.

Simplicity of the Gospel: Relevant – not Relativistic

In more than one respect, T. L. Osborn's story is about a man who was ahead of his time. It's about a ministry that was sent to give us an earnest representation of what was going to finally hit-home for this day and hour for every believer. The focus and heart of his ministry has been *"Jesus in people"* and *"Jesus in every believer"*. T.L.'s ministry is different; it is *"about you"*–God's creation *everywhere*. And because of that, his ministry has sought to be sensitive and purposeful in getting the message of Jesus Christ *"to you"*–where the people live,–socially, economically, nationally, and religiously…in the most pertinent and effective way he could without compromising God's Word.

Simplicity, clarity, accessibility and applicability were obvious criteria for the messages that T.L. and Daisy preached to the world's masses. Jesus used simple, common illustrations and familiar terminology when He ministered to people. When asked, "What's God saying?" Dr. Osborn responds, "Well, read Matthew, Mark, Luke, and John and you will hear the message of God that is to be sent to the world."

T. L. stated in his book, *God's Love Plan,* "The Christian religion is bogged down with theological complexities. Society has almost relegated God and miracles to legend and superstition. Instead of relating God and faith to people and their needs, many relate Him only to church sanctuaries." The need in ministry to be *relevant,* not *relativistic,* has been something that T. L. Osborn has not only understood and embraced, but has literally pioneered for his day and age. Being relevant, has to do with being applicable to the behavior and beliefs characteristic of a particular social, ethnic, or age group. Being relevant means bearing upon or connected with the matter in hand–pertinent.

While the primary goal of the Church today is not cultural relevance, but rather drawing people to Jesus, cultural relevance should certainly be an objective. Cultural relevance is a powerful instrument used in drawing people to Him. T. L.'s "slanting" and "modifying" for the success of the youth revival in the United States in the late 1960's and into the 1970's were illustrative of becoming relevant for the sake of the gospel.

Relativistic, on the other hand, means that something is dependent upon external conditions for its specific nature, size, etc., as opposed to being absolute or independent. The gospel, itself, is not dependent upon a culture to determine its content. It does not change as societies change, when it comes to what is accepted as trendy, fashionable or status-quo. A relativistic church will water down the gospel to make it fit the culture, rather than let the gospel remain the absolute truth. In a relevant church, the gospel remains unchanged, but the methods of administering the gospel change in order to be more relevant to the people they are ministering to. T. L. has understood and embraced this, and has also implemented this with great skill. Being relevant and not relativistic has helped make Osborn Ministries International a sustaining ministry.

Adapting to Change

T. L. Osborn's success is based on his understanding that God's message is unchanging. In a world of change, he has managed to continually present an unchanging message to those who have never heard the fundamental message of the gospel. There is a difference between growing and maturing in our understanding of the gospel and yielding to the pressure of having a "new" message to be successful in ministry. It is easy to get caught up in the world's way of doing things. There's always something "new" and "improved" in our world today. We have embraced the idea that all these changes are "better". As Christians, we are growing and maturing in our knowledge and understanding of the gospel, and in that respect we are experiencing something "new".

When we refer to "something new or better," it's not a matter of this wave of God being better than those T. L. Osborn has ridden in times past. God continues to take us from glory to glory, to a fuller and greater revelation of Himself. God is not changing; *we are.* As a result of T.L.'s ministry, we will be better equipped to understand, experience and handle a message that is powerful and unchanging.

Some simply prefer the security and comfort that comes with being familiar with the way things have been done in the past. They don't want to transition from one move of God to the next. They know the words to all the songs of a certain move or they know all the "Who's Who" of a particular move. They are well-acquainted and well-versed in how the Spirit of God has generally flowed or how ministry has generally been administered in this particular move. They prefer settling down and clinging to the old way of doing things. They have set patterns of thought and behavior. They are content in only watching the new thing that is taking place around them and being critical. All these things have hindered the Church from fulfilling its purpose on the earth.

T. L. Osborn, however, has remained flexible and has been willing and able to transition when needed, and to do so quite effectively, while remaining anchored in the unchanging Word and power of God. He has been bent on "moving with God's cloud," not missing what God was doing in the present hour. Any changes that T.L. made were for the sake of God's changing emphasis, changing needs, or relevance. He never gave in to relativism or compromised the Word of God to please anyone.

T. L. has usually stayed ahead of God's moves or waves, because he has been a pioneer and that's what pioneers do. They go ahead of the crowd and blaze a way in the wilderness and forge new trails. Osborn was not one to stand pat. Where tradition and caution have characterized many orthodox ministries, Osborn has often set the trends, established the pace, and stayed in the forefront of evangelism by sheer faith and divine audacity. He constantly did something new.

T. L. has known when to observe what others are doing and copy it, if that's what worked. That is being a copycat in a good sense. He has even gone so far as to observe what the world was doing and adapted that for the gospel, if that's what worked. Even Jesus stated in the parable of the unjust steward that the *"master praised the dishonest (unjust) manager for acting shrewdly and prudently; for the sons of this age are shrewder and more prudent and wiser in [relation to] their own generation [to their own age and kind] than are the sons of light"* (Luke 16:8 AMP).

On the other hand, T.L. has also known when to have courage, be bold, and break molds when things did not work or no longer worked. This has been illustrated by the Osborn's implementation of praying for the sick en masse, as opposed to sticking with long healing lines and praying for the sick one at a time. During their open air meetings, T.L. and Daisy boldly declared that Jesus *will* heal and perform miracles.

Another remarkable illustration of being bold and daring, innovative and pacesetting, as well as being flexible and willing to transition, is found in T. L.'s ministry move in the late 1960's. He did another new thing when he diverted his attention, for the time being, away from the mission field and became involved in a youth revival in the United States. During the mid-1960's, the hippie subculture, which was originally a youth movement, had arisen. Its adherents did not follow the teachings of their elders. They rejected them for a different culture with its alternative lifestyle, radical beliefs, and unusual behavior, which included flagrant use of illegal drugs for expanding their consciousness, finding revelation within, and enjoying their experiences of ecstasy.

T.L. barnstormed the country delivering a three-lesson series designed to save modern youth. It began with a lesson entitled, "Conversion," billed as a mighty sermon for teen-agers on declining moral standards, then continued with a sermon entitled "God Is NOT Dead," a devastating answer to atheism and false theology, and concluded with a film featuring his overseas work, entitled, The Healer of Trinidad. T.L. used the "One Way" slogan, which became the mark of a national youth revival.

T. L. purposefully changed his method of delivery, slanting every message in language that makes sense to young people. He stated, "Many of the vandals and sex-perverts who run our streets today like wild animals, will be voted into state and national offices tomorrow. We'd better talk on their level, while we still have the chance."

It was a crucial time for emphasis on youth, so T. L. also put his focus there. He changed his vocabulary and his appearance, which included growing a beard and modifying his wardrobe to be able to appeal more and relate better to the younger generation. He urged his old-time followers, "Think young in your faith". T. L. Osborn, a youthful man in his mid-forties, came on as hip to the youth scene. He had moved with the revival to appeal to a quite different audience.

T. L.'s message on soulwinning, as presented in his book entitled, *Soulwinning*, revolutionized the church in the 1960's. It shifted the believer from the pew to the streets, sharing their faith with others. He proclaimed, "Hey, you don't have to wait for your preacher to do it; you do it!" It was groundbreaking, as he challenged the churches and individual believers: "You can't just be in your little church, under your steeple, and sing your songs, and be good…and win the world. You have to get out there." It had the flavor of what today is called "marketplace ministry." T. L. had already coined that expression, decades before it was common phraseology in Christian circles.

Throughout his ministry, T.L. has maintained a balance between knowing when to observe what others are doing and copy it, when to step out of the box and break molds, when to be bold and daring, or when to move when God moves "New" for T. L. Osborn has had to be for the sake of kingdom work. He was sensitive when it came to knowing when to change and when to transition, as well as *when not to*. He was very much his own man, but, even more, he has remained God's man—not to be bought or sold or to go with the flow for the sake of religious acceptance or the approval of man or anything else. And this has also made for sustaining ministry.

LaDonna stated, "That is one of the things that has caused this ministry to be so focused and, to me, very effective…because it's not doing more new things; it's doing the same thing to more new people; therefore, you touch the world."

Organization…Organization…Organization

In addition to a lot of fearless dedication and hard work, Osborn Ministries International has been a sustaining ministry because of something called "organization." There has to be organization for carrying out the complex details of a national evangelism crusade. Such details include clearing customs, dealing with border officials, choosing and contracting the crusade and/or seminar venue, getting shipments of evangelistic materials brought in, acquiring permits, getting papers signed, and meeting deadlines.

The crusades ideally have been planned with the knowledge and approval of the national government. If possible, they have started with a meeting with the president of the nation, to give him a thorough perspective of their purpose in coming to his nation. Sometimes they also met with other government officials, pastors, or pastoral associations. They also had to deal with the press, in order to organize and supervise publicity.

When it came to organizing these national evangelism crusades, knowledge, understanding, and spiritual sensitivity have been required on T. L.'s and Daisy's part, in regard to local and national strategies, processes, methods of operation, systems, programs, tactics, maneuvers, formulae, designs, grappling with the intrigue and intricacy of diverse governments and the present political climate, and working with nationalities, traditions, cultures, and religious postures.

T.L. and Daisy saw the need, as missionaries, to be ambassadors, so they stepped up to the plate to become global gospel diplomats, allowing themselves to be trained and polished, acquiring both natural and spiritual skill, perceptivity, wisdom, and expertise in handling negotiations and people, as well as in acquiring and managing the needed finances.

He Has Modeled Servanthood Leadership

T. L. Osborn has modeled *undergirding*, instead of *lording-over*, leadership in the body of Christ. He has modeled being touchable and personable, instead of elitist. He came in the spirit of a *servant-leader* and has been sold out to raising up, equipping, and releasing *all* believers to fulfill their potential and to realize their destinies in God. T. L. Osborn has modeled servanthood leadership worthy of imitation. As a result, he has made Jesus more real and being a Christian more desirable to the Christian world, as well as to the unsaved world who is looking in and searching for something real.

T. L. Osborn has demonstrated the veracity of the following scripture:

> *You know that the rulers of the Gentiles lord it over them,*
> *and those who are great exercise authority over them. Yet*

it shall not be so among you; but whoever desires to become great among you, let him be your servant. And whoever desires to be first among you, let him be your slave—just as the Son of Man did not come to be served, but to serve, and to give His life a ransom for many (Matthew 20:25-28 NKJV).

T.L. has been willing to be at the forefront of more than one movement; however, in both spirit and deed, he has modeled that being at the front is not synonymous with being high on a pedestal and better than the rest. *"Their lives are perpetual fashion shows…They love to sit at the head table at church dinners, basking in the most prominent positions, preening in the radiance of public flattery"* (Matthew 23:5-7 MSG). T. L. Osborn has exposed and discouraged controlling and domineering, competitive and ambition-gone-awry, and elitist Christianity, which makes for non-lasting, non-enduring ministry.

Jesus treated everybody the same. He regarded the lowest the same as the highest. He gave the same attention to beggars and lepers as He did to priests and dignitaries. T.L. has also demonstrated this throughout his ministry. Claiming no special anointing or call, he has been respected and remembered as being, "touchable." LaDonna recalls:

> *The young people, especially those who have grown up in the church, are truly sick of all the hype. They are sick of the polish, the plastic, the commercialism and the celebrity focus. This younger generation just wants to know if someone is real. The things about my father that evoke compliments from them, simply amaze him.*
>
> *He just comes in and sits in the middle section of the church and participates in worship. The children come*

over to him, like he's a normal person. People who come merely to see him are amazed that he's so touchable.

"Oh, you act like you really love people," some have commented to my father, as though they were quite surprised. Of course, he really loves people. That's our message – how much God loves people. Why wouldn't we do that and be that way if that's what we preach? Jesus did and taught – and in that order. (Acts 1:1.) I mean, my father just can't figure out why people would expect him to act any differently. But young people, oh my goodness – this is what impresses them.

T.L. also eradicated the word *esoteric* from the Christian vocabulary. *Esoteric,* means to be understood by or meant only for a select few. In essence, T.L. has given the body of Christ blueprints, by example and great gospel literature such as *The Best of Life* and *You Are God's Best,* for what is available to every believer. T. L. has made the words of 1 Peter 2:9, *"But ye are a chosen generation, a royal priesthood,"* real for the everyday person. We are *all* royalty.

The following encounter, recounted by a young minister from the hills of Tennessee portrays this principle so well. He followed the ministry of T. L. and Daisy Osborn, since his youth. When he was eighteen years old, he was privileged to be the guest singer in a meeting where they were the special speakers. Today, he is forty-six and a seasoned leader and a highly credible voice for this new generation. His encounter with T. L. and Daisy Osborn was unforgettable. It impacted and changed his life and ministry in a most distinct and positive way.

"We have one message – Christ and His ministry to forgive, heal and restore people to fellowship with God. Every person is included in God's great love-plan. This is the GOOD NEWS that Christ wants told!"

– T.L. & LaDonna Osborn

When Dr. T.L. saw Jesus alive in a vision in 1948, the ministries of T.L. & Daisy and their entire family – for generations to come – were forever changed. The healing power of Christ and His resurrection LIFE is the Osborns' central message.

Raised on the platforms of global miracle evangelism, Osborn daughter Dr. LaDonna's worldwide ministry is also marked by supernatural healing miracles. Why? Because Jesus and His ministry are the same TODAY as in Bible days.

Tens of thousands of weary Congolese gather to hear a message of hope from Dr. LaDonna. Thousands believe on and accept Jesus Christ after hearing the Gospel, and marvelous miracles of healing are witnessed daily.

Dr. LaDonna Osborn is experiencing BIBLE DAYS in Point-Noire. "The blind receive their sight, and the lame walk ... the deaf hear ... and the poor have the Gospel preached to them." (Mat 11:5)

Just as in Bible days, "Dr. LaDonna goes and preaches everywhere, the Lord working with her and confirming the word through the accompanying signs." (Mk 16:20 paraphrased)

The cripples are walking. The blind are seeing. The deaf are hearing. Cancers are disappearing. Hundreds of physical healing miracles are confirming the message of God's love and saving plan for people.

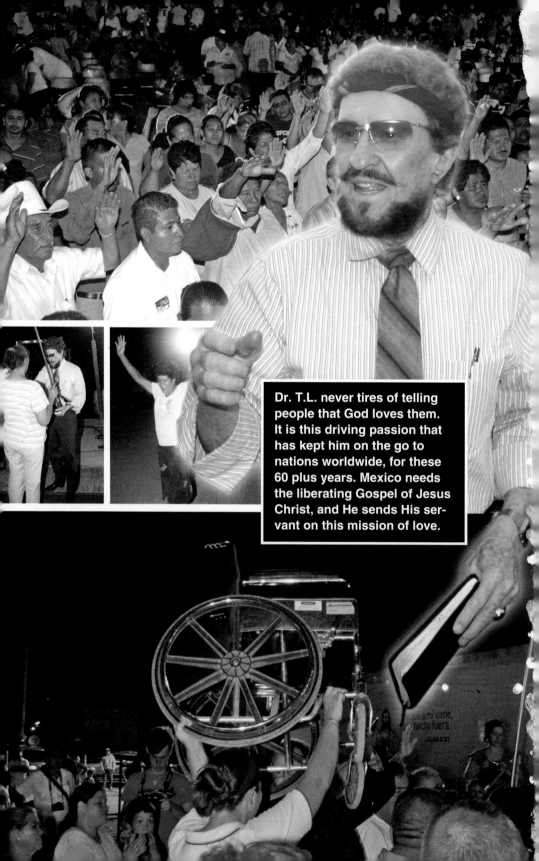

Dr. T.L. never tires of telling people that God loves them. It is this driving passion that has kept him on the go to nations worldwide, for these 60 plus years. Mexico needs the liberating Gospel of Jesus Christ, and He sends His servant on this mission of love.

The young minister shares:

I had just finished singing to a packed house. The air was electric with excitement and faith for the impossible, in anticipation of what great miracles we were all about to witness and experience. As I stepped down from the very same stage they were about to occupy, the honorable guest speakers—T. L. and Daisy Osborn—enthusiastically jumped to their feet and walked toward me. They reached out their hands to shake mine; and with the biggest smiles, firm, tight handshakes, and a hug, they greeted me. T. L. said, "T E R R I F I C job!" followed by similar comments from Daisy, in her charming, lady-like way. I was swept away by this most-humble gesture on their part. This is how I was introduced to the legendary, world-renowned missionaries, Drs. T.L. and Daisy Osborn.

I could not dismiss the royal air, which at the same time consumed and exuded from them. They were sophisticated, confident, poised, and magnetically charismatic; the perfect gentleman and the perfect lady, with a modesty that was glamorous. They were the most beautiful display of well-dressed humility I've ever seen. But neither could I dismiss their obvious love and high regard for humanity. They were kind, genuine, respectful, polite, and appreciative.

It was something to both behold and experience—how they had a way of taking the admirable attributes that were so much who they were and inspiring you and making you feel like you were the one with those outstanding qualities. I saw firsthand, up close and personal, how they perceived and treated one human being after another the same—royally—regardless of one's education, background, or status. T. L. and Daisy approached each and every individual, with whom I saw them interact, with the same effort and polish and attentiveness that one would approach someone of superior status, such as a president, king, or queen–by wearing the best apparel and being impeccably well-groomed and using the best social skills and bearing oneself with utmost kindness and respect.

Airing nothing of egotism or arrogance, always courteous, cordial, and personable, they had a way of convincing every man and woman present that he or she was of high esteem. The value they place on you is one you cannot explain, but it sticks with you. You come away from their presence feeling as though you were the one they came to see! They were masters of communication who seemed to understand and connect with all people. Exceptionally wise, two of the most highly-intelligent people I have ever met, of definite conviction and clarity of mind, they chose their words with precision. You were convinced that these two were true, real, and to be taken serious. Just as Jesus said that when you saw Him, you saw the Father (John 14:9), to see T. L. and Daisy Osborn was to see Jesus of Nazareth, "anointed... with the Holy Ghost and with power: who went about, doing good, and healing all that were oppressed of the devil; for God was with him" (Acts 10:38KJV).

Five

Teachings

by

T. L. Osborn

Chapter 15

Seven Secrets of Success

In the midst of worldwide psychological fragmentation, Dr. T. L. Osborn's life and writings express what the philosophies and psychologies of people have not been able to. His life and writings distinguish him from philosophers and sermonizers. The principles he shares are not derived from what he has merely read, but from applying what he has learned throughout his ministry. He shares principles that he has put to the test, as he has presented them in face-to-face teaching sessions, among Buddhists, Muslims, Shintoists, Hindus, animists, fetish worshippers, Christians, and atheists. Loyalty to common sense and practicality tremendously enhance Dr. Osborn's credentials as a lifter of people; he believes in adhering to ideas that are only useful when they benefit people and meet human needs. They must provide solutions and be workable in real life issues.

All that remains to make the rendering of T.L.'s legacy complete, to the extent that his legacy can be confined to the pages of one book, is to share a little more of the essence of the "unique" messages, that through this man and his wife, have lifted needy human beings to new levels of dignity all around the world–the kind of truths that anchor a ministry and cause it to last.

In his book, *The Best of Life,* which was geared to an American audience, is a powerful seed-message for the new, emerging generation. It is part of T. L.'s legacy. And, thus, a synopsis of its content is provided in this chapter.

What You Can Get out of This Book/Message

T.L. Osborn has written this book to show you how simply, quickly, and easily you can get what you want out of life. There are just a few basic secrets to discover. They are within your reach. No special education is necessary. With these seven secrets, or principles, you can achieve your highest goals.

- *You can win over inferiority and mediocrity.*

- *You can become a problem solver.*

- *You can surmount poverty–get out of debt and off of welfare or social aid–and enjoy the good life.*

- *You can start over right where you are, and discover abilities in you that you never dreamed were there.*

- *You can enjoy a super-lifestyle with dignity and self-esteem.*

- *You can hook up to a dynamic energy that will make you a constant winner.*

- *You can break any destructive habit.*

- *You can discover the surest connection for prosperity, happiness and longevity.*

- *You can use the master key to life's best and open the wide gates to prosperity and fulfillment.*

- *You can experience The Best of Life.*

The Principle of Self-Value:
EVERYBODY IS A REAL SOMEBODY

Secret #1: You are created in the image of God, to be like Him, to manifest Him in human form. You are made for life and love – for power and prosperity- for success and dignity. God made nothing inferior. He is first class all the way. He created you unique. You are exceptional – one-of-a-kind. Before you were born, you existed in God's mind. He knew this world would need you at this time. He planned you with a special purpose that no one but you could fulfill because no one on earth could do what you are here to do.

An insane man was brought to one of our teaching meetings overseas. Fifty thousand people were there. He was known as the running maniac. His hair and beard were long, disheveled and flea-infested. His body was filthy. His rags barely covered his nakedness.

God never created anybody to be unable to think and act normally, or to live in shame and disgrace. I did not know that the insane man was in the audience as I planted the seeds of human value in the mind of the people. There is a miraculous power in truth. I believe words are seeds. They have ability to produce what they say. They are energizers.

I told that audience, "Each one of you is beautifully and wonderfully made–in God's image. Every individual among you is special. You do not have to be second class. You are each unique. God who created you like Himself, put you here for a purpose so special that no one else on earth can do what you are here to do."

God Made No One for Failure, Poverty, Sickness, or Shame

Those word-seeds had power. There is a remarkable statement in the Bible about the power of Jesus' words: *"As He was teaching, the power of the Lord was there to heal the people"* (Luke 5:17, paraphrase mine). That has to be what happened to the insane man who was brought to our meeting that day.

We taught that crowd the essence of my message in *The Best of Life*. We emphasized that God made no one for failure, poverty, sickness or shame; *that everybody is a real somebody in God's eyes*. I urged that audience to personally accept the fact that each of them was a special creation of God and to begin believing that by cooperating with God, any person could realize the best in life.

In some miraculous way, those seeds of truth penetrated that insane man and his mind was healed and his life was transformed. Before those teaching sessions were over, that man was perfectly normal. He was clean, groomed and wearing a suit. He attended every meeting, listening, learning and developing into a remarkably balanced gentleman. He found good employment and became a positive influence in his community. He is a living example of one who rose from emptiness to meaningful living.

No human being was ever created to be inferior. God never planned for anyone to be lonely, defeated, unhealthy, destructive or despondent. God created YOU in His own image, to live His life, to walk and to talk with Him, to think, plan and act with Him.

The Best Possible You

Created in God's image, you are His kind of being! Accept your self-value. See the picture of yourself as God's masterpiece—regardless of your present state of affairs. The seeds of greatness are in you. By accepting this first principle, you are causing those seeds to begin growing in you right now while you read.

Your God-given value does not depend on special genes from superior parents. Your worth, before God, is not measured by your assets, the color of your skin, super intelligence or formal education.

Created by God, you are a part of God. It is right that you esteem what God esteems and value what God values. The Bible says You are God's workmanship. (Ephesians 2:10.) The man who wrote most of the Psalms was wonder-struck by how God made human persons:

> *You have made people a little less than God,* [King James Version—"angels"; original Hebrew, French, and certain other language versions—"God"] and

> *You crown them with glory and honor. You have given them dominion over the works of Your hands; You have put all things under their feet.*

Psalm 8:5-6, paraphrase mine

The bottom line of positive and stable self-esteem is when you can say, "I accept the value that God has put on me." When you do that, you will then cooperate with God to develop the BEST possible you in this world.

Self-value will rid you of all jealousy because you will never again want to be anyone else.

Self-value will wipe out inferiority because you are in God's class of being; and He, in you, is greater than any person or any power outside of you. (1 John 4:4.)

Self-value will eliminate fear of failure or defeat because nothing can stop you and God working together.

Self-value will give you courage because you discover that with God at work in you, you become indomitable.

Self-value will cause you to stand up tall, to square your shoulders, to look out into the future with new confidence, to walk with a steady stride, and to rise to the level of the importance for which God created you.

Seeds of Greatness Are in You

In Genesis 1:27 KJV, the Bible says that God created people in his own image. Then it is repeated, *"In the image of God created He him; male and female created He them."* Genesis 5:1 adds that you were created in the likeness of God. God created human persons as much like Himself as any child can be like its natural parents. God planned that whatever could be said about HIM, could be said about YOU. The Bible explains the lifestyle and plan God designed for you and me: *"Be fruitful and multiply, and replenish the earth, and subdue it: and have dominion over...every living thing"* (Genesis 1:28 KJV).

As this powerful principle takes root, you begin to see and respect yourself as a member of Divine Royalty. God's family is supposed to represent Him and reflect His lifestyle on earth. When you recognize your value, you cause the seeds of greatness to germinate in you. Keep those seeds watered by thinking on them and reaffirming your value until your attitude and conduct are transformed. You stamp your own value on your life by your very own thoughts, words and actions.

You Are God's Starting Point

Keep the picture of God's kind of being in your mind. Self-value and self-esteem are the noblest garments you can wear. Once you accept your own value with God, you will be able to value others. As you care about yourself, you will care about others. Everything from God is channeled through you. The stronger God can be *in you,* the more He can lift others *through you.*

The more love that fills you, the more love you will discover being expressed through you. Poor people cannot help poor people. Down people cannot lift down people. Only happy people can make others happy. Only positive people can make others positive. You are God's starting point.

The greatest possible achievement in life is to be the terrific person God created you to be. To disregard that noble purpose results in frustration, unhappiness and deterioration. The reason there is so much loneliness, depression, drug and sex abuse, insecurity and even suicide is because people do not value themselves.

Your thinking is like electricity that can be captured, harnessed and channeled into creative productivity for yourself and for the good of others. The most powerful concept you can lay hold of is that *God is in you.* Your life is the very breath of God. God's life in you means His love is in you, without limit; healing, lifting, and blessing you *and others through you.*

Recognize Your Roots

When you recognize your roots in God and see yourself as His intended habitation; when you discover how easy it is to experience God in you, you will actually have a rebirth of self-worth–your very life becomes the miracle of God's Life breathed into you.

People cannot tolerate life without dignity. They will withdraw into rooms and close the blinds. They will become recluses from society, or lay down in ditches or gutters and gradually die–the victims of lonely and purposeless abandonment.

Welcome the Friendly Voice

For thousands of years, there has been a barrage of conflicting voices that frighten people away from God. Traditional religious doctrines and orators say, "No! We must stress the basic fact that humankind is *bad!*" Humanism has tried for centuries to make a more attractive appeal based on logistics and reason. Seeking to placate the conscience of people, they cry, "Humankind is *good!*"

Both arguments miss the point because they focus attention upon the *human person in itself.* Rather than to argue either that

"People are bad" or that "People are good," the positive option transcends all human assessment and builds on the foundation that *"God is good!"* If God is good, you can be good. Since He created you in His own image and likeness, you can have dignity and *self-value.*

I have been criticized because I do not stand before audiences and expose or assail or condemn the sins of people. A human person who has not found the way to God is already conscious of guilt and condemnation. I choose to point you to God who is *good.* He loves you in whatever state you may be, so much so that He paid the supreme price of giving His own Son, Jesus, to redeem you from all sin by suffering the penalty for your sin, *in your place*–and He did it before you ever knew you needed it.

So welcome the *friendly* voice that does not attack and condemn you, but that honestly gives you hope by reminding you that God is there, powerful, loving and caring. Welcome the *friendly message* of the gospel that tells you that God created you to be exactly like Him; that your purpose is *to be Him in action;* that He so valued you that He paid an infinite price to redeem you from inferiority, deterioration and sin.

Your conscience condemns you. Sermonizers threaten and frighten you. Your own habits and life-style undermine you. You may be alone, afraid and guilty. Now this *friendly voice* lifts you by reminding you of your origin in God, of your design for success. Your purpose is to be an achiever. You are God's creation.

60-Second Secret

I am valuable, because I am created in God's class of being.

I am vital because God's plan involves me.

My heritage is to have God's best, to enjoy His companionship and to use His wealth and power for the good of myself and others.

I am created for life, love, power, prosperity, success and dignity.

The seeds of greatness are in me. God never created me to be a "Nobody," but a real "Somebody."

I therefore recognize my self-value, that God designed me for His lifestyle and I now know that He planned life's best for me as His child.

I shall no longer discredit or demean or destroy what God created in His own image and values so much.

I welcome *God's friendly voice.* He reminds me of my divine origin, of my high purpose, and of His Love Plan to help me achieve, enjoy and share His best in life.

The Principle of Identity

Now that you have discovered your value, you are ready to identify with this God in a personal encounter. This second principle, that I call identity, is the most powerful key, because it is the one that opens the gates to God's riches, health, success and blessings. This brings us to Secret #2: Understand *WHO* Jesus Christ is;

WHY He came, *WHY* He was put to death, *WHY* He came back from the dead and *HOW* He lives today. Then identify with Him in a personal way because He is your link with God and success.

God's plan was to reproduce Himself in Adam and Eve and to have companionship with them. Adam and Eve were not required or forced to respect God any more than you are. God made one single restriction to measure their faith and confidence in His dream for them. He said, *"You may eat from every tree in the garden except the tree of knowing good and evil…the day you eat from it you will certainly die"* (Genesis 2:16-17, paraphrase mine). They were expected to have confidence in what God said and that is all that He expects of you and of me.

If Adam and Eve trusted in God's integrity, they would live and prosper with Him forever. If they abused His trust and disbelieved His Word, the process of deterioration would begin and they would die. Their lack of trust in the integrity of what God said was later called "Sin."

Two-Way Friendship

The friendship between God and the human persons had to be two-way. God would need to be sure that Adam and Eve wanted Him, like He wanted them. Satan heard of God's dream and conceived a scheme to induce Adam and Eve to betray God's trust. And they did, both eating of the forbidden tree. God spelled out what the results would be: There would be no grounds for a relationship with God. Adam and Eve had exercised their free wills and had, by their action, disregarded and disbelieved what God had said. The good life ended.

The integrity of God required the full measure of His law. Otherwise, His Word could never be trusted. That was the beginning of suffering, disease, pain, hate, lust, envy, murder, jealousy, loneliness, guilt, poverty, hunger, destruction and death. Sin had entered the human race and would be passed on to all generations.

The fundamental sin that severed God's relationship with humankind was not murder or adultery or lying or stealing or hatred or abuse. *It was the assumption or philosophy or attitude that God did not mean what He said.* When that position is taken, deterioration sets in like a cancer and is terminal.

When you do not trust God, you do not trust yourself–or anyone else. When you decide that God has no integrity, your own integrity is abandoned. Conscience is calloused. Dignity is deprecated. The human person deteriorates and dies. The light goes out. There is only darkness. Could that be society's problem today?

Love's Idea

God never abandoned His dream for you. God is love, and love never quits. He found a just and legal way to absolve mankind from the penalty of death for their sins and restore humankind back to an intimate relationship with Him. *Substitution* was the legal answer. In order to provide a substitute who had no sin of his own, God gave His own Son. Jesus was born by a miracle conception. Jesus was not born of human seed that was infected by sin. Not only His conception, but His life among people must be sinless, in order to be *your Substitute.* He was subjected to the same temptations of sin as any human person is. He resisted sin and proved that God's original plan could work–that humans could choose God's Word and never dishonor His integrity.

Under the most trying circumstances, Jesus believed God's Word. He was in every respect tested as we are, yet without committing any sin. (Hebrews 4:15.) Your penalty of death was assumed by Him, and you were legally absolved of the penalty. *Since no debt can be paid twice or no crime punished twice, you were restored as though you had never done wrong.* You are no longer guilty before God and need never be judged for any sin that you have ever committed. The judgment you deserved was put on your substitute, in your place, and that judgment can never be imposed on you again. This is the crux of God's love in the Bible that we call *Salvation*.

You and God Can Come Home

God's love plan depends on your willingness to identify with the one who died as your substitute. This is your key to *Life's Best*. This involves your will. You have the right of choice. You are free to accept the validity of what Christ did on your behalf, or to reject it as superstition or irrelevant or insignificant. God's love plan depends entirely on faith, just like He required Adam and Eve to trust His integrity.

The record of your sins was credited to Christ's account. Then He assumed your guilt and bore the judgment that you deserved. In exchange, His righteousness was credited to your account and you were declared "righteous" in God's eyes, forever.

When does this happen? When you decide to *identify* with what Jesus Christ did, and when you believe that He assumed the judgment for your sins in your place. When you do that, you will experience a miracle. Christ opened the way for God to come to you and for you to come to Him.

Good Things Happen

First: You are re-born, re-created, restored to God and made new. You become a child of God. (John 1:12.)

Second: You receive a new spiritual life, the miracle life of God through Jesus Christ in you.(2 Corinthians 5:17.)

Third: You receive total peace—freedom from anxiety, hypertension, fear, guilt, and condemnation. Jesus said, "Peace I leave with you, my peace I give unto you" (John 14:27). "Being justified by faith, you have peace with God through your Lord Jesus Christ." (Romans 5:1.)

Fourth: You are restored to friendship, fellowship, and life with God—the way you were designed to live on this earth. (1 John 1:3.)

Fifth: Your physical body is affected so much by this new inner peace with God that your sicknesses disappear and you experience new physical and mental health. "You will serve the Lord your God, and He will take sickness away from the midst of you" (Exodus23:25). "The Lord forgives all of your iniquities; He heals all of your diseases" (Psalm 103:3).

The Way to Life's Best

First: Believe you are valuable, as God's creation.

Second: Know that distrusting God's Word is the original and basic problem.

Third: Understand that disavowing God's integrity results in death.

Fourth: Believe that God valued you too much to let you die.

Fifth: Know why Jesus came and died as your substitute.

Sixth: Identify with Christ's death, burial and resurrection.

Seventh: Believe the gospel and receive Jesus Christ in person now.

Second 60-Second Secret

I identify with Jesus Christ in a practical way. He is my model of purpose and achievement—my way to the best in life.

I know God's original plan was for happiness, health and fulfillment without inferiority or condemnation—like Adam and Eve whom He created. But they disregarded His plan. That was the origin of human problems.

To save me, Jesus assumed my wrongs and died in my place. Then He returned with new life from God, which He offers to me.

I identify with Him because, since He assumed my penalty, I am able to receive the new life of God which He brings to me.

It was Love's idea not to let me die in emptiness, but to pay for my wrong and to restore me to God's lifestyle, for which I was originally created.

Now I am at home with God again, and He blesses me with life's best through Jesus Christ. I have regained dignity. I am restored as God's child.

The Principle of Desire

Your *yearning* power is more important than your earning power. People who win in life concentrate on what they desire and ignore any limitations they may face. First, dream beyond what seems possible to you. Second, desire what you dream about. Third, drive for your dreams. A common characteristic of all winners is they deeply *desire* to win.

The force of intense desire in you has a miraculous way of releasing powerful energy, creativity, and an almost supernatural pull toward what you yearn for. What do you want out of life—with all of your heart? Is it wrong to desire to do things, to be something, to have something?

Religion has emphasized surrender, humility, suffering, and poverty. It has sanctified resignation, submission, relinquishment, and abandonment, but it has neglected the virtues of positivism, development, faith, productivity, success and accomplishment. Common sense tells us that God did not intend the wealth He created in this world to be monopolized by those who ignore Him. He created it for the pleasure, the usefulness and the fulfillment of those who honor Him and walk with Him.

Sincerely desire the good things God has created in this world. Believe they are placed here for you–in partnership with God– to enjoy and to use for the betterment of your world. Know that your desire for good is God's desire being expressed in and through you.

No Limit to Your Source

A primitive villager who scratches the soil with a sharpened piece of wood, does not know to desire a steel plow. Once he hears about it, new ideas fill his mind. His ambition is fired. He sets himself to acquire better tools–and a better life. The purpose of God's Love Plan in the Bible is to show you His better way.

This message, *The Best of Life*, is to let you know that God wants you to know that it is not wrong to desire progress and better living. You were born to enjoy life's best. You were born to live in God's dream with His lifestyle. You have the miraculous capacity that no other creature has–to think and plan, to ponder and imagine, to believe and progress. When you recognize God in you and discover that His desires for you have never changed, you begin to dream a new dream–to envision the lifestyle for which God created you. You begin to rise, to climb and to grow.

As your new vision gets clearer, that dream creates a yearning, deep desire for life's best; and you begin to dare to tackle life, to harness the abilities in you, and to go for the top. Faith is desire turned God-ward. God wants you to realize that within you is the possibility to shed the cloak of failure, to escape the negative syndrome of discouragement, to break the demoralizing dogmas of defeat, to get out of the boredom of conformity and to go for life's best—whether the "average" person does it or not.

One of the most vital facts you will discover is that *God wants you to have good things*—the BEST in life—but He must wait until you *desire* them before He can give them to you. When a blind man cried out to Jesus, He stopped and asked him, *"What do you desire for me to do for you"* (Mark 10:51)? He desired his sight, and he received it. That is the way God works. He desires that you have and enjoy His BEST; but until you desire what He desires, He must wait to give it to you.

Jesus said to a woman who intensely desired Him to heal her daughter—and who would not give up—*"Let it be as you desire"* (Matthew 15:28). And the girl was healed. *"When you delight in God, He gives you the desires of your heart. You will inherit the earth. God will exalt you to inherit the land."* (Psalm 37:4,9,34.)

Religion "spiritualizes" God's blessings. It promises that when you get to heaven, you'll be rich. God's desire is that you inherit the earth—NOW. He created it for you to enjoy and to use in *this life*.

It Is Right to Desire the Best

The true message of the Bible is Good News. Let me share three blessings from God which are GOOD:

(1) *Peace with God is GOOD.* You were never created for guilt and fear. God's Love Plan offers inner peace and tranquility. He wants you to have that happiness, but He waits until your desire matches His desire.

(2) *Physical health is GOOD.* You were never made to suffer pain, disease or disability. God's Love Plan for you includes healing and soundness. He yearns for you to walk in His boundless health. But He must wait until you desire His health in you.

(3) *Material prosperity is GOOD.* You were never created for poverty and deprivation. God's Love Plan for you includes prosperity, success and abundant living. He wills all of His abundance and blessing for you. But He must wait until you tire of poverty. When the fire of desire burns in you for His lifestyle, then things begin to happen for you.

Jesus said, *"Whatever things you ask when you pray, believe that you receive them, and you will have them"* (Mark 11:24).

Religion has focused on the negative side of human desire so much that people are impregnated with the idea that *desire* is carnal and must be suppressed. When I researched what theologians had to say about *desire,* I found volumes written about the evil of desire. It is condemned, judged, censured and penalized.

I knew that to desire riches or wealth or any other thing out of greed, jealousy, avarice or lust was wrong and destructive. I knew hundreds of reasons to warn about *evil* desire. But I know very little in theology that encourages people to *desire* the *good* things that God has created on this planet. Religious piety and negativism about anything material has practically obstructed the positive viewpoints of the abundant life.

Many years ago I learned that if I want what God wants, then that desire is holy and good– and I will have it. And God wants restored what Adam and Eve lost in the Garden of Eden. He wanted Adam and Eve to be happy, healthy, productive, and live in abundance.

The Good Life Is God's Idea

Your desire depends on your knowledge of God's desire. He desires for you every blessing He originally created for human beings on this earth. He wants to give this world back to you to rule, to dominate and to enjoy. He accomplished that when Jesus assumed the judgment for all of your sins. *"All [things] are yours, and you are Christ's and Christ is God's"* (1 Corinthians 3:22-23). *"The desire of the righteous will be granted"* (Proverbs 10:24).

We are created with desire. David said, *"My heart and my flesh cries out for the living God"* (Psalm 84:2). *"My soul thirsts for [God], my flesh longs for [Him]"* (Psalm 63:1). Our spirits *yearn* for God—for peace, for tranquility, for meaning and for achievement. Our flesh *desires* the physical and material provisions God has created for us—water, food, air, comforts, success, wealth, abundance, health, happiness and fulfillment. If those desires are suppressed and not allowed to motivate us, we will die in nothingness and emptiness, without purpose or significance.

We are what God is in us. *"As He is, so are we in this world"* (1 John 4:17). The very principle of desire is vital to faith.

Walk Tall—Success Is for Now

Religion in its many brands invariably links poverty with godliness, suffering with piety, burdens with humility and lack with holiness. Emerson, the great American philosopher, said that from the time he was a lad, he wanted to write an essay that would deal with traditional theology which indoctrinates people against desiring material success, achievement and prosperity.

He explained how a preacher talked about life and the Last Judgment as though every issue would have to await its outcome until then. By this doctrine, the preacher ignored the fact that you reap what you sow and get what you strive for, *even here in this life.* Mr. Emerson was shocked at the preacher's doctrine, for he emphasized that only the wicked should be successful in this world and that good people should prove their humility and piety by living lives of misery.

But then the preacher extolled the fact that God would balance the scales at the great Judgment Day. Then and not before, the wicked would get their deserved misery and the righteous would inherit riches. But it was all spiritualized. There was nothing for the righteous here and now—in this material world. In other words, Mr. Emerson said that the preacher applauded riches for the righteous—*in heaven,* but he deplored the thought of material prosperity for them *here and now.*

He said, in essence, the preacher is teaching the Christians to say: "In this material world, we will submit, and suppress our desires and live like paupers, while the wicked revel in their sinful material luxury.

"But once we get to heaven, we will no longer cower in submission, suppression and deprivation. We shall stand up and revel in all of the riches that the wicked have here on earth."

In other words, "It is a sin to be rich here and now. We who are pious shall not sin now, but we shall sin in heaven; we would like to sin now, but we shall get our revenge later."

To young Emerson, this was nonsense. Though he understood little about the Bible, it seemed illogical to him that the wicked should prosper and that the righteous should be poor. Why not the opposite? The Good News is the opposite. Now–here on earth–is where the wealth God created can be put to work for the good of life and the good of people. One of the greatest sins might be to refuse to discipline ourselves, apply our talents and achieve material success–here and now–when it can mean so much in helping people.

Jesus came to save us from the negativism of religion that condemns, demoralizes, threatens and negates human personhood. Religion has always been cruel, esteeming laws as being more sacred than lives. Jesus healed a poor man with a withered hand. The religious crowd yelled, "It's the wrong day! Leave his hand crippled! Respect the Sabbath!" (Mark 3:1-6.) They cared more for their law than for a poor man's crippled hand.

Jesus raised a man from the dead who had been in his tomb for four days. The religious crowd never glorified God, but recoiled and took counsel to kill Jesus, lest the people follow Him. (John 11.) They were so preoccupied with their control over people's minds and the absoluteness of their religious doctrines that even the restoring to life of a man who had been dead for four days did not affect their dogmatism. They preferred to ignore the miracle and kill the Master, rather than to risk losing their manipulating influence over the people.

They brought a woman to Jesus who had been taken in the act of adultery. The religious crowd wanted to stone her to death for breaking the law. Jesus treated her like a lady and restored her self-esteem by forgiving her. (John 8:4-11.) That is what He did for you and for me.

Jesus came across a naked maniac–a wild man. The religious crowd had no interest in him, but left him to his torment. Jesus restored his mind and gave him a position of honor. He sent him to ten towns of the Decapolis to represent Him personally. (Mark 5:1-20.) What an honor!

Jesus met an unclean leper. The religious crowd left him to his fate. But Jesus cleansed him so that he could have honor and dignity as a respected citizen again. (Mark 1:40-45.)

Jesus never, ever put anyone down–except religious people who used their religion to put people down. Religion is usually a put-down–a standard by which one is judged or condemned. But Jesus Christ is a *Lifter* of people, a *Healer* and a *Restorer* of human persons.

He wants to restore your faith in life, if circumstances have broken your will. If you are poor, He wants you to have hope and to believe the Good News that good things in life are for you. If you have been blind to your value, to your potential, or to the possibilities around you, Jesus Christ will open your eyes to see a dozen solutions to problems you thought were insurmountable. Your ears may have been stopped. Perhaps you missed the answers in life. The Lord will miraculously open your ears and you will hear what counts for life's best. You may have been demoralized until you withdrew in failure and humiliation. Jesus will stand up inside of you and cause you to walk tall in life, and succeed where you failed before.

Help Yourself to God's Lifestyle

To believe in God is to believe in Good! God wants you at peace. God wants you healthy. God wants you happy and prosperous. Are you willing to be prosperous and successful? Are you willing to assume the responsibility of administering wealth and success for your own good and for the good of people?

The crippled man blamed others for his thirty-eight-year plight. He said that no one would help him to get well. Jesus said, in essence, "Help yourself! Get up! Carry your bed! Walk!" The man got up and walked and was whole again. That is what God says to you and to me. Decide what you desire and resolve to possess it! You can have or do or be anything that you *desire*.

Until you desire what God desires, His goodness cannot materialize in you. This principle of *desire* is vital because your action is motivated only by what you want. When there is no desire, no choice is made, no decision is taken and no action is performed. Without the "want to" there is no "will to."

Third 60-Second Secret

Since I am created like God and since He is now alive in me, my desire for good in life is His desire expressed through me.

It is right for me to *desire* to be, to have and to do the good that God created me for.

Happiness, success, health and prosperity are God's original plan for me. He has never changed His mind. His love plan is my blueprint for life's best.

My desire is my faith turned heavenward.

I will never allow religious piety and negativism about material blessings to stifle my desire for God's abundance. No member of His family is created for mediocrity or poverty.

I believe in God's Plan of Love that restored me to Him, so that now, my desire is His desire at work in me. I believe in *good* and desire *good* because I believe in God. It is right that I enjoy His best.

The Principle of Decision

The fourth vital principle to get the best out of life concerns the use of your *Power Secret*. **You** alone control it. No one but you can use it. It is indispensable to your success.

Your Power Secret is your right of choice and your ability to decide what portion in life you will resolve to possess; what you will settle for; what level you are content with; how high you want to climb; how rich you want to be; to what extent you want your business to grow; what kind of lifestyle gives you fulfillment; how long you want to live; how much power you want to control; how much respect you want people to have for you and what goals you want to reach.

You—and no other person, organization, influence or agency—have control over your own choices and over the decisions that you make in life. *"For it is God who works in you, inspiring both the will and the deed, for his own chosen purpose"* (Philippians 2:13, paraphrase mine). God in you gives you the *desire,* the *opportunity,* and the *power* to be, to have, and to do as much as you want. He leaves the decision up to you. You—and you alone—are in charge.

You Are Deciding for Yourself

Decisions and choices are verbalized by two of the shortest words in the English language: "yes" and "no." The Bible urges us to use these words judiciously. Say only "yes" when you mean "yes," and "no" when you mean "no." (James 5:12.)

T. T. Munger says, "The heaviest charged words in our language are those briefest ones, 'Yes' and 'No.'" People who have left their mark upon the world have been decisive. Those who are irresolute, always lingering between two opinions, not knowing which course to take, have no self-control and are doomed to be controlled by others.

Decisive people do not wait for favorable circumstances, nor submit to opinions or influence which negate or demoralize value. Decisive people create circumstances. They establish trends. They bend opinions and make them serve positive purposes.

The indecisive are always at the mercy of those with whom they last talked. They never belong to themselves, but are in the control of whoever captures their attention. Like a twig or a chip floating near the edge of a stream, they are caught by every weed or bush and are whirled in little circles while their energy is dissipated and their strength is wasted.

The winner in life is a *Decider*. Winners are well-informed. They make clear choices; then they resolve to put those choices into action. Like Caesar, they commit all and burn their ships behind them so that retreat is made impossible. Satan himself cannot stop such a one from possessing the best out of life. The only power Satan can ever have over you, to break, discourage, demoralize, destroy or defeat you is through the negative suggestions or ideas that he can plant, or use someone to plant, in your mind.

Your Power Secret of choice and the right to decide for yourself what measure of life you will settle for, is the power that no one can take from you. It is not circumstances, but your choices and decisions that determine who you are, what you have, what you do and where you go in life. Daisy, my wife, said, "Every morning when I get up, I choose to be happy, to savor life, and to make it count for me, for people, and for God." That is why she was always an inspiration, an achiever and a positive influence around the world.

How Much Is Enough for You

Your decisions define what you want in life. You can decide to win if you choose to win, desire to win and are committed to win. You can never fail until you choose and decide to give up. The law of sowing and reaping guarantees that you will reap the harvest of each choice or decision you make and of each thought you think. Your life is the sum total of your choices and decisions.

Amazing things start happening in life when you decide and choose what portion in life you resolve to possess:

- *Ideas begin to come to you as to how you can reach out and achieve whatever you have decided upon.*

- *Opportunities come your way that were not available before.*

- *People, organizations, companies or businesses will be there to help you at the right time and in the right place.*

- *You will discover new friends, whose cooperation will be available and vital to you.*

- *Fears and doubts will vanish like dirty smog.*

- *You will become aware of the new you who becomes successful, valued and respected.*

- *Vitality, strength and enthusiasm will swell up inside of you.*

What portion of life will you decide to possess? What are your limits? Are you worthy of the best? In your opinion, what do you deserve?

What are God's limits inside you? How much is He worth, living in you? What does He deserve as He lives in you? How much is too much for Him?

Can God be separated from His power when He comes to live in you? Is God any different in you than the way you think of Him in the Bible? Does He lose His power and miraculous ability when He comes to live in you? Does He reduce Himself to your standard, or does He raise you to His standard?

How much of the goodness and abundance and beauty of this planet will you allow God to share as He lives in you? Will you limit Him by the measure of your opinion of yourself? Or will you measure your opinion of yourself by the measure of God in you?

The Bible says, *"Behold the kingdom of God is within you"* (Luke 17:21 KJV). God's kingdom is everything that God is–His nature, His power, His love, His health, His wealth, His abundance, His ability, His virtue, His righteousness and His life.

A Beggar Can Become a Master

Our world is marked at every level by people who had no advantages, little or no money, no help and no means of achievement. But they sensed destiny at work in them. They became aware of their own value and they tackled impossibilities with decision and faith. And they never quit. They succeeded. To them, every problem became an opportunity, every obstacle was turned into an advantage, and every difficulty became a growing experience.

A man by the name of Sanford Cluett found a way to keep cloth from shrinking. That discovery brought him over five million dollars a year in royalties alone. Henry Ford believed in the knowledge he had and decided: "I will build a car cheap enough for anyone to drive and own." He never quit, and that idea brought more wealth to him than any other person of his time received. A man by the name of Raymond Yates listed over two thousand inventions that were urgently needed at the time. The knowledge to solve those needs, plus thousands of current ones, was and is in God; and He is in you and in me. So our part is to proceed and to get the best out of life.

You and God can meet those needs, and that achievement can help take you to the top. You hold your *Power Secret*.

Week after week, in factories, offices, and businesses, millions of people continue to resign themselves to the sterile drudgery of tradition because they have accepted the status quo. They have never used their brain power to think creatively and discover a better way. By realizing the value of a human person and the potential of anyone who thinks, decides, and acts, a beggar can rise to become a master.

You Are a Branch of God

A businessman was praying about the masses of people on the earth who are still unaware of these truths. He asked God, "What are You going to do about it? Are You going to let them die?"

He said God answered him: "Son, I have done all I can do. I gave you Jesus. I gave you His Name. I gave you His power, His love, His authority. Now it's up to you!"

You see, the kingdom of God is within you. You are a branch of God's power and love, of His creativity and abundance. Everything that is in the vine comes up into you and is manifested through you. *"When you abide in me and I in you, you bring forth much fruit"* (John 15:5, paraphrase mine). *"It is God who works in you"* (Philippians 2:13).

But it all depends on your willingness to use your *Power Secret*–your inalienable right to choose and to decide how much and what of life you will resolve to experience. Failures are simply the casualties of the world of thought. You only fail when you think failure and decide to accept failure. To fail, you must first quit. To quit, you must decide not to continue.

You are much bigger than anything or anyone who tries to stop you. Never give attention to impossible situations, problems or obstacles. As fast as difficulties loom in your way, transform these tough problems into opportunities to get ideas for solving them. Nothing is a greater advantage to you than a problem, once you draw on God and His wisdom to solve it. You then have expertise that is marketable. It is the ability that others will pay to benefit from.

Since most people do not try to solve their own problems, they search for a specialist. You can be that specialist! What's more, you can charge a good price for your services; and people will gladly pay it. So decide to do what has produced millionaires for centuries:

Find a problem and solve it.

Find a desire and fill it.

Find a need and meet it.

Find a hurt and heal it.

You and God Win Together

Since God is at work in you and you have chosen and decided to get the best out of life, problems and impossibilities are the material to assist you on your way to success. You and God can solve anything. *"Greater is He that is in you than he that is in the world"* (1 John 4:4 KJV). Solve your problems and you will solve the problems of others.

Lift your lifestyle and you will lift others.

Love yourself and you will love others.

Believe in your value and you will believe in the value of others.

Your Power Secret can change your world.

If the world around you does not satisfy you as it is, you and God can re-create it:

1. *Choose* the idea of what you want.

2. *Discover* the power of God at work in you.

3. *Believe* in the creative force of God to do anything.

4. *Write* down and repeat often, what you want.

5. *Desire* it deeply, believing that your desire for good things is God's desire in you.

6. *Decide* on what in life will satisfy you.

7. *March forward,* with God at work in you, until your world is transformed.

Moses decided on his course in life. He made a *choice*. (Hebrews 11:24-29.) He purposed to allow God to work in and through him, and a burning bush experience so affected him that he transformed two million slaves into a powerful nation for God. What a loss to society if Moses had not chosen God's way and decided that his people must not be slaves any longer! Their success depended on Moses' commitment. Only when they won, did Moses win. In company with God, he never wavered because he had made a choice, and he stuck to his decision.

When you align your choice with God's choice and your decision with His, you and God win together. No power or opposition can stop you and Him as partners.

God Depends on You

When Abraham Lincoln entered the Black Hawk War, he went as a captain but returned as a private. His business failed, and the very tools he depended upon to make a living had to be sold to pay his debts. The first time Lincoln tried for the Legislature, he was defeated; as he was in his first attempt to become a congressman. When he tried for the office of Commissioner of the General Land Office, Lincoln failed again. Then he failed when he tried for the Senate. He also failed to get nominated as Vice President. But Abraham Lincoln never did quit. He became President of the United States and is recognized as one of the greatest leaders our nation has ever had.

Thomas Edison, in his ten thousand attempts to invent the light bulb, denied that he ever failed. He just found thousands of ways it would not work. He was committed. He and God never quit. The electricity was there all the time. Edison allowed God to help him harness it.

President Grant, at thirty-nine, was chopping and delivering wood for a living. But his choice was noble and his decision was lofty. Nine years later, he was elected President of the United States.

Thousands of so-called "nobodies" have chosen the *good* life, decided on the best, and have risen to lead nations, build fortunes, and establish institutions for the betterment of humanity. When you choose, decide and act with God at work in you, nothing can stop you and Him *together* from succeeding.

Twenty-five thousand cases of failure were analyzed. The glaring evidence showed that lack of decision was the principal cause for defeat in every case. Four out of five graduates from our schools of higher learning have not yet decided what they want out of life. Statistics prove that, at the age of sixty-five, only one out of a hundred graduates will be rich.

Several hundred success stories were analyzed. In all cases, those who had succeeded had made clear choices, had informed themselves as well as possible, and then had decided and committed themselves, and had achieved their goals. The majority of people who fail are deeply affected by, and therefore subject to, the opinions of others. There is nothing more plentiful, and of less value, than the opinions of people who are not successful.

You have a brain and a mind of your own. You are at the controls of the greatest *Power Secret* on earth for your life—your right of choice and decision. Manage it or be manipulated by the whims, the opinions, and the negative influences of other people.

You are far too vital and of too great a value to be subjected to or manipulated by others who, once you are down, will walk off and leave you and forget that you ever existed. God is not that kind of partner. He believes in you, trusts you, wills His best for you, and identifies with you. He makes your house His palace; he depends on you, created you, reaches out to you, and lives with you.

All things are possible with God in you. (Matthew 19:26.) Choose what you want in life and *decide* to experience it. Use your own *Power Secret*. Think for yourself and value your own ideas. Accept all that God is in you and believe in His love, His power, His presence, and His abundance. Act on the fact that God is in you, and reach for the stars. Stand up tall, like God. March to the sound of His music. *Go to the top with Him!*

Fourth 60-Second Secret

God has given me a *Power Secret* which I alone control. It is my right of choice, my ability to decide how much I want out of life, how high I want to climb, how rich I want to be, how long I want to live, how much power I want to have, or what goals I want to reach.

I inform myself, I set my targets, and I achieve my goals *because I choose to win*. I have decided that God and I cannot be losers.

I recognize God at work in me. He does not reduce Himself to *my* standard. He raises me to *His* standard.

I have chosen and have decided to get life's best because I *am* God's best. He created me in His likeness—first class all the way. His Mastership is in me. The only person who can limit me is the one who makes my decisions. I choose life, success, happiness, health and prosperity. I have *decided* to say "yes" to God's best because that alone glorifies Him, fulfills my life, and makes my world better.

The Principle of Wealth

The fifth secret in essence is: Recognize the wonderful fact of God's riches, that He has created such an abundance on this planet that there is plenty for you of whatever you can need or desire, and that it belongs to you because God created it for the material blessing of His children who do His will. From the beginning of creation, God set Adam and Eve in the middle of total affluence, beauty, health, wealth and happiness. God placed man and woman in a veritable paradise of bounty, generosity and material wealth. And it belongs to you as your estate!

Never allow religious sermonizers to whittle you down to the level of an unworthy indigent before your Heavenly Father. You are made to enjoy God's abundance. He has created plenty for you.

There is no shortage, no limit. *"No good thing will [God] withhold from those who walk uprightly"* (Psalm 84:11). *"For as you know Him better, He will give you, through His great power, everything you need for living a truly good life: He even shares His own goodness with us"* (2 Peter 1:3 LB).

You Are Tapped into God's Plenty

Shortage exists only in your mind; limits exist only in your thoughts. God knows no scarcity. You are created (then recreated) to be one with God, sharing all that He is and has. *"[God's]divine power has given to us all things that pertain to life…[with] exceedingly great promises [by which] you may be partakers of the divine nature"* (2 Peter 1:3-4).

Religious tradition teaches that it may be God's plan for you to live in poverty, helpless, defeated, inferior, and humiliated; that such conditions may be a blessing in disguise to teach you humility and godliness; that you must not resist sickness and disappointment which may draw you closer to God; that you may be required to lead a meager existence; that physical suffering, financial limitations, and submission to defeat and failure, can be the influences which develop virtues of humility and holiness in you.

But those circumstances are a form of hell on earth, and you don't have to go through hell to get to heaven. They are foreign to God's dream for you.

Jesus talked about treasures, which moths and rust corrupt and which thieves steal. The treasure or wealth that God brings to your life cannot be taken from you. No thief can steal it. No moth or rust can destroy it. The abundance that God gives to you is spiritual wealth, but it will produce material wealth at your house, because when you know that you are in rapport with Divine Royalty, nothing is too good for you.

The only way you can be poor or unworthy is not to recognize Christ and His power at work in you. The only way you can feel guilty or afraid is not to recognize that Jesus assumed your judgment and left you justified forever before God, with no reason to ever sense guilt, fear or condemnation again.

The only way you can ever feel inferior or subservient is not to recognize your self-value as one of God's children, made in His own image. You have been redeemed by Christ, and you are a believer. You are restored to His level and status of life. Now His quality becomes your quality. His wealth becomes yours. He created plenty for everything that you can desire, need, use and enjoy.

See Yourself in God's Class

When you discover God's kingdom in you, you begin to recognize that you were not meant to be poor or inferior. You are in God's class of being. All that He has and all that He is, is yours. *"[The Lord] daily loads us with benefits"* (Psalm 68:19). *When you seek the Lord, you will not lack any good thing.* (Psalm 34:10.)

The High Purpose of Material Plenty

Naturally, material wealth hoarded and selfishly guarded, never produces happiness. You can never know life's best with the cancer of greed and lust for material wealth consuming you from within. That is not God's best. But when you recognize The Big

Connection–that you are in rapport with God, that His kingdom is in you, and that you and He are united in His Love Plan to lift, to heal, and to bless people–then material wealth has godly purpose. God wants you to know The Big Connection in order to do big business with Him–to live the *big* life, to utilize His material provisions to lift your *big* world on a *big* scale.

The idea that has made millionaires is to find a need and meet it, to find a desire and fill it, to find a problem and solve it or to find a hurt and heal it. When you taste the blessing and the joy of being able to help and to lift others, then God's wealth in your life has divine purpose. This gives meaning to love, to power and to material blessing.

God Has Big Ideas for You

God's kingdom is big business. You are a part of a big Love Plan. David said, *"When I consider Your heavens, the work of Your fingers, the moon and the stars which You have ordained, [I am amazed]"* (Psalm 8:3). Why did our Lord make billions of stars? Wouldn't a few thousand have sufficed? If He wants you limited or impoverished on this earth, why such an extravaganza in the heavens?

How could God want you to live in deprivation when He created so much wealth all around you? Why did He make such huge mountains and so many of them–full of treasures? What purpose would it serve if His followers are to live in scarcity and insufficiency? Why did God create such vast oceans and fill them with such wealth, if He wants His people to exist in meagerness?

Why did He create so many huge trees? Why such vast deserts, such lush jungles, such enormous plains, and such rich valleys? And why so many of them? No parsimonious, tightfisted God could ever have created the abundance that you live amidst. *"Who is so great a God as our God?"* (Psalm 77:13). *"How great are Your works!"* (Psalm 92:5). *"Great are Your tender mercies"* (Psalm 119:156). *"The LORD has done great things for us"* (Psalm 126:3). *"Great is our Lord, and mighty in power"* (Psalm 147:5).

When you consider God's Big Connection, your mind stretches, your imagination enlarges, and you think *big* thoughts–you get *big* ideas. And when you think *big*, then you talk *big* and you act *big*.

Throughout our world ministry, whenever my wife Daisy and I faced impossibilities and our faith was tested, we got away from limited horizons and went to the mountains or to the desert or to the ocean, and we contemplated the greatness and the generosity of our Father. Our minds were *s-t-r-e-t-c-h-e-d* to God's infinity. We realized that our Lord had created all of earth's abundance, and we were in His class of being.

Contemplating God's abundance helped us to draw courage and renewed faith to meet our task. We learned to release Jesus within us to stand up tall in our boat and to calm our storm. Knowing that God has *big* ideas for us, we have always been re-energized to think *big* with Him.

When we were in the Papua New Guinea mountains, teaching those precious people these secrets, I was intrigued by the Pidgin English translation of 1 Timothy 1:12 which, with my adaptation to make it understandable to you, goes something like this:

"The Big Fellow that belongs to me, Jesus Christ; He gives me strong power. He thinks I am good enough to do all of His works and He put me in this big work of His. For this I thank this Big Fellow, Jesus, who lives inside me now." Clearly, the Papua New Guinea people have captured the essence: God has *big* ideas for you and for me.

Someone asked Helen Keller, the renowned blind, deaf, and mute author, "Isn't it awful to be blind?"

She answered without hesitation, "Not half as bad as it would be to have two good eyes and never to see anything!"

Electricity was here all the time, waiting for someone to get the *big* idea of harnessing it for the good of people. The air waves, with their miraculous power to carry words and pictures around the world, have been unchanged for millenniums, awaiting our search for and discovery of them for the good of humankind. Most great discoveries have come from things which everybody thought they knew about, but somebody pondered until the *big* dream was born. The great fortunes which have made millionaires out of ordinary people have come from opportunities which were available to many, but which somebody did something about.

All of God's created nature is your estate. His wealth is stored here for you. It is abundant.

The fifth secret to getting the best out of life is not a responsibility thrust upon you; it is your response to God's ability at work within you.

You Are Seeded for Abundance

One of the most successful men of this century recounts the speech that his stepmother made soon after she married his father and came to live in their poverty-stricken home. She gathered the family together and announced that the place they called home was a disgrace and a handicap for the children. She reminded them that they were all able-bodied and that there was no reason for them to accept poverty. She reasoned that if they remained as they were–resigned to their circumstances–the children would do the same.

Although for the time being she did not know how they would break out to freedom from poverty, she made it clear that they would make the break successfully, regardless of the time it might take or the price they might have to pay. With pride, she announced that she would see to it that those children would be impregnated with the drive to master poverty, which she regarded as a disease, adding that any time poverty is accepted it becomes almost terminal.

She assured them that, although being born in poverty was no disgrace, "it most decidedly IS a disgrace to accept this birthright as irrevocable." She reminded them of their fortune to be born in the wealthiest nation on earth, where possibilities abound for any person who has the drive to observe and to accept them. She added that, if circumstances were not favorable, then they would create new and favorable circumstances.

She notified that family that poverty was like creeping paralysis; it would eventually suffocate the desire for success and liberty; it would stifle the drive for an improved lifestyle and would debilitate individual aspiration and enterprise. She vowed to make sure that those children would become "prosperity conscious" that they would expect life's best!

The speech that woman made that day broke the grip of poverty upon that family as it seeded faith for a better lifestyle and started them on the road to *The Best of Life*. I believe this message will break the influence of poverty, inferiority, poor health and disappointment in your life forever. There is no limit upon you except the limit that you place upon God who lives in you.

I have observed the disastrous effect that a theology, negative about material blessings, can have upon people and even nations. It is amazing how many people are programmed for failure and poverty. They have resigned themselves to do without what they want, to never feel good about themselves, and to accept their present role as permanent. No one has to do that.

God's Generosity

I love the Oklahoma hills and streams where I played as a child. I love to walk among the strong oak trees, ponder the miracle power of the soil where I worked as a barefoot boy, and walk alongside the clear brooks where I went fishing as a lad. I pick up a single acorn at the base of a huge oak tree, and I hold it in my hands. I look up at the huge oak tree, and I know that it grew out of that small seed. Jesus spoke of the wonder of growth in the mustard seed. (Matthew 13:31.)

All of the technological miracles of humankind could never produce that strong oak tree, or make that tiny mustard seed grow to such proportions. But God could and did. And it was easy for Him. There among nature I receive the message: The greatest power that exists cannot be measured by a meter, or analyzed, or seen; but it is real and it produces—*and it is at work in me.*

I walk beside the river and think about the millions of people I have taught or will yet teach, face to face, across this planet. God says, *"I will open rivers in high places, and fountains in the midst of the valleys"* (Isaiah 41:18 KJV). I want people to look at God's created abundance that surrounds them and see with their own eyes the wealth with which they are connected.

As I ponder nature's wealth, I pray that I can help people recognize God's abundance around them; that I can cause them to rid their minds of stingy, negative, and poverty-programmed theology and religion; …that I can help them discover The Big Connection and recognize that material blessings, happiness, health, success and abundance are God's gifts for everyone who believes in Him.

You will be abundantly satisfied. (Psalm 36:8.) You will know the love of Christ…and be filled with all the fullness of God. (Ephesians 3:19.) He will give rain to your seed, so you may sow the ground; and the bread of your increase will be plenteous. (Isaiah 30:23.) He will make all grace abound toward you; that you may always, having all sufficiency I all things, abound to every good work. (2 Corinthians 9:8.) His will is abundantly above all that you ask or think, according to His power that works in your life. (Ephesians 3:20.)

I bend over and pick up a handful of soil. There in my hand is the essence of what produced the corn we harvested in the autumn and the "stuff" that produced those huge oak trees that I love so much. Rich soil! Another element in my world of wealth! God created it—so abundantly.

I sit down on a boulder beside the stream and remove my shoes to splash my feet in the cool water like I did in my youth and I hear another message. *Water! A miracle!* From the beginning of God's abundant creation, water has been the miracle worker. What stories it could tell if it could talk to us. Ever since this planet became the habitat for human persons, water has been the life-giving servant to all. The thirst of billions has been quenched by it. It has been transformed into steam to power humankind's mechanized world, and is then faithfully returned to its liquid form to serve again. What a rich partner—water! It is so much like God—never quitting, never ceasing, never retiring, and never stalemating.

I walk out to a grassy slope and stretch out in the sun and consider this part of God's creation. And, lo—another message of abundance! What power! What wealth! What an energy source! Without the sun's incalculable energy, that small acorn could never have germinated in the rich soil; and those minerals, mixed with water could never have been converted into that giant oak tree, or yellow corn, or intricate fern leaf, or rich fruit, or beautiful flowers.

I remembered how the prophet said: *"But unto you that fear my name shall the Sun of righteousness arise with healing in his wings"* (Malachi 4:2 KJV). Without the sun, the brook where I played as a boy never could have existed and those fish never could have lived. And without the Son of Righteousness in my life, I never could have experienced the wonders of His grace in my own life and upon so many millions of needy people to whom I have witnessed.

There is so much of Him shining—so much energy, so much salvation, so much healing, so much new life. The supply is infinite. The hope of our world depends on Him and on His living presence. Without Him, humanity would be trapped in nothingness, emptiness and unfruitfulness.

I get up from the grass and start back to the city. Everywhere I look, everything I see is pouring out God's message of abundance. I stop by the brook and pick up a single pebble; and again, I hear the message. The pebble seems dead and motionless, but it is not. It is made of molecules and inside each molecule are myriads of atoms, each of which is actually a little universe in itself.

Within every infinitesimal atom are worlds of electrons which move at speeds inconceivable to the human mind. Within that small pebble, there exist all of the basic materials that one would find if the stars could be examined microscopically. While that pebble seems dead, it is really a highly organized family of units of endless energy. It is not a solid mass as it appears to be. Each electron is actually separated from another by a space larger than itself.

What a study in life! That small pebble looks so ordinary, yet all that is in the universe is at work in it. And that makes me think of God at work in me–and in you. All of the creative power and energy that He is, right now is energizing your life and my life. We are living miracles by the creation of God.

Fifth 60-Second Secret

I recognize that the abundance which God has created is proof of His goodness and great generosity.

There is plenty for my needs and my desires.

Since the wealth of this earth was created by our Father, it is good and not bad. It was not intended for the monopoly of unbelievers but for the use of those with faith in His Love Plan.

It is no disgrace to be poor. It is a disgrace to believe in poverty.

God created me for abundance. It is right that I enjoy life's best.

I refuse religious bigotry that condemns wealth and sanctifies misery. God created plenty. There is no shortage for His family.

In God's Love Plan to lift, to heal, and to bless people, material wealth has divine purpose.

As His partner, I vow never to accept poverty, but to stand up and to believe for God's best in life–because I am part of His big plan, and His material blessings are part of my birthright.

The Principle of Vision

The miracle of sight must be among the most awesome wonders of life. The delicate mechanism of the eye is astounding. Yet it is not really what you see with. Your brain is what sees.

With your eyes closed in sleep, you may watch entire scenes of faces or places or happenings with such perfect detail that you can never forget them–yet they did not appear in the material world. What you "saw" in your dream was a vision created by your brain.

You have the ability to see in different ways. Your brain receives the image of what materially appears before your eyes. Also, you have the power to "see" by forming mental pictures which do not exist materially. You can project positive or negative possibilities, scenes and situations.

Fear or worry is the negative use of your imagination. You project situations which have not occurred and the same feelings are experienced as if they were real–anxiety, headaches, an upset stomach, a rise in blood pressure, acceleration of the heartbeat, rapid breathing, constriction of arteries, etc. If your imagination can be used in negative, destructive ways, you can also deliberately use it in a positive, constructive way and get positive results.

Worry and fear are fed by negative information–by *seeing* negative scenes. Faith, poise, confidence, and assurance are nourished by positive information–by *seeing* positive scenes. I have trained myself to see God at work in me, to see His faithfulness, His generosity, His power, and His abundant Life. I see Him; and I have courage, assurance, peace and happiness.

This sixth secret is to help you discover the value of your ability to *see*–to *imagine*, to *think*–and to draw such a source of strength and power from God at work in you that nothing can stop you from getting everything you want in life. An idea, a concept, a thought, or a vision is something you see with your mind–a mental picture. Your thoughts are the pictures which you personally choose to project in your mind.

The visions which you see and ponder wield an almost miraculous influence upon you and your lifestyle. The phenomenal law of life, irrefuted for centuries, is that *you become whatever you envision.* The "you" you see is the "you" you'll be! Every page that you read of this message is projecting the picture of the potential new "you" upon your mind and spirit. The seed of the new "you" is being planted and it is beginning to produce after its kind.

In five steps, secret number six is:

FIRST: Get a clear vision in your mind and spirit of the unique "you" that God has created and that Christ died to redeem, with the unlimited potential that His presence in you represents.

SECOND: Gather all of the information you can, from the Bible and elsewhere, to support that uplifting vision of the *"you"* that God made in His own image.

THIRD: Reject every thought, concept, counsel, image, or vision that in any way diminishes, devaluates, demoralizes, depreciates, discredits or depresses your vision of the "you" that God made to walk and to talk with Him.

FOURTH: Refocus and re-project your picture of the "you" created by God and redeemed by Christ, and hold that vision of the new "you" in your mind and spirit until you forget what the old self was like.

FIFTH: Become acquainted with that transformed new "you." Believe in Christ at work in your new being. Act according to the new, re-created "you." You will actually become that updated new "you" that is now redeemed by Christ and that is at one with your Father in heaven.

Learning and applying these five steps will affect the way you talk and act. You will go out the same door as before, but the world will look different to you. You will walk down the same sidewalk, but the way you walk will change. There will be certainty and decisiveness in your steps. You will carry your shoulders differently. Your health will improve. You will sleep better. People will admire you, and you will inspire the best in them.

Whenever you meet or mingle with people in offices, factories, marketplaces, churches, clubs, homes, or wherever, they will treat you with greater respect and esteem. They will have confidence in you. You will be more convincing, attractive and likeable.

Beyond Humanism to Unlimited Miracles

To achieve this phenomenal transformation into the wonderful "you" that God has created, base your vision on information that is valid and proven. The Bible is the most proven and the most reliable information available anywhere.

Philosophers, psychologists, professors of psychosomatics, mental science, and psychic religions have evolved remarkable statements, clichés, theories, and formulas which appear to be helpful, inspiring and productive. But without the miracle of being restored to God through Jesus Christ, self-improvement is limited to nothing more than psychological humanism. While this self-help process of the mind can motivate improvement in lifestyle and circumstances, it cannot touch the supernatural, creative realm of God's domain in you through the redemptive work of Christ.

The secrets I am revealing to you go infinitely beyond humanism and mental science. They relate to God in a supernatural lifestyle. When you discover the facts of (1) your *identification* with God, (2) your *relation* with His Life-source, and (3) your *potential* with Him at work in you, you realize God's miracle, creative power at work within you—which is actually His kingdom in you— and nothing is impossible when you and God become partners.

With God at work in you, ideas that come to your mind which are good for God, good for people, and good for you are messages direct from Him. If they are *i-m-p-o-s-s-i-b-l-e,* that is even more proof that they are from God, because they exceed the limits of humanism and have room for God–they require a miracle.

Lifted to Dignity and Self-Esteem

The picture that you perceive of yourself that is projected from the Holy Scriptures is the seed of God's faith at work in you. Your power to think is your power to have faith. Your faith and your hope are the vision or the picture that you see in your mind or spirit, based on what the Bible says. It is the picture that represents the miraculous possibilities that exist with God at work in you.

This new "you" is made possible because the principle of your sin has been dealt with by Jesus Christ, in your place. Since He paid the penalty for all of your sins, nothing you ever did can stand between you and God to accuse you, or threaten you with judgment, or fill you with guilt, fear, or inferiority. Consequently, the new, restored, and recreated "you" that God paid so much to redeem can stand up and become a living representative of Him at work in human form on this earth. This is the only way God can fulfill His original dream for you.

A young Kikuyu tribal girl heard us teach these principles. She was a village "nobody," a Kikuyu female, uneducated, with no cultural worth beyond the dowry her father would collect and her childbearing and wood-carrying ability for the man who would own her as his wife. Following the teaching that we shared during our seminar, Jesus appeared to her in a vision. He told her to go explain the Bible promises to people and to pray for them, and that He would go with her and work through her and bless the people.

Across her nation she journeyed on foot, on bicycle, by cart, and by other means of primitive conveyance. A stream of miracles followed that girl until the crowds became so large that policemen had to protect her while she taught and prayed for the people. She learned what Jesus Christ did for her and how God wanted to live in and through her. She received a new vision of herself, recreated in God's image, with God at work in her through Jesus Christ.

Her ministry has grown until she has traveled across Scandinavia, America and Africa, helping people in Christ's name. She was a female "nobody" who was transformed into a powerful woman of God who has been received like a queen wherever she has journeyed with the gospel.

Forming a New Image of Life

God will do wonderful things through you when you see your potential in Him. As long as you think you are a nobody and see a nobody in your mirror, you will walk, talk and act like a nobody. The average person tends toward indoctrination–creeds, guidelines, limits, and absolutes which are established by others. The average person is programmed by culture, religion, educators, family, and peers... by television, by the newspaper, by their organization or club or community.

Once others categorize you and fit you into the mold of their making, if you accept their opinion and live like you think they think you should live, that is what I call being indoctrinated. People who submit to this manipulation seldom ever rise beyond the level that is pre-programmed for them by others. Once you are indoctrinated, your mind is fixed and you stop thinking creatively. This is why religion often stunts personal growth. (I said "religion"–not vital Christianity.)

Many religious doctrines are outdated. Sermonizers limit god to the sixteenth century English and make Him sound like a prophet from antiquity. But God is very much alive in the now and has never changed. He speaks your language and is speaking today in many ways, continuing to impress upon you that He values you and wants you to get the best out of life.

You and God can change the predominate, day-and-night concept of life that you have allowed to take form in your mind and that exactly matches the way you are living today. God must wait until you are willing to think new thoughts, to formulate a new image of life, and to see a new vision of yourself based on His Love Plan for you.

Miracles Are Waiting in You

Ideas, thoughts, and visions are seeds. When they are based on God's Bible Love Plan, they are miracle seeds; and they will yield or produce after their kind. (Genesis 1:11-12.) A morbid mind filled with sick thoughts will produce a morbid, sick body. Mental discord produces physical discord. Develop faith in God's Love Plan and in His ideas about you, and you will drive out the devil of pessimism, the great breeder of disease, failure, and misery in human lives.

Take control over the pictures you allow to formulate in your thinking by being sure that they conform to God's image of you. *"We behold...the glory of the Lord and are changed into that same image"* (2 Corinthians 3:18 paraphrase mine). Concepts of weakness, failure, or poverty are destructive and demoralizing. They will reduce you to their level. They are your deadliest enemies—vicious thieves of your happiness, health, success, and abundance. Resist as you would demons the ideas that you are poor, unworthy, limited, weak, or inferior. Those ideas are lies! You were born to succeed, not to fail.

Idea-power and vision-power are seed-power. In your own brain are ideas of power just waiting to be born, to grow, and to procreate. You have the capacity for over three billion ideas, according to scientists. It is said that, at best, we use only ten percent of our thinking power. That means that God who is at work in us is being allowed to accomplish, at best, only ten percent of what He created us for.

Seeing Life's Best at Your House

In certain nations, perfectly born infants are deliberately blinded or their legs and arms are broken, twisted, and left to heal in deformed positions. The gods are supposed to be pleased for a member of the family to be crippled and to spend his or her life as a beggar.

Traditional religion often does that to the human spirit. Born into God's family healthy and perfect, the eyes of the mind are blinded to God's miraculous, abundant lifestyle. Attitudes are twisted and warped by pious ideologies and sanctimonious doctrines. The facts are that God created birds to fly, fish to swim, and people to be happy, successful, healthy, and productive.

God told Abraham to look as far as he could see and promised him that whatever he could see, he would possess. (Genesis 13:14-15.) That is why He wants your vision clear so that you can see His abundance and possess life's best.

A blind Hindu was led to our meetings in South India among some seventy-five thousand people. As I talked about God's love and what Jesus Christ did to redeem us to God, he was astounded. Having never heard the gospel before, he wept and told God that he believed what I was saying. The man said that he experienced a sensation like warm water washing his entire spirit, mind, and body. Overwhelming peace swelled up in his heart, and when he opened his eyes to look up toward God in thanksgiving, they were as clear as the eyes of a new-born child. God had healed his blindness.

A baby boy was carried to our meeting in Africa. The child was born without eyeballs. The mother heard our teaching, and new faith was born in her heart. Standing amidst some sixty-five thousand people, she listened; then she prayed earnestly to God for a miracle, and the child was marvelously healed. Small eyes formed in the boy's empty sockets, and he could see. By the following day, perfect, beautiful eyes had been formed in the child's head and he was normal. Almost anyone in the provincial capital of Nakuru could take you to that village because they know about little Simeon.

God wants you to have physical eyesight; and he also wants you to learn to see spiritually–to imagine and to envision the wonders of His promises and of His Love Plan for you.

Now I See a Brand New Me

The tramp in the park sees the chauffeur-driven Rolls Royce go by, carrying the man with the tall silk hat, and bemoans, "There, except for ME, go I." Pogo Possum blurts out in the comic strip,

"We have met the enemy, and they is US!" Solomon said centuries ago, and all sages, philosophers, and prophets agree, as a person thinks in the heart, so is he or she. (Proverbs 23:7.) The comedian's line, "What you *see* is what you get!" has a far deeper meaning than the suggestive analogy implies.

A Gypsy family in France brought their boy to our meetings. He was born club-footed. They carried a new pair of shoes with them because they had listened to our teaching about God's Love Plan until they could *see* their son walking with normal feet, wearing normal shoes. One night, as thousands were listening, the lad's feet became as straight and normal as mine. With tears of joy, the father told the audience what had happened and the people rejoiced as they watched the lad put on his new shoes and walk with pride for the first time in his life. The family's *vision* was fulfilled.

A Filipino man sold his little house to buy a ticket to the city where we were teaching a great multitude of people. He was dying of a terminal disease but he had heard about the wonderful things that were taking place, and he believed that God would restore him. When friends urged him not to sell the house, he replied, "I'll be cured. I'll come home well, and I'll build another house. If I lie here, I will die."

He saw himself well again. The picture he held in his mind of God healing him was the seed of its own fulfillment. He was wonderfully restored, and thousands of people were inspired to have faith when he told the crowd what he had done.

Your imagination is a great aid to the release of your faith-power when it is based on God's promises in His Love Plan. Jesus said, *"Unless one is born again, he cannot see the kingdom of God"* (John 3:3). One needs to experience the new birth in order to see God at work in a human person. Perhaps you never considered yourself as the domain of God from where He reigns, saves, blesses, restores, and prospers people. Maybe you thought He does all of those fine things from heaven. The essence of the Christian message is the wonder of Christ in you. (Colossians 1:27.) It is the miracle of the kingdom of God within you. (Luke 17:21.)

When Christ lives in you, your new life is really His life in you. You say, "Jesus, here is my brain; think through it. Here is my face; glow through it. Here are my hands; touch with them. Here are my eyes; see through them. Here are my ears; listen with them. Here are my lips; speak through them. Here is my heart; love through it."

Sixth 60-Second Secret

I see myself in God's image, redeemed by His love and restored to Him as He created me to be. I believe God is alive and at work in me. I act on that premise and I release His power in me. The seed of His faith is in me. He fulfills His dream through me.

I resist, as I would a demon, any idea that I am limited or inferior. I reject every thought or influence that discredits my vision of the new "me." Pessimism only breeds disease, failure, and misery. I will allow no one to program my life, categorize my value, or rate my potential.

God at work and alive in me lifts me to the level of super living. Nothing is impossible for Him in me. My house is His domain. He gives me dignity and self-esteem. No creed, religion, or person can control my vision of the new "me." I see me like He sees me with His best in me.

The Principle of Action

Action is the proof that you believe what you say. It turns knowledge and trust into power and achievement. It is the great awakener of excellence. The seventh secret of success is: Recognize that life's best is plenteous and available to you when you put your new knowledge about yourself and God into action. Real believing is always proven by decisive action. The process of achieving faith is: (1) knowing, (2) analyzing, (3) choosing, and (4) deciding. Then the climax of faith is (5) action...claiming God's best because you know it belongs to you. The greatest secret to the success of our world ministry has been action. We act because we believe.

What is the secret to dynamic *a-c-t-i-o-n?* God is alive and at work inside you. It is God who is at work in you causing you to be willing and to do His good pleasure. (Philippians 2:13.) Look unto Jesus, the author and finisher of your faith. (Hebrews 12:2.) Always see Him in action through you. As the art instructor said, "Keep your eyes on the model; don't watch your hands."

Acting on the "Yes" in Life

Knowledge only becomes power when you act upon it. Many people who can quote sacred scriptures or the philosophers often contradict all they have memorized by their conversation and their actions. Knowledge is meaningless until enthusiastic commitment and decisive action transforms that knowledge into power for the good of yourself or your loved ones or your community.

The most natural thing in the world is to act on what you believe in. You buy an airplane ticket and commit your life to that airline company when you board the plane, without examining its equipment or its performance record. You prove your faith by your action.

You put your money in the bank—money that you worked hard to save—without examining the bank personnel's credentials, and usually without verifying the bank's success record. You trust your lawyer, butcher, grocer—and what about your physician? Or your insurance company? You act positively because you believe in these institutions and people. You live a "yes" in life. You can get nowhere living a "no."

Some people wonder if they can trust a power that is invisible, but the greatest powers are invisible. Love and joy cannot be seen or measured; yet they are powers that produce some of life's best treasures in the form of happiness, peace, and contentment. The sounds of a radio and the images transmitted to your television screen are invisible to your sight out in the open air, yet the lives of millions are regulated by them. Electricity is not something that you can go out and touch in midair and analyze, yet it keeps society functioning. Law is invisible, untouchable; yet you are governed by it.

Releasing God's Creative Power

A single drop of fresh dew on a rose petal was microscopically photographed for a television special. Inside that tiny globe of moisture was an entire world. Infinitesimal creatures could actually be seen mating, eating, moving in organized patterns–all in a drop of fresh dew on a rose. Female species were actually photographed in the act of giving birth. That tiny drop of dew was, in itself, a microcosmic universe of life. The depths of the seas or the mountains, the infinity of the universe or of life in a tiny drop of dew has not even begun to be comprehended.

Faith is seeing the unseen and acting upon it as though it already existed in tangible form. We call those things which be not as though they were. (Romans 4:17.) We look not at the things which are seen, but at the things which are not seen. (2 Corinthians 4:8.) Things which are seen were not made of things which appear. (Hebrews 11:3)–or we could say, "What we see was made of things we cannot see."

This means that the *unseen* world is more real than the *seen* world, because *seen* things were all made of *unseen* things which existed in God's unseen domain before He materialized them in our seen world. Everything that you desire already exists in God's domain. It is only waiting for you to know about it and to believe it, then to transform that knowledge and faith into power by *a-c-t-i-o-n*. *"Faith is the substance of things hoped for, the evidence of things not seen"* (Hebrews 11:1).

Your action that corresponds with knowledge of God's Love Plan and The Big Connection–coupled with faith in God to bring this to pass, working through you–releases the same creative power of God that was released when He created the world, divided the Red Sea, provided manna from heaven or water from a rock. Your faith in action releases the same power that was released when Jesus healed the cripples, restored the blind and deaf, fed the multitude, and raised the dead–or when Peter and John lifted a cripple to his feet, or when Paul raised a dead man or told a lame man to walk.

Start–and You Will Go Places

Jesus told the crippled man who was brought to Him in Mark 2 to take up his bed and go his way. (Mark 2:11.) The man did not hesitate because of his paralysis, but he did what Jesus said to do; and his *a-c-t-i-o-n* released the creative power of God to materialize his miracle. He was made whole. They brought a man to Jesus who had a withered hand. Jesus told him to "stand up." Then He said, *"S-t-r-e-t-c-h* forth your hand." In other words, "Do something!" The man put forth all of his energy to do as Christ had commanded, and his hand was restored.

In practically all of Christ's miracles, there is the clear lesson that one must act–must do something in order to obtain what one desires. It may seem impossible, but do it anyway because God is at work within you. Your action by faith releases God's creative power within you for the impossible. *"The things which are impossible with men are possible with God"* (Luke 18:27).

Heaven is never reached by the person who does not act. You honor truth by putting it to work for you. The songwriter underscored this principle in this verse:

A bell is not a bell 'til you *ring* it.

A song is not a song 'til you *sing* it.

Love in your heart is not put there to stay,

Love is not love 'til you *give it away.*

Expand–S-t-r-e-t-c-h Yourself

Jesus was always an action person. Most teachers explain things. Jesus did things. Jesus was not a man of theory or a promoter of religious doctrine. He was not a philosopher. He was a man of action. One translation says that God is the energizer within you. (Philippians 2:13.) It says that the same God does all the energizing. (1 Corinthians 12:6.) God empowers you with strength by His Spirit. (Ephesians 3:16.)

As long as you treat this knowledge as a philosophy or a theory, and wistfully dream about what it may mean to you someday, God's power will not be manifested in your life. *"Now is the accepted time; now is the day of salvation"* (2 Corinthians 6:2). *Now* is when you are what God says you are. *Now* you have infinite value. You are identified with Christ *now*. *Now* your life is different, changed, transformed. You are a new "you." The miracle-Jesus lives at your house *now*.

Expand–*s-t-r-e-t-c-h* yourself. Believe! Then put action to your faith and release the power that produces God's best in your life–*now*.

D. L. Moody said, "I like the way *I am doing things* more than the way you are talking about them!"

I call this principle: Action TNT, meaning *Action–Today, Not Tomorrow*. The winning crowd does not wait on things to happen, or wonder at things that happen. They make things happen. God cannot act until you act. The ball is in your court. The next move is yours. No one else is responsible. Not your parents, your boss, nor your community.

The apathetic and the cowardly lament each failure with lazy submission, moaning, "That's the way the ball bounces!" or, "That's the way the cookie crumbles!" But the believer *takes charge*. The action person says, "I'll bounce my own ball!" or, "I'll navigate my own vessel!" The believer *makes* things happen!

Pine caterpillars have been placed end-to-end in a circle, with food in the center. They will follow each other until they die of starvation, with plenty of food within smelling distance. The greatest waste is to permit one's life to be spent under the influence, domination, or leadership of someone who is negative. Associate with big people. They influence you to think big. Little people make you feel and think little. They retard your progress and destroy your self-esteem.

The only person who restricts your progress or obstructs your happiness, health, success, and prosperity is the one who negatively influences your decisions. Life is up to *you*—no one else.

Someone said that it is not the size of the dog in the fight, but the size of the fight in the dog that determines the winner.

"In all labor [action] there is profit, but idle chatter leads only to poverty" (Proverbs 14:23). A renowned artist was asked to make a speech at the unveiling of his marble sculpture. When the veil was withdrawn, his only words were, "There is my speech!"

Seventh 60-Second Secret

Action is the proof of what I believe. By action I transform my knowledge into power, turning my possibilities into realities. All things are possible when I act with God at work in me.

Action produces the rich fruit of God's best in my life. It releases His power in me. It awakens excellence in me. Mediocrity, failure, and weakness belong to those who are afraid to act.

I shall never allow religion or tradition to stifle my desires, to cloud my dreams, or to benumb my ambitions. God is everything good that I can desire or need. When I act, He acts to materialize His best in my life. He is my energizer.

I am resolved to go for life's best. God says "yes" to my finest dreams.

Chapter 16

The Message that Works

The life and ministry of T. L. Osborn have been dedicated to those–

Who are weary of condemnation,

insecurity, confusion, and guilt;

Who feel alone and without personal value;

Who desire forgiveness for wrongs committed

against God, against others,

and against themselves;

Who face problems, pressures, and dilemmas,

and who crave practical answers;

Who want a new lifestyle of happiness, health,

purpose and blessing;

Who have been frustrated by doctrines

of evil spirits in Christians and need

to know they are secure in Christ;

Who need healing for the whole person,

mental, physical, and spiritual.

A major aspect of T. L. Osborn's ministry is the message he preaches. In the '90s, he wrote a book called *The Message that Works.* He had been in ministry long enough and had experienced such success all over the world, that he could boldly say, "*This* is the message that works!" The truths contained in this literary rendering are fundamental guidelines for gospel ministers, beacons of inspiration for Bible students, and vital seeds of miracle blessings.

LaDonna shared on behalf of her father and Osborn Ministries International,

> *It is the message of the gospel that makes the difference and my father has emphasized that in this book. He lays out the gospel; and, for us, when we talk about its message, we're not talking about one of many topics…as in, this is square one and then we'll go on to square two. The gospel is the* essence *of the Christian faith.*

> *When you get saved, you* really *need to understand its message—and everything else is built on its truth. To us, the gospel is the foundation of everything; so if any other topic is not compatible with the framework of its message, then you're off-track.*

> *There are already built-in boundaries in the Word for all of our beliefs and teachings.*

Must Be Rooted in the Redemptive Work of Christ

There is no magic in the concepts that Dr. Osborn teaches. They are strategic, dynamic, pragmatic, and biblical. When he says "biblical," he means that they are rooted in the redemptive work of Christ. More than one concept has gotten off-course; such as healing, giving, the gifts of the Spirit, church structure or leadership, or so-called spiritual warfare and intercessory prayer. They have gotten off-course because they have been rooted in ideology–doctrine or belief–that is not accountable to the redemptive work of Christ.

Dr. Osborn teaches that the *Good* News is "The Message that Works." He attributes the long success of his global ministry to the teaching of this message. The message is simple, but fundamental. Through this message, people are acquainted with: (1) their origin in God, (2) satan's deception, (3) Christ's death and resurrection, and what that means, and (4) the reality of His life in believers today. Who was Jesus? What did He do? Why did He do it? Whom did He do it for? Those are the essentials. And as Christians grow in truth, they should re-visit everything they believe in light of this, which is the essence of God's plan for man.

The Seed–Better Than the Touch

T. L. Osborn announces to the multitudes the facts of the gospel. The people listen. Faith is created in their hearts by the good seeds that are planted in their lives. When they embrace Jesus as Savior, their lives are transformed; and in tens of thousands of cases, their sicknesses and maladies are miraculously cured. The seed, which *"is the Word of God"* (Luke 8:11), procreates its own harvest in the lives of those who believe the truths that they hear. Most of the great miracles that Dr. Osborn has witnessed have taken place while he was preaching and teaching the gospel.

Whether spoken audibly or expressed in print, truth has the same seed-power and accomplishes the same results. That is why so many thousands of people have been miraculously healed while reading the pages of his book, *Biblical Healing*.

In attendance at one of the Osborn meetings, was a deaf man who was unable to hear the teaching. T. L. gave him a copy of *Biblical Healing*–along with a personal note urging him to read it to help him to have faith, and telling him to then come back for prayer. He was so disappointed by this delay, that T. L. proceeded to pray for his healing without him understanding the truths on which biblical faith is based. When his ears did not open, the man returned home very despondent.

Two days later, he returned to the meeting rejoicing and with perfect hearing. He said that as he read the pages of the book, he received a new living faith, and was instantly healed of his deafness.

T. L. has asserted time and time again, "The miracles and wonders, that I have witnessed for so many years, have not taken place because of special prayers or special anointing, but because the seed of the Word of God has been sown in the hearts of the people. The life of God, in the seed of His Word, produces its healing wonders in the people."

"[Jesus] cast out the spirits with His Word, and healed all that were sick" (Matthew 8:16 KJV). If demon spirits do not leave the people while Dr. Osborn is preaching, then during the mass prayer for the multitude, he adjures them to leave–"we cast them out in Jesus' name." In nations around the world, insane people, cripples, paralytics, diseased victims, and all kinds of oppressed and sick people have been instantly healed while T. L. and his wife have taught the truths about Christ and God's Word.

Dr. Osborn tells the people: "Do not try to have enough faith to receive miraculous blessing. Just allow the seed to be planted. It will produce harvest in your life. You can experience your miracle while listening and pondering these truths."

In his ministry to multitudes, he never touches people when he prays for their healing, although he teaches that it is scriptural to lay hands on the sick. (Mark 16:18; Luke 4:40.) Laying hands on suffering people in a multitude can potentially provoke public injury, panic, and even riot.

God's Good Plan

God created Adam and Eve and placed them in a garden of abundance, where everything that He made was pleasant and good. (Genesis 1:31; 2:9.) They were His companions and they experienced His fullness. In God's redemptive plan for human lives, He still wants every person to have happiness and pleasure, energy and strength, peace and love, tranquility and joy, health and dignity, and an abundance of real living. But a tragedy interrupted rapport between God and people. The result is that now this world is filled with people fighting depression, struggling to meet obligations, plagued by disease and loneliness, abandoned, insecure, and frustrated by problems without solutions.

Many have made irreparable mistakes and have engendered enemies. The psychological diseases of resentment, animosity, pride, jealousy, dishonesty, and hatred have obstructed success and destroyed happiness in millions of lives. Remaining in this chapter is the direction Dr. Osborn takes in providing the answers to the questions, the solutions to the problem, and the cures for the diseases. This is only an earnest of what he shares in his book, *The Message That Works.*

God Is on Your Side

God has made provision for every need or desire that you experience. Start believing that He cares as much for you as He does for anyone else. Despite whatever makes you seem to be unworthy, God is on your side. A small grain of faith can start a miracle in your life today.

The Garden of Eden exhibited the lifestyle and circumstances for which God designed you. Realization of that which has been made available again through the sacrificial love of God's Son will put you on the road that leads back to the paradise that was forfeited so long ago by Adam and Eve. Jesus Christ came to re-demonstrate what God wants us to have. He opened to us the door of His limitless mercy and abundance, through His death on the cross. Every miracle He performed was an example of what God wills for every other person in similar circumstances.

Jesus—The Way Back to God

When Jesus encountered people who were troubled by sins committed against themselves, against their neighbors, and against God, He performed a *spiritual* miracle in their lives—He forgave them. (Mark 2:5-7; Luke 7:47-48; 19:8-10; John 8:3-11.) When He came in contact with people who were suffering diseases or who were crippled or paralyzed, He performed *physical* miracles—He healed their bodies. (Matthew 8:16-17; 9:35; Mark 6:55-56; Luke 4:40.) When He found people who faced material needs, He performed *material* miracles—He provided for them, even when it required a creative miracle. (Matthew 14:15-21; 17:24-27.)

Jesus said, "[Satan's] purpose is to steal, kill and destroy. My purpose is to give *life* in all its fullness" (John 10:10 LB).

STEALING is taking something that belongs to someone else. Satan has done that by conditioning people's minds to accept poverty, fear, sickness, defeat, and problems. Through this negative process they have been cheated out of God's bountiful provisions.

KILLING is cutting short someone's life. The devil has done that to millions through disease and fear, and want and distress, tension and failure.

DESTROYING means to spoil and render useless something of value. The plagues of loneliness and poverty, of sickness and evil, of fear and insecurity have destroyed the influence and happiness of millions whom God intended to be blessed with His fullness.

Jesus came to reveal God to us and to show us the kind of life He wills for us. (John 5:30; 6:38; 14:8-9.) He came to solve our problems, forgive our sins, heal our diseases, give us success, walk with us, surround us with good things, give us energy, and fill us with His *love* and real *life*.

Spiritually, God wills that we have peace, tranquility, faith, hope, love, creativity, and abundant living. *Physically,* He wills that we enjoy healing, energy, physical strength, and vigorous health. *Materially,* He wills that we experience success, achievement, prosperity, and access to the Divine Source of all material provisions.

Through Jesus' death on our behalf, He became *The Way* for us to come back to God. (John 14:6.) And He became *The Way* for

God to come home to us so that He can share with us His abundant life. (John 14:23; 2 Corinthians 6:18.)

Connected with God

Traditional religion has fostered a limited concept of God's relationship with people. It suggests that intimacy with Him is reserved for those who live in poverty and self-abasement.

The seed-truths in this message can extricate you from the religious syndrome of mediocrity that has been handed down from negative pontificates of past centuries.

To fulfill God's plan in life, one needs to grasp *His purpose—His will*—as Jesus did, and learn to be aware of one's infinite value. Fifty-seven times in the Gospel of John—in every chapter except three—Jesus spoke of how he was sent by the Father. His life had divine purpose. Ours does, too.

When Jesus Christ lives in us, He becomes our new *Life*-source that not only engenders blessings in our lives, but also in the lives of those around us. Our thoughts and our words have the mysterious power of creating the situation that surrounds us. They are seeds that we sow. They inevitably procreate of their kind.

This message can help you become aware of God's high opinion of you. You can discover your roots in Divine Royalty. You can learn to think of yourself as God thinks of you, and to talk about yourself as He does in the Bible. You need not *try* to make this happen. It will take place as these truths take root in your thinking.

As you read and ponder this message, be conscious of God's love and of the ransom He paid for you. Be sensitive of how much it has cost Him to make His life available to you. Respond with a hearty "Yes!" to each truth as you grasp it.

These are the concepts that will render ridiculous the outdated religious notions that link poverty to godliness, burdens to humility, and suffering to sainthood. Life can be fresh, empowered by God's ideals. New, miracle energy can flow into your being as you gain knowledge of the remarkable lifestyle that He wills for you.

It's Not Too Good to Be True

When Moses was ready to possess the rich land that God prepared for His people, he sent twelve spies to investigate. (Numbers 13; 14.) The majority of them took one look at that wealthy land and fled. They said in essence, "It is too good to be true! It flows with milk and honey! It is too rich for us! Besides, giants are there! We saw them! We felt like grasshoppers! They could destroy us!"

They thought that way. They talked that way. They acted that way. Consequently, they reaped that crop. They never inherited the blessings God intended for them to share. They died in despair.

Only two men saw things like God sees them. Caleb and Joshua saw a land of blessing. Their assessment was: "This is a good land full of abundance. Since we are God's people, we can take it. He wants us to be enriched by His best." The source of their faith was God's spoken Word. They acted on it and they inherited the Land of Promise.

Caleb and Joshua believed that rich land belonged to royalty. They were not content to leave it in the control of wasters. They were connected with God by their faith–and He prospered their way.

That can happen to you. If embraced, these seeds of truth will grow in the soil of your heart and will produce a rich harvest in your life.

God Is a Good God

I wish all the world could know how good God is. The Bible says that the Lord is gracious and full of compassion. (Psalm 86:15; 111:4; 112:4; 145:8.) Jesus was everywhere moved with compassion. (Matthew 9:36; 14:14; 18:27; Mark 1:41; 6:34.) Another Bible verse says, *"His compassions fail not"* (Lamentations 3:22). Thirty-three times in the book of Psalms it is stated, *"His mercy endureth forever."*

Another remarkable verse states, *"For You, Lord, are good, and ready to forgive; and abundant in mercy to all those who call upon You"* (Psalm 86:5). God says, *"I will rejoice over [you] to do [you] good…with my whole heart and with my whole soul"* (Jeremiah 32:41 KJV). God has a very big heart and soul, and it all rejoices over you to do you good.

Unfortunately, many people think of God as a dominating master who lords it over people with a whip, afflicting and punishing them with sickness, suffering, poverty, and failure. But this is not true. God wills that people enjoy His lifestyle of happiness, success, and blessing–physically, emotionally, spiritually, and materially. The biblical concepts in *The Message that Works* will help you forget the negative way you may have formerly thought; they can obliterate from your mind outmoded and negative thought-patterns.

We Take It One Step Further

God is a good God. It's no small thing to understand that God loves people; therefore—and this is where we take it one step further—*people are valuable to Him*...not because of who they are, not because of anything they do, but because they essentially are valuable to God, even in their most destitute state. You see, we minister to hurting people like beggars that smell, with flies swarming around them—of no value to society, to their families, to themselves. But we see them as so precious to God—the fingerprint of God is on each one; and His whole desire and passion is for their sake. This makes for such a different view of God than His just wanting people to worship Him...as though everything God made was so that He could be stroked. That is such a narcissistic idea of who He is!

Even the idea that God is horrified at sin, so He shed His blood so that sin could be removed...because He can't stand sin because He's so holy—what an odd and degrading way to "sum up" God. We hold this contorted view of God ourselves, and then we paint this picture of Him to the world. Absolutely, God is holy. And absolutely, God hates sin. We read in Hebrews 1:9 that He loves righteousness and He hates iniquity. But this isn't what God's redemptive plan is really about. It's about people whom He loves and wants to return to Him in relationship and fellowship and, even more—to pour His very life into so that they, like He, can live like royalty...Divine Royalty.

We Need This

How important is this message of Dr. Osborn's in a day of explosion of truth, faith, the Word—a day when young people can quote tons of Scripture, but still feel like they don't measure up. They still fell like they're not getting it right. They can't remember all the steps, all the formulae—let alone be able to follow through with them—so they're still riddled with guilt.

Since Bible days, deceivers, seducers, false teachers, vain talkers (2 Timothy 3:13; Titus 1:10), and heretics (2 Peter 2:1) have disturbed, confused, and disquieted Christians—those Christians who lack knowledge of what Christ accomplished for them. Uninformed believers are vulnerable to misguiding voices. Through worldwide electronic and fiber-optics media, Christians of this generation are obliged to cope with an unprecedented bombardment of *"divers and strange doctrines"* (Hebrews 13:9 KJV).

We have been easy targets of the enemy due to little or no understanding of what the redemptive work of Jesus is. In days gone by, the experience of many was that human beings could never be truly valuable. Even the Christian was still a sinner, never able to measure up. Again, caution must be taken that *all* of our concepts are rooted in this essence, this basis, this foundation of God's plan for human beings—Christ's redemptive work on behalf of *all* mankind. Understanding this is vital. Not understanding it can be deadly. *The Message that Works* does just this—*it works*…to arm us with the truth in this regard.

Another interesting observation in regard to what Dr. Osborn has taught for scores of years is that, in light of Mark 16:20, which tells us that Jesus confirms His Word with signs following, Dr. Osborn's message has indeed been confirmed with amazing signs of healing and miracles on an astronomical scale, and not just for a crusade here and there, but consistently, continually for scores of years. His simple, clear unchanging message of the *Good* News–the redemptive work of Jesus Christ–has met with God's unchanging approval.

Chapter 17

God's Love Plan

"I don't think you could ever hear a message by my father without being overwhelmed by the love of God," LaDonna stated.

T. L. Osborn's book—*God's Love Plan*—draws attention to the *love* of God being at the core of salvation. LaDonna continued to share once more on behalf of her father and Osborn Ministries International:

> *God's plan of salvation isn't about righteousness—not really.*
> *At least it isn't about our aspiring to righteousness—how can we*
> *ever claim to be righteous apart from what Jesus accomplished*
> *at Calvary? We are utterly incapable of living the glorious lives*
>
> *God wills for us. But He made that possible through Jesus'*
> *atoning blood.*
>
> *The plan of salvation isn't about sin either—not really. Some*
> *think the main gospel message is: If you're a sinner, you die…*
> *you go to hell! No! It's not about God's judgment, His rules, His*
> *holiness—not really!*
>
> *The real essence of the message that works is God's love plan.*

It's all about love.

God is love! His plan is love! It's about the love of God that He desires to pour into people's lives. They can know His love and therefore know Him.

God's plan was motivated by love. Jesus' action was love in demonstration. His care for us now—His shepherding of our life—is only love. So that's a point that just heals people. When you begin to see salvation as love, you are so much quicker to go share that with somebody else. Everybody needs love.

There is no message in this chronicling of T. L. Osborn's legacy that is more encompassing or more descriptive of what his mission in life has been, than the love plan. Proclaiming and demonstrating God's love to humanity has indeed been the enduring focus of his ministry to millions. The idea, the truth that *God is love, Love created us, and we are meant for love*—is the essence of what T. L. has brought home and bequeathed to a world in need of purpose, peace, power, provision…and hope…for its journey. In all of his teaching, preaching, writing, and recording, T. L. Osborn has emphasized that love is the greatest power. The following teaching has been taken from T.L.'s book, *God's Love Plan*.

Love is God's Greatest Idea

Love is the greatest idea ever to come from God to human beings. *"There is faith and hope and love, but the greatest of these is love"* (1 Corinthians 13:13 paraphrase mine). The Bible says, *"God is love"* (1 John 4:8). You are created by God, so you are the product of love. That means that you are made for love. You are not made for hate or fear.

You are made for life, not for death. You are made for health, not for disease. You are made for success, not failure. You are made for good things, not for bad things.

God loves you so much that He paid a big price—the price of His Son—to have you near Him. When Jesus came to this earth, everything He did underscored how much God values people.

Love Has Healing Power

One day a leper came to Jesus. The disciples said, "Get him away. He is unclean." But Jesus said, "No, let him come. He has faith." (Mark 1:40-42.)

You see, the purpose of Christ's coming was to help people, to save and to bless them. Love caused our Lord to reach out His hand and touch that leper, and his flesh was instantly healed.

Love Causes Rejoicing in Dance

In our crusade in Zaire, two blind women were healed. What a love gift that was from God. Throughout the night they danced in the streets of Lubumbashi, telling the people about their healing.

Love Sets the Poor Among Princes

I saw this poor man, clad in rags, near the Lugogo Stadium, supporting himself with two poles, staggering on trembling, un-coordinated legs, struggling all alone as he headed toward our crusade grounds. The red dust was thick and stirred by the frantic press of people—some carrying lame and sick folks and some leading the blind. But Damiano's lonely figure of despair kept my eyes riveted his way.

As I watched him from our car window, the Lord whispered to me, *God raises the poor out of the dust, and lifts the needy out of the dunghill; that He may set them with the princes of His people.* (Psalm 113:7-8.) I saw the entire nation of Uganda in that forsaken, unloved, desperate man–alone, without hope or faith.

Daisy and I had come to this dejected, vandalized, and brutalized nation to tell them, "Uganda, God loves you! God values you! God paid for you! He needs you! If you will believe on Him and reach out to Him, He will save and heal you and give you a new beginning!"

When I reached the platform, I was still thinking about that staggering, struggling man. The Lord impressed me to call for him and to make an example of him before the multitude–to underscore the fact that God paid the same price for each person and loved each one equally, regardless of how poor or sick or sinful anyone may be.

When I went to the microphone, I described the man to the people, and they found him and helped him to the platform. There before the multitude, I used him as an object lesson. I said, "Even if you are poor, in rags, alone and sick, God values you. He has sent Daisy and me to tell you He needs you! He paid for you! Trust Him, call on Him, and He will save and heal you; He will give you His new life and a new beginning!"

The people clapped and wept at the same time. I called the poor man by his name, Damiano. I said, "You are special to God. You've begged and crawled long enough! I bring you good news! You are not forsaken. Jesus paid for you. He needs you! In His name, I love you. Only believe!"

I told the people, "What God does for this man, He will do for every Ugandan who believes!" I told Damiano about Jesus; I led him in prayer to be saved–and he accepted Christ. Then I pulled him to me and I loved him. I called out with a loud voice, "Oh, you spirit of infirmity, leave this dear man forever, in Jesus' name!" Then I held Damiano and imparted God's love and the healing presence of Jesus Christ.

I took the two poles from his hands and said, "Damiano, you've staggered long enough. Animals crawl, but you are a man in God's image! Let's go! Walk! Jesus heals you! You are no longer a beggar! You are valuable! You are a child of God, with dignity and new life!"

Damiano walked, taking long steps! Then amidst tears, he broke into a glorious smile! The miracle was done! He flung his arms around me in a grasp of love and gratitude. I'll never forget that embrace. A beggar had become a prince in God's family!

I said, "Damiano, thank you for your love! Daisy and I are richer now because you are our new brother."

This man was worth all that we did to bring God's love and miracle power to Uganda. For Daisy and me, that was God's number one job–to go to the forgotten, the lonely, the unloved, the disinherited, the sick, the fearful, those in despair–to go in Jesus' name and to help them discover their value to God and to humanity, to lift and heal and save them and to give them dignity, pride, and salvation.

I told Damiano, "Sit in my chair. You are one of God's choice people now!" As he sat there, smiling and happy, he looked like a prince.

We arranged for Damiano to have good food, a bath, a bed, and new clothes. The next day he came looking like a re-created wonder of God's love and power. He embraced me and laid his head on my shoulders. We were new friends! My new brother had been raised from despair to become a member of royalty through the compassion and powerful love of Jesus Christ.

Love Has Transforming Power

As Jesus climbed out of a boat one day, a wild man came running from among the tombs. Night and day this poor creature screamed and cut himself with sharp stones. He was tormented and possessed by demons. Jesus spoke to the evil spirits and they came out of the man and he was healed. (Mark 5:2-8,15.)

That is what Christ came for. He never wants a human person to live in shame or fear or disgrace. He values people—every person—and He will do whatever you need in order to develop your finest potential as a God-person, successful, happy, healthy, and valued.

Gagged, Strapped, Chained, and Locked in a Hut

A young man was brought to one of our crusades who had been attending a medical college, studying to become a doctor. For some reason his mind snapped, and he became insane. His classmates took straps of iron and bound his hands and feet, then chained him so he could not escape because he was a menace even to himself. They took him back to his village, where his family kept him strapped, chained, and locked in a hut with a door made of crossed poles, wired together, to allow ventilation.

The young man's food was tossed to him like one would feed a dangerous animal. He would lunge at people and try to bite them as they passed his hut. Someone had kicked him in the mouth and knocked out his front teeth.

Four men brought him to the crusade, with his ankles and wrists bound with the chained iron cuffs. They also gagged him to prevent him from biting someone. Jesus came to that man while we were teaching God's Love Plan to the multitude. The demon spirits that had tormented him went out of him, and he became perfectly normal. He resumed his studies at the university and became a living witness of God's big Love Plan.

Love Is Never Mad at You

A prostitute was brought to Jesus one day. Self-righteous people said, "Let's stone her to death. She is an unclean woman." (John 8:3-11.)

But Jesus said, "Wait a minute. God did not send His Son into the world to condemn the world, but to save the world." (John 3:17.) You see, He values each human person. He forgave this woman's sins, made her pure and clean again, and restored her self-dignity and self-esteem as a lady. It is impossible for Him to accuse or judge or condemn you. His value of a person is so great that He seeks to lift and bless you, and to help you become all that your Father created you to be.

A Prostitute Abandoned to Die

In one of our crusades, a young woman who had practiced prostitution since she was a teenager, was hauled to the meeting in an old wheelbarrow. Some Christians found her wasting away on a straw mat in a tiny adobe hut where she had been abandoned to die. She had a large, cancerous tumor of the womb. She was a terminal case, rejected by society, and not even thirty years old.

At first she objected to coming to the crusade, because she was sure there was no hope for her ruined life. She felt guilty and ashamed for her many years spent as a prostitute. The Christians shared that God had not sent His Son to condemn her. They placed pillows in the old wheelbarrow and hauled her to the meeting. Her emaciated body resembled a sallow, skin-covered skeleton, except for her swollen, cancer-ridden abdomen.

Lying there in the wheelbarrow under the open sky, she listened to our teaching. She discovered that God loved her and valued her as she was–that He was not mad at her. She heard us teaching that God loved her so much that, during all the years she had lived in prostitution, He had kept on loving her and had never given up on her.

I remember well my subject that night. I had shared that when we accept what God had accomplished for us, we can receive Him into our lives and that when He comes to live in us, His life transforms us and creates in us a new person. I shared that His life heals our sicknesses and regenerates us spiritually, mentally, and physically.

That woman accepted her pardon and forgiveness and received Jesus Christ into her life by faith. Lying there, weeping and thanking God, she looked up at her friends, reached out her bony arms to them, and was raised up on her feet for the first time in months. She suddenly realized that her tumor had disappeared and that her legs and arms had become strong.

She was not only forgiven of her sins and restored to dignity in God's family, but she was also miraculously cured of cancer. She marched through the press of people and up the steps of the platform, and with tears streaming down her cheeks and with those bony arms raised toward heaven, she shared what God had done.

Afraid of God

A Syrian trader, who had lived most of his life in Ghana, attended our great crusade in Accra and heard about God's big Love Plan for the first time in his life. He was a single man who lied and cheated in business and whose abusive and immoral lifestyle included exploiting African girls to satisfy his sexual pleasure.

Finally he lost his health, being inflicted with a paralytic stroke which left the right side of his body useless. In that condition he attended our crusade, finding it almost too much to comprehend that God valued human beings so much that He gave His only Son to redeem them to Himself. But he kept coming and listening, finally realizing that Jesus Christ actually died in his place, having assumed his own guilt and having suffered the legal punishment for all of his sins. He came to realize how much God loved and valued him, that God had created human beings in His own image, to walk with Him and to live His lifestyle and that God had never abandoned His dream to have people close to Him.

He cried out to God and experienced an indescribable peace that came to him. "I was no longer afraid or guilty." The man had been afraid of God. Regaining his composure from the weeping and thanking God, he realized that all of the paralysis had disappeared. He rubbed the right side of his face that had been twisted, and it was perfect. His right hand, arm, and leg were totally restored. The man was saved and healed in the same instant. He was greatly moved by the knowledge that he was pardoned, redeemed to God, and restored to dignity.

Promiscuity Leads to a Crippled Son

A man who attended one of our meetings had been born in a very poor home and was uneducated. As he struggled in life, he began to steal as a young man. He carried on promiscuously with girls in his neighborhood. He used them, and if they resisted, he abused them. Then shame and guilt began to cloud his life.

Finally he married one of the girls. But he was not satisfied. He continued his promiscuous lifestyle, and soon he was the victim of a venereal disease. A little baby was born to his marriage, but its legs were not normal. They never moved or developed.

Guilt depressed him. He knew that he had been responsible for bringing disease to his wife–that it had now affected his child. As he tried to conceal his guilt by drinking, he developed ulcers, then cirrhosis of the liver, and before long, cancer.

There was little food on the table. Tensions mounted. Nerves were on edge. Then the man's joints began to tighten as the pressures of life intensified. Before long, he could not lift his arms. It was painful for him to walk. Then he was obliged to use crutches.

Unemployed, afraid, resentful, guilt-stricken, and angry, he hated himself–and he hated God. In that despondent state, he heard of the crusade where we were teaching the gospel. At first he presumed that we were foreign soothsayers or charlatans deceiving people. But then he asked himself, *What can I lose?*

So he hobbled to our public meeting on his crutches. His wife accompanied him, carrying their little crippled boy in her arms. There they listened as we taught God's Love Plan, the gospel, to that field of people.

As that man stood there on his crutches looking at his little boy who could not walk, he thought to himself: *My wife and I have none of that. We fight and hate each other. We are sick. We have little food. We are poor. We are fearful. We are lonely. We are angry.*

When I talked about Adam and Eve trying to live without God in their lives, after the fall in the Garden, resulting in hate, lust, envy, problems, and sickness, this man thought to himself, *That's why we are lonely. That's why I am in trouble. That's why my little boy cannot walk. That's why I am about to die of cancer. That's why my body is filled with pain. That's why I am full of remorse. That's why my wife and I are nervous. We are out of touch with God. Our sins have separated us from Him.*

As I continued with God's Love Plan, explaining that the Good News is for each one who has sinned, each one who is sick, each one who lives with guilt, each one who is condemned, each one who is poor, each one who has failed, each one who is affected by an incurable disease, that man nudged his wife and said, "That's the answer. That explains Christ's death. That's the gospel I never knew about. That's not just a religion. That affects us and our problems."

Yet he continued to wrestle with his own logic: *This must be too good for me. I am too far gone. My heart is too sinful. I am too sick. My child was born this way. Nothing can help us. We are without hope.*

He continued reasoning: *I know what brought on this cancer. It was my lifestyle, my rebellion. Did Jesus suffer that for me? Jesus was too good to do that.*

I continued to emphasize that the gospel is the power that brings salvation to everyone who believes. (Romans 1:16.) "Only believe," I said. "All things are possible if you can only believe." (Mark 9:23.)

As I kept teaching, that man decided, *I will believe what Mr. Osborn is saying. I do believe it.* He and his wife found themselves weeping together, embracing each other. Suddenly he thought of his little son. He told his wife, "Put him down. I believe his legs are changed. Put him down."

The little boy was perfectly whole. His little legs functioned and had become strong for the first time in his life.

Then the man noticed that he did not have pain in his shoulders. His crutches were not hurting him as he leaned on them. There was no pain in his knees. He dropped his crutches aside and discovered that while he had received peace and joy in his spirit, the Lord had healed his arthritis.

The family walked home together. The happy mother fixed some food. The father ate and realized that his stomach had no pain, the suffering from stomach ulcers was not there. His side felt good too, because the swelling was gone. He pounded his side–the cancer was obviously gone, too. He was a new man: physically, mentally, and spiritually.

Love Does Not Discriminate

I can tell you that people are basically the same worldwide. They commit the same sins, experience the same needs, sense the same guilt, suffer the same diseases, and instinctively search for the same peace, regardless of race, sex, color, nationality, or background.

When people really understand God's big Love Plan, they react with the same overwhelming satisfaction—from the stoic and traditionally calm American Indians, Eskimos, and Japanese to the placid and poised Buddhists.

We have proven what the Bible says: *"For there is no difference...the same Lord over all is rich to all who call upon him, for whoever calls on the name of the LORD shall be saved"* (Romans 10:12-13).

Buddhist Nunn Finds Peace in God's Love Plan

During our crusade in southern Thailand, a seventy-four-year-old Buddhist nun attended. She was placed in the temple when she was only a girl and had consecrated her life to serve the temple. Our teaching meetings were conducted out under the shade of a huge coconut palm grove. The sound from our loud speaker horns reached her ears.

She slipped away from the temple and bought a piece of cloth in the marketplace with which she could conceal her identity, since her only clothing was a nun's habit. She stood in a shadowy area at the edge of the field to avoid recognition.

That night I spoke about God's big Love Plan and how the good news of what Jesus did on the cross is for us. This old woman had never heard those gospel facts in all of her life.

She came to mine and Daisy's cottage the next day. We sat for two hours out under those beautiful palm trees as she tried to tell us, through the interpreter, what had happened. She explained how she had received Jesus Christ and had been made new inside. She said, "All of my life, I searched for peace. The only thing I knew to do was to work hard in the temple and to serve the priests every way possible.

"I soon learned that everyone in the temple was searching for the same peace that I sought, but they were all unsatisfied. The others were as unhappy as I was. I often wondered if there was anything else I could do to find peace in my heart. Many nights I wept for hours in the darkness when no one could see me. I felt guilt, but I knew no way to find peace."

This dear old woman went back to the village of her people to tell them about Jesus. It was not long before she was teaching groups of them about God's big Love Plan and, together, they built a bamboo and thatch meeting house which soon became a thriving church in that village.

From Alaska to Argentina, from Calcutta to Calabar, from Moscow to Manitoba...whether the people are red, brown, yellow, black, or white...whether they are educated or illiterate... whether they are rich or poor, they all respond to Christ when they see His unchanging compassion.

A Great Era of Flaming, Miracle Evangelism

Dr. T. L. Osborn made it a point to say, "One of the most challenging statements in the Bible concerning the last days is in Matthew 24:14. Jesus said, *And this gospel of the kingdom shall be preached in all the world for a witness unto all nations; and then shall the end come.'* This prophecy from the lips of Jesus, foretells a great era of flaming, miracle evangelism that proclaims Christ as Lord with evidence to the people and nations of the world, including Muslims and Hindus."

T. L. Osborn, while passionately hating the demonic belief systems of false religions, has modeled passionate and unconditional love for his fellow man who is held in bondage by them. It took more than sheer commitment for this to happen. It took love for the Hindus and the Islamic people—love that was willing to throw off any shackles of racism and any religious spirit regarding them. He has been able to maintain a fine-tuned, sensitive balance due to his understanding of God's Love Plan. It will take that kind of love-motivated, fine-tuned, and sensitive—to fuel and bring to fruition this great era of flaming, miracle evangelism that Jesus prophesied about in Matthew 24:14.

Chapter 18

Victorious Prayer

Dr. Osborn says that everywhere he goes people question him about his prayer life. When he teaches on the subject of prayer, he points out that prayer, like any other concept of the Christian faith, must be rooted in the redemptive work of Christ. When prayer has gotten off-track, T. L. states that it was because it was not rooted in Christ's atoning work on the cross.

T. L. and Daisy started out in ministry as good Pentecostal folk; and a story that he finds helpful to share is how, as he and Daisy began to better understand the gospel, they had to learn how to pray differently.

Prayers that Bear No Fruit

When we began our ministry, we spent hours on our knees daily, beseeching God for blessings that He had already provided, and begging Him to do so many things that He had commissioned us to do. In our passion to please Him and to win souls, we even went to India as missionaries. But without understanding God's plan of redemption or the blessings that Christ's death provided, we were unable to convince people of ancient religions about the gospel. Without miracles, we offered little more than a Christian philosophy.

In less than a year, we returned to the United States, heartbroken and embarrassed by what seemed to us to be a failure in our mission. Although we spent hours on our knees, seeking God for needed answers, our manner of prayer did not harmonize with biblical truths. For over a year, we struggled to reform our thinking and our attitude about prayer. As we searched for knowledge concerning the miraculous, God saw our struggle and the Lord Jesus appeared to us. Following that awesome experience, we began to discover in the Scriptures the blessings that Christ had provided through His death, burial, resurrection, and ascension. We became aware of Satan's total defeat by Christ, and we learned about God's promises to confirm His Word by miracles.

Prayers that God Will Not Answer

We realized that the two things we prayed for the most would never be answered by God because, (1) we were asking Him to do what He had already accomplished through Christ's sacrifice, and (2) we were asking Him to do what He had already commissioned us to do.

These and other biblical discoveries posed a major dilemma for us. We were fanatical about prayer. If we failed to spend hours on our knees each day, we felt condemned and unworthy to minister. As we discovered redemptive truths, however, we realized that our way of praying did not correspond with God's Love Plan for people. We were pleading for Him to do things that He was already passionate to do.

For example, at the time I was learning about mass prayer, I became aware that Jesus wanted people healed more than I did. I went past pleading with Him, "Heal them *for me,* heal them *for me!*" It was a spiritual breakthrough to realize how truly passionate God was about healing, and to come to the realization that this wasn't about me and my ministry. It was about God's love for people.

Before we launched our first healing crusade in America in 1948, I went into the basement of our home where I prayed and fasted for three days (without a drop of water or a crumb of food). I was interceding for God to heal the sick FOR US when we would lay our hands on them in our upcoming meetings. After three days, I seemed to hear the echo of my voice. But it was in the form of a question: *Heal them–FOR WHOM?*

I stammered, "Heal the sick FOR US, O Lord, when we lay our hands on them."

And the voice came again: *For WHOM?*

Then the light turned on in my spirit as I pondered: Two thousand years before we became interested in healing sick people, God was so moved with compassion for sufferers that He sent His Son who gave His back to the smiters. They ploughed his flesh like a farmer ploughs furrows in a field (Psalm 129:3), and by those stripes we are healed. (Isaiah 53:5.)

There I was, fasting and praying for God to have enough interest in sick people to "heal them–as though He was not as interested in them as we were. I was interceding and fasting, but

I was ignoring redemptive truth. Our part is to give the gospel to our hurting world and to give it with faith. Then the people have the opportunity to believe it, and God confirms it. Salvation is His idea. Healing is His idea. He gave His Son and His Son gave His life to make possible these redemptive blessings of the gospel.

As Daisy and I grappled with inconsistencies between our praying and God's redemptive provisions, we resolved to reform our prayer life, regardless of how awkward it might prove to be—which became a very difficult challenge. Why? Because language becomes routine, automated. It flows from our lips almost without thought. We were pouring out supplications to God with automated phrases, verbalizing empty, traditional prayer concepts that were not in accord with the truths of redemption.

It was embarrassing to interrupt my pleadings to God and to say, "Wait, Lord. I didn't mean what I just said. I was rambling. *This* is what I meant to say." Then I would force myself to articulate exactly what I had intended to say. What a challenge!

Daisy and I struggled with our miserable, automated verbosity for over a year. But by persistence, we finally conformed our prayer vocabulary to God's redemptive provisions. We learned to say what we meant, instead of rambling in a torrent of sacred phrases and platitudes like religious gurus.

Must Be Rooted in Redemption

Prayer has been complicated and ritualized by religion. When understood, biblical prayer is as natural as breathing. But too often it is an agonizing cry for divine help, a barrage of desperate pleadings, or a torrent of meaningless verbiage.

For prayer to be meaningful and fruitful, the redemptive blessings that Christ provided for believers must become living realities. My purpose is to motivate that result. That's why I shared how Daisy and I were lifted from the boredom of long, monotonous, pleading prayers into a family relationship with the Father.

Prayer, in its most biblical essence, is simply one's relationship with God. The basic concept of prayer, expressed in Hebrew and Greek Scriptures, is never begging and pleading for blessings and gifts, and it never suggests "spiritual warfare" or conflict with evil spirits. When Daisy and I made that discovery, our prayer times became spiritual feasts instead of ritual boredom.

Principles and Priorities

Prayer is a time of communion and fellowship with the Father, not a time to besiege Him with a barrage of solicitations and petitions. Jesus said, *"Your Father knows the things you have need of, before you ask Him"* (Matthew 6:8).

Prayer is integral to the believer's relationship with God, every hour of every day. As Daisy and I comprehended the meaning of redemption and the biblical ministry of the believer, we faced a serious dilemma: If we did not need to pray for God to do what He had sent us to do, then how were we to pray, and what were we to pray for?

The Lord's Prayer

The simplest and most basic concept of prayer that even a child can emulate is when Christ said, *"After this manner pray ye"* (Matthew 6:9 KJV). His words make it clear that a believer's rapport with the Father is the same as His.

The logic of Christ is simple. He compares prayer to the relationship between a parent and a child. To illustrate that, he says, *"If a child asks for bread, what parent would give him or her a stone? If they ask for a fish, would a serpent be given instead"* (Matthew 7:9-10 paraphrase mine)? His concept is fundamental. He says, *"Ask, and it will be given to you, seek, and you will find, knock and it will be opened to you"* (Matthew 7:7).

Most New Testament teaching about prayer was addressed to people who were not yet knowledgeable about the blessings provided through the death of Christ. The gospel facts that engender confidence in prayer–in communicating with the Father–are knowing about: (1) redemption, (2) why Christ died, (3) what His death accomplished, (4) how His death and resurrection affect the believer, (5) Christ's total triumph over Satan, (6) the meaning of each fact of redemption to all who embrace the gospel, and (7) the believer's standing before God–holy, unblameable and unreproveable in his sight. (Colossians 1:22; 1 Thessalonians 3:13.)

It required time for early church believers to grasp the significance of these facts and to embrace and apply them in their new Christian faith. Once these provisions are understood and assimilated, prayer becomes a relationship, a communion, and a time of rapport with God. That is why the prayer that Jesus taught is so simple.

The Lord understood the purpose of His coming and of His death for us. He also knew all that would be provided through His sacrifice. The way He taught us to pray was principally attuning our spirit to His will and confessing our rapport with Him in His Love Plan for the world.

How Jesus Taught Us to Pray

The prayer that Jesus taught is not a torrent of pleadings and claims for His blessings, nor is it a battle-cry against evil spiritual powers in the cosmic realm. Note the simplicity and the broad scope of the prayer that Jesus told us to pray, then observe the dignity and the oneness with the Father that His words project.

When you pray do not use vain repetitions as the heathen do. For they think that they will be heard for their many words. Your Father knows the things you have need of before you ask Him. In this manner, therefore, pray:

Our Father in heaven,

Hallowed be your name.

Your kingdom come.

Your will be done

On earth as it is in heaven.

Give us this day our daily bread.

And forgive us our debts, as we forgive our debtors.

And do not lead us into temptation, but deliver us from evil.

For yours is the kingdom and the power and the glory forever. Amen.

Matthew 6:7-13

Victorious prayer is following *His* example. His prayer begins by contemplating one's relationship with the Father. As His child, created in His image, we reverence the hallowed Name conferred upon us as believers. We express harmony with His will, agreeing that His Kingdom is now extended through us.

We confess His faithfulness to provide for our daily needs. We appropriate His forgiveness by the measure that we forgive others. We express our trust in His deliverance and guidance in times of temptation and evil.

As we close our prayer, we contemplate three preeminent truths: (1) His kingdom plan in which we are purged of our sins so that He can now live and express Himself through our lives (Hebrews 1:3); (2) His power of Love that is now manifested in our hurting world, in and through us as His interpreters and representatives; and (3) His Glory that is bestowed upon us as His co-laborers who are redeemed so we can continue the ministry that Jesus began.

There is no hint of pleading for blessings, power, or gifts. There is no suggestion that we struggle against spiritual powers. His prayer consists of positive statements—mostly of confessions of intimate trust in God, assertions of harmony, confidence, commitment, receptivity, agreement, and rapport with Him and His will—never with a hostile attitude, never suggesting conflict with demons, never assaulting evil principalities in the spirit world, and never focusing on claims for blessings.

This Is How I Pray

When I kneel before God's throne of grace, I drink from His presence and I absorb His life and compassion, so that I can represent and interpret His fullness to people. (Hebrews 4:16; John 1:16.) Seven prayer priorities have been my guiding light for years. They have kept me focused on God's will. They have helped me escape the pitfalls of religious boredom. They have kept me happy, with a positive outlook and a productive outreach to millions of people worldwide.

1. *This is how I pray.* On my knees, I worship the Lord and I commune with Him. I meditate on His Word and on His ideas. Then I attune my spirit and my emotions to His Holy Spirit for action in His will. I align my plans with His.

2. *This is how I pray.* I adapt my perception of people to what His redemption has made possible for each individual. I absorb His love so that I can witness for Him effectively. I thank Him for His gifts and for entrusting me as His interpreter.

3. *This is how I pray.* I correlate my spirit with His attitude toward people. I reform my notions to harmonize with His Word. I assimilate His faith, hope, and love expressed in the Scriptures. I

ponder His dreams to be enacted through me. I contemplate how much He needs me and believes in me as His associate in reaching people.

4. *This is how I pray.* I pour out my plans and my concepts before Him, then I listen for the response of His Word and of His Spirit. I conform my agenda to His guidance so that I can always be involved in fulfilling His will.

5. *This is how I pray.* I drink from His Spirit. I am inspired by His vision. His love and compassion infuse me so that He can speak effectively through my lips, touch with my hands, walk in my feet, embrace with my arms, hear with my ears, and see with my eyes. He said, *"I will dwell in you, and walk in you.... I will be a Father to you, and you will be my child"* (2 Corinthians 6:16,18 paraphrase mine).

6. *This is how I pray.* I rejoice in the presence and power of Christ alive in me. I re-commit myself as His witness, knowing that He always causes us to triumph (2 Corinthians 2:14.) This is the way I wrestle against principalities and spiritual wickedness in high places. This is how I fight the good fight of faith. This is the way I prepare myself to persuade people about Christ, as the apostle Paul did. (Acts 13:43; 18:4,13; 19:8; 28:23; 2 Corinthians 5:11.)

7. *This is how I pray.* I thank the Lord Jesus for fighting my battles and for winning the spiritual war on my behalf. (Isaiah 40:1-2.) He has triumphed on my behalf. He has delivered me from the power of darkness, and has translated me into the kingdom of His dear Son. (Colossians 1:13-14.) He has spoiled

principalities and powers, and has made a show of them openly, triumphing over them. (Colossians 2:15.) I rehearse those triumphs and thank Him that as His co-worker and interpreter, He has made me more than a conqueror through Him who loves me. (Romans 8:37.)

Prayer–A Time of Conditioning

For me, prayer is visiting with the Father while He conditions my spirit for effective living and ministry. Prayer is re-thinking His Word, visualizing His plan, conceptualizing His objectives, remembering why Christ came and what He accomplished, pondering what He sends me to do, and contemplating afresh His defeat of Satan.

Prayer, for me, is visualizing the Holy Spirit at work within me, which is what makes my gospel witness effective. It is recognizing my calling, my position, my rights, my mandate, my reasons for believing and for being His partner and friend. (Romans 5:10-11 LB; Colossians 1:21 LB.)

When I witness to the unconverted, I share the Good News joyously–with faith, hope, and love–because I know that I am transmitting the Person and Spirit of Jesus Christ to those for whom Christ died. That is the mission of the corporate church– the body of Christ; and that is the mission of each individual believer. And prayer–rooted-in-redemption, victorious prayer–is vital to this assignment.

Chapter 19

The Real Fight of Faith

It was a time when much was being taught and modeled as "spiritual warfare." And for someone who has ministered to literally millions upon millions and has witnessed thousands upon thousands of deliverances including the deliverance of the wildly insane and those bound by spirits of deafness and infirmities of all kinds, T. L. Osborn wanted to go on record as to what he saw to be *true* spiritual warfare.

LaDonna disclosed that her father had never written a book to counter anything that was going on in the contemporary Christian world.

If you would try to corner him and say, "Well, So-and-So is teaching this. What do you think about that?" he would never answer. He would never argue. But for once he was going to correct error as an apostle of the church–though he would never say that about himself. But that's the way I saw his message on this particular subject in his book–*The Message that Works.*

This amazed LaDonna, because when it comes to her father, everybody is his friend. She recounts, "He just smiles...you know, he's a peacemaker. He just does his thing and lets you do your thing. He doesn't feel like he has to correct anybody. But on that one issue–spiritual warfare–he was going to set the record straight. But in getting to his point, he first lays out the gospel...because every concept of the Christian faith must be redemptive-based."

So, in a day when an important Bible concept was being abused, T. L. Osborn saw fit to help correct that abuse.

God and Satan Are Not Equals

An infinite legacy is bequeathed to Bible believers. God's Word promises, *"In all these things we are more than conquerors through Him who loved us"* (Romans 8:37). It also promises, *"'No weapon formed against you shall prosper; and every tongue which rises against you in judgment you shall condemn. This is the heritage of the servants of the LORD, and their righteousness is from me,' says the LORD"* (Isaiah 54:17).

In light of this infinite, redemptive-founded legacy, I have occasionally, upon returning from ministering in other nations, been bewildered–and at times appalled–by concepts that I hear pontificated publicly. Great emphasis has been promulgated, for example, about "spiritual warfare." The label has become lucrative for public marketing, motivating countless books, broadcasts, and digital recordings that proliferate in our world.

The "spiritual warfare" term has been generally misused. There are various renditions of a message on this subject that are based on philosophical premises that are unscriptural. Teachers and preachers conjure up images of the forces of God (being Christians) and the forces of satan (being evil spirits and rulers of darkness) pitted against each other as contending powers that are so nearly equal, that the conflict is only won if Christians engage in "spiritual warfare" and pull down enough strongholds. (2 Corinthians 10:4.) To visualize satan's power to be so great, that when he is pitted against God's people in a struggle, the struggle may be lost if Christians do not "wrestle in prayer" long enough–this negates Christ's victory and gives undue credit to the enemy.

This is not what Paul taught. Whatever view is held of "spiritual warfare," it must be compatible with redemptive truth and with what Paul was addressing.

Limited Understanding of Redemption

Take prayer, for example. Prayer is a biblical and valid ministry in the church. Paul emphasized it (Ephesians 6:18; Philippians 4:6), but he never told Christians to struggle against devils as though evil spirits can impede or interdict access to the Heavenly Father. This concept indicates a limited understanding of redemption.

Daniel's experience in the Old Testament is cited as an example of how rulers of darkness and spiritual wickedness in high places can hinder or impede a believer's prayers from being answered. Daniel had set himself to pray for twenty-one days on behalf of his nation. A messenger (angel) was sent from God to tell Daniel *"from the first day that you set your heart to understand…your words were heard; and I have come because of your words"* (Daniel 10:12). The messenger went on to say, *"But the prince of the kingdom of Persia withstood me"* and *"Michael, one of the chief princes, came to help me"* (v. 13).

This example is understood and used today by some to encourage Christians to struggle against the "prince of the powers of the air" and "spiritual wickedness in high places," as Daniel did. They are told that their prayers may not prevail due to spiritual hindrance by emissaries of satan. But, the theory goes, if they intercede long enough, then angels may join in the conflict, as they did for Daniel, and their prayers can finally be effective.

That was an Old Testament example. When Daniel struggled for those three weeks, Jesus Christ had not yet conquered satan and his demons. He had not yet wrenched from the evil one, his dominion over believers.

Concepts Incompatible with Redemptive Truth

Christians who are narcissistic in their view of spiritual warfare (self-aggrandizing–seeking to attract attention to their own spirituality) miss the point. They are influenced by voices that contradict redemptive truth and that assert concepts that are incompatible with Paul's revelation of the new creation in Christ.

From Bible days until now, young believers have been confused and disquieted by the voices of those who lack knowledge about, or who demean what Christ accomplished in His death and resurrection. Paul alerted Christians to beware lest anyone spoil them through philosophy. (Colossians 2:8.) He spoke of those who are proud and destitute of the truth. (1 Timothy 6:4-5.) He said that vain talkers would subvert whole houses *"for filthy lucre's sake"* (Titus 1:10-11 KJV), and would *"make merchandize of you"* (2 Peter 2:1-3 KJV). They peddle their *super-spirituality* at great financial gain from the uninformed people they deceive. Modern, digital media gives them the ear of millions. It is vital that Christians be aware of their rights in Christ and that they become secure in their knowledge of salvation through faith in God's unchangeable Word, so that they can stand against satan's deceptions without wavering.

Redemption Is a Finished Work

In Christ's vicarious death and resurrection, satan was stripped of authority over believers. (Colossians 1:12-14; 2:15.) The liar, the defeated one, no longer has ability to interdict the prayers of God's children. Jesus says, *"Ask and it will be given to you... For EVERYONE who asks receives"* (Matthew 7:7-8, emphasis added).

Redemption is a finished work:

> *Christ being come a high priest...by His own blood He entered into the holy place, having obtained eternal redemption for us...[He is entered]...into heaven itself, now to appear in the presence of God for us.*

Hebrews 9:11-12,24 KJV

> *Seeing then that we have a great high priest, that is passed into the heavens, Jesus the Son of God, let us...therefore come boldly unto the throne of grace, that we may obtain mercy, and find grace to help in time of need.*

Hebrews 4:14-16 KJV

> *And if we know that He hears us, whatsoever we ask, we know that we have the petitions that we desired of Him"* (1 John 5:15).

Taking Paul's Words out of Context

This popular concept of struggling in prayer against evil spirits and powers is based on Paul's counsel to Timothy, to the Ephesians, and to the Corinthians.

- *"Fight the good fight of faith"* (1 Timothy 6:12).

- *"Put on the whole armor of God, that you may be able to stand against the wiles of the devil. For we wrestle not against flesh and blood, but against principalities, against powers...against spiritual hosts of wickedness in heavenly places"* (Ephesians 6:11-12).

- *"For the weapons of our warfare are not carnal but mighty in God for pulling down strong holds"* (2 Corinthians 10:4).

Paul was encouraging young believers, reminding them that Jesus had spoiled those principalities and powers and had made a public show of their defeat; that He had triumphed over them. (Colossians 2:15.) Christ won the victory over satan's evil influence and now gives us the victory. (1 Corinthians 15:57.) He always causes us to triumph. (2 Corinthians 2:14.) Knowing this is what gave them and also gives us spiritual stamina to stand up against opposition to the message of Christ.

Identifying with Jesus Christ

When Paul said to *"fight the good fight of faith"* (1 Timothy 6:12), he was talking about identifying with Jesus Christ in His triumph over satan. Christian believers need not struggle to conquer an enemy that has already been defeated. They are to carry their witness with boldness and courage, believing that Jesus, who triumphed over satan, is at work in them, and that He is greater in the believer than satan is in the world. (1 John 4:4.)

Satan's oppressing spirits will relentlessly tempt and pressure Christians, deceiving them, tricking them, and diverting them by delusions and chicanery—*"wiles."* (Ephesians 6:11.) They will oppress the bodies of Christians with pain and disease and their minds with negative and doubtful thoughts that contradict God's Word. The believer's recourse is to *"resist the devil [with the facts of the Word of God], and he will flee from you"* (James 4:7 KJV). That is why Paul said, *"Cast down imaginations, and every high thing [thought] that exalteth itself against the knowledge of God, and bringing into captivity every thought to the obedience of Christ"* (2 Corinthians 10:5).

Evil Spirits that Cannot Be Cast Out

A believer cannot exorcise evil spirits who persistently entertains negative and doubtful thoughts that satan's emissaries plant in his mind. A believer cannot exorcise spirits of discouragement, fear, or doubt. Those symptoms are the result of one's thoughts—negative, thoughts that contradict redemptive fact. Such "spirits" must be overcome through a resolve to embrace the facts of the Word of God. When it comes to weaknesses, temptations, and influences of the enemy that any believer may deal with, they are to be overcome, not cast out. (Romans 12:21; 1 John 4:4.)

Christians cannot run to their believing friends when they feel discouraged, frightened, or oppressed, counting on them to drive evil spirits out of them. Those evil "imaginations" must be "overcome" by steadfastly believing God's Word.

Believers cannot exorcise the "spirit of gluttony" from someone who is obese because of over-eating, or the "spirit of drunkenness" from someone who consumes addicting intoxicants. These destructive propensities are to be overcome, not cast out. *"Be not overcome of evil, but overcome evil with good"* (Romans 12:21 KJV). This is Paul's counsel. He never suggested that we cast evil tendencies out of people. Those predispositions are to be overcome; and in doing so, spiritual growth results.

Paul was urging believers to deal with those negative influences themselves. They concern people's thoughts. Discouragement and fear are the result of thoughts that contradict God's Word.

When Christians choose to think wrong thoughts, they can be deluded by the enemy. Everyone has the right of choice. He or she can choose to change their thoughts. Paul said, in essence, "You don't need to run to stronger believers, asking them to drive out the spirit of discouragement or fear. Your part is to bring into captivity every thought to the obedience of Christ. You are to cast down fearful imaginations and every thought that exalts itself against the knowledge of God. (2 Corinthians 10:5.)

Thinking God's Thoughts

Analyze your thoughts. If they contradict the facts of redemption, then simply change them. Think redemptive thoughts. Think of what God says. Ponder it. Rejoice in it. Talk it. Communicate it. Believe it. And act on it. Discouragement will dissipate like a toxic fog before the sunshine.

Wherefore lift up the hands which hang down, and the feeble knees; And make straight paths for your feet, lest that which is lame be turned out of the way; but let it rather be healed. Follow peace with all men, and holiness, without which no man shall see the Lord: Looking diligently lest any man fail of the grace of God; lest any root of bitterness springing up trouble you, and thereby many be defiled.

Hebrews12:12-15 KJV

Finally, brethren, whatever things are true, whatever things are noble, whatever things are just, whatever things are pure, whatever things are lovely, whatever things are of good report; if there is any virtue and if there is anything praiseworthy—meditate on these things.

Philippians 4:8

And be not conformed to this world: but be ye transformed by the renewing of your mind, that ye may prove what is that good, and acceptable, and perfect, will of God.

Romans 12:2 KJV

The Message that Works was written to help accomplish this. Each of a person's basic needs is provided by God's redemptive provisions. As he grasps them, embraces them, speaks them, and acts on them, God will confirm them in his life. A person cannot experience Christ's victory if he identifies with and gives credence to negative and contradictory thoughts that are sown in his or her mind by the enemy. To be a winner with God, one has to identify with Christ's victory over satan. When He won, we won. We are in Him. He is in us. Now He always causes us to triumph. (2 Corinthians 2:14.)

Pagan Rituals to Exorcise Spirits

Prayer is a vital part of the believer's armor. But prayer and any idea of "spiritual warfare" that is not based on knowledge, can be fanaticism. Pagans pray and cry, scream and pound their chests, as they contend against evil spirits which they believe they must appease or exorcise. They offer blood sacrifices with the beating of drums and emotional dancing, all orchestrated by mediating witchdoctors with their boring incantations, as they officiate at these tribal rituals.

Almost every religion that we have encountered in nearly a hundred nations fosters strange concepts about demon spirits. The people are preoccupied with the presence of evil spirits, which they visualize as the source of destructive disasters, diseases, and evil upon themselves and upon their communities.

Their biggest defense against these evil powers is to bring animals or fowl for a priest or witchdoctor to sacrifice while they cry, yell, agonize, rebuke, and contend with these demonic powers, voicing curses against them, interceding and thinking to exorcise them from their midst. The unconverted world is full of such practices that express pagan faith in demons. That is why, when I come home to my country, I am appalled when I hear leaders preaching or teaching in ways that breed faith in demon spirits and spiritual insecurity among Christians.

The armor that Paul says for us to put on includes prayer and supplication. But biblical prayer must correlate with the rest of the Armor of God: (1) truth, (2) righteousness, (3) peace, (4) faith, (5) salvation, and (6) God's Word. Prayer or "spiritual warfare" without knowledge about these other elements can be the expression of superstition. But prayer (and any ideas of "spiritual warfare"), focused with the knowledge of truth, righteousness, peace, faith, salvation, and God's Word, becomes the vital link between the believer and God.

Two Concepts of Prayer

The following two notions about prayer contradict the truths of redemption:

1) The belief that Christians must "wrestle" against "principalities, powers and the rulers of the darkness of this world" *within the church*. That is not where these principalities and rulers of darkness exist—unless Christians concede place to them. Satan has no right to impose his destructive works in the lives of believers who have been washed from their sins in Christ's blood (Revelation 1:5), and who have been delivered from the power of darkness, and translated into the kingdom of God's dear Son. (Colossians 1:13.).

2) The belief that by prayer and intercession, Christians can wage "warfare" against satan, and bring down his power in unconverted, non-Christian areas of the world. We must remember that satan has the right to rule his own subjects. God never imposes His dominion over people, demons, or even satan. Jesus did not and could not; therefore, believers cannot.

In the lives of believers, Jesus is Lord. The only power that satan can wield against Christians, is the power that they concede to him by embracing ideas that are not biblical. He cannot impose his dominion against a believer's will. Neither can Christians impose the gospel against the unbeliever's will.

In the unconverted world, satan is the ruler. The only real power that Christians can wield is to witness to them of the gospel. When the witness of Christ is given, satan's subjects have the right to believe the gospel, or not to believe it. Satan cannot interdict their right of choice. If they choose to believe it, then he must relinquish his rule over them.

By the same principle, Christians cannot enter satan's territory and impose God's message or His will on people. If unbelievers reject the Good News, the believer has no option other than what Paul did when he was rejected—he gave his witness to someone else, or in another locality. (Acts 13:51; 17:32-33; 18:6-7.)

Even Christ Himself, *could do no mighty work* in His hometown of Nazareth *because of their unbelief.* (Matthew 13:58.) And when Jesus looked over the city of Jerusalem, He lamented, *"O Jerusalem,…how often would I have gathered thy children together, as a hen doth gather her brood under her wings, and ye would not"* (Luke 13:34).

Regardless of how many Christians unite in what is called "intercessory prayer" for a person, an area or a region, God never imposes His rule against the will of unbelievers. Christians cannot bombard the heavens with their "intercessions" and "spiritual warfare" and impose the gospel message in an area against the will of the people. People's right of choice to believe or not to believe will never be ignored.

In the Garden of Eden, God did not thwart the will of Adam and Eve to doubt His word and to believe satan's lie. He did not interfere in people's right of choice during the ministry of Jesus. He did not in the early church. He does not now. He offers His salvation as a gift. The believer's part is to publicize God's offer, and the hearer's choice is to accept or to reject His gift of life.

When God created people, He gave them a free will and He never abrogates their right of choice. Paul said, *"...to whom ye yield yourselves servants to obey, his servants ye are to whom ye obey; whether of sin unto death, or of obedience unto righteousness"* (Romans 6:16 KJV). Peter said, *"Of whom a man is overcome, of the same is he brought into bondage"* (2 Peter 2:19 KJV). The Living Bible says it like this: *"For a person is a slave to whatever [or whoever] controls him or her."*

That is why Christians cannot reform people by casting evil spirits out of them. (I didn't say that there is not a time or place for Christians to cast out devils; I said Christians cannot reform people by casting evil spirits out of them.) What they can do is teach God's Word to people, then people can embrace or reject His truths. They can conform their thinking to God's plan and resist the enemy, overcoming temptations and negative suggestions; or they can choose to ignore God's way. That is their right of choice, and no one can impose God's good life agenda against their will.

The Power of the Gospel

Demons know the gospel and its power. They know that their only means of resistance is to prevent the gospel from coming to the attention of their subjects because, if the unconverted come to know the truth, the truth will make them free. (John 8:32.)

We do not *win* lost souls by struggling in prayer to defeat evil spirits and to bring down Satan's strongholds in their lives. We defeat principalities of darkness by informing people about the delivering truths of the gospel. That is the power that pulls down satan's strongholds and that opens the way for the lost to receive salvation.

Unconverted people, who are ignorant of the gospel, will not be brought to Christ simply through the prayers of believers. The believer can pray for laborers to be sent into the harvest. (Matthew 9:38.) But the unconverted can only be saved through faith. (Ephesians 2:8.) That faith comes through, hearing the Word of God. (Romans 10:17.) They hear that Word when believers share the gospel with them.

Paul asked, *"How can they call on Him in whom they have not believed? and how shall they believe in Him of whom they have not heard? and how shall they hear without a preacher [or messenger]?"* (Romans 10:14, paraphrase mine).

Helping by Prayer

Paul spoke of *"helping together by prayer"* (2 Corinthians 1:11). He was on the front lines and needed the Christians to help him in prayer. Prayer for what? He urged the believers at Thessalonica to pray *"that the word of the Lord may have free course"* (2 Thessalonians 3:1, KJV). Why? So that the gospel would not be hindered or would not be rejected by the people.

Paul did not engage the Christians to pull down the strongholds of the rulers of darkness by prayer, exercising authority to demand satan's surrender so believers could impose the Christian faith. To bring Christ's salvation to the unconverted, Paul knew that he must inform the enemy's subjects of the gospel which is *"the power of God unto salvation"* (Romans 1:16).

Paul knew that if he could do that effectively, his gospel witness would have "free course", and the people would hear it and believe it. When they did that, satan's strongholds would be pulled down, and his rule over their lives would be ended, because satan cannot hold people captive against their will to receive Jesus Christ as Lord.

Victory Is Won

There will be no more lost battles at your house—nor at ours. Devils may roar and threaten, but John said that when we are born of God in a new birth, that wicked one touches us not. (1 John 5:18.)

We are no longer losers in life's battles. *"Thanks be to God, who gives us the victory through our Lord Jesus Christ"* (1 Corinthians 15:57).

The death of Christ signaled that all of our sins have been remitted and that Satan can no longer condemn us—we are translated out of his dominion. Satan knows this; and, therefore, when we resist the devil, he flees from us. (James 4:7.)

"If God be for us, who can be against us?" (Romans 8:31 KJV). *"Who shall lay anything to the charge of God's elect? It is God that [already] justifieth us"* (v. 33 KJV).

When God raised Jesus from the dead, He took from Satan the keys of hell and of death. (Revelation 1:18.) His triumph over satan was our triumph. Now because He lives, we live also. (John 14:19.)

Our adversary is conquered. Sin and evil, disease and suffering, poverty and failure have been defeated by Christ for those who believe His gospel. We are now privileged to be His partner, His associate in life and in ministry.

Overcomers in Victory

"Now is come salvation, and strength, and the kingdom of our God, and the power of his Christ; for the accuser of our brethren is cast down, which accused them before God day and night. And they overcame him by the blood of the Lamb, and by the word of their testimony" (Revelation 12:10-11 KJV).

Now we are triumphant. Satan no longer defeats us because He whose name is called the Word of God (Revelation 19:13) dwells in us (John 14:17); and we have redemption through His blood. (Colossians 1:14.)

Our Lord says that *"all power [all authority] is given unto me in heaven and earth...and lo, I am with you always, even unto the end of the world"* (Matthew 28:18, 20 KJV). So we can say, *"The life which I now live in the flesh, I live by the faith of the Son of God, who loved me, and gave Himself for me"* (Gal. 2:20 KJV). *"All things are ours...and we are Christ's, and Christ is God's"* (1 Corinthians 3:21-23, paraphrase mine).

Jesus came to give us abundant Life. (John 10:10.) He abrogated our enemy's authority; and, now, we only think of satan as a defeated foe. His power and jurisdiction over us are finished. We are delivered. We are saved. We are free. When satan tries to touch us now, he touches redeemed property. (1 Peter 1:18; Revelation 5:9.)

God's Will Revealed

A Christian believer would never question God's will to save someone. In the same way, it is God's will to fulfill every provision that has been bought and paid for through the death, burial, resurrection, and ascension of Jesus Christ.

Seven divine, redemptive blessings are now ours:

1. Our dignity is restored because Jehovah-Tsidkenu, "the Lord our righteousness," has imputed His divine virtue to all who embrace Jesus Christ as Lord and Savior. If condemnation or guilt besieges you with accusations about past sins, remember that you have been washed from your sins in Christ's own blood. (Revelation 1:5.) God sees you only in the light of His righteousness.

2. Our peace is recovered because Jehovah-Shalom, "the Lord our peace," becomes our peace, when we believe that Christ Jesus endured the judgment and paid the penalty for our sins. If despair overwhelms you and you sense accusation or confusion about your spiritual standing before God, remember that Christ is your peace.

3. Our signals are refocused because Jehovah-Raah, "the Lord our shepherd," provides perfect guidance and direction for those who embrace Him as Savior. If problems arise and decisions must be made, when you stand at the fork in the road and you need to know which route to take, Christ, your shepherd, is always there to provide the guidance that you need.

4. Our health is renewed because Jehovah-Rapha, "the Lord our physician," becomes the healer of all of our diseases. If sickness assails your physical body and you are threatened by disease that may be incurable, you count on the life of Jesus your physician, at work within you, restoring your health.

5. Our prosperity is regained because Jehovah-Jireh, translated "the Lord will provide," has covenanted to supply all of our needs. If economic circumstances defy you and you wonder how to make ends meet, think about your Creator, your Father, who is the creator of all riches, and how He now lives at your house and His wealth is available to you as a family member.

6. Our friendship is renewed because Jehovah-Shammah, translated "the Lord is present," promises: "Lo, I am with you always, and I will never leave you nor forsake you." (Matthew 28:20.) We are friends of God. If you feel lonely or afraid, you hear Christ say that He is with you always and will never leave nor forsake you. You know that He is present as your best friend and companion.

7. Our victory is retrieved because Jehovah-Nissi, "the Lord our banner," gives us the victory through our Lord Jesus Christ who destroyed the works of the devil, and who always causes us to triumph. If the enemy bombards you with lying accusations and threats of defeat, you remember that the Lord is your victory. Satan must now deal with Jesus Christ when he attacks or tempts you.

Jesus is yours. You are His. You and He are friends and partners. Together, you are an unbeatable team–INVINCIBLE.

You have become a winner. God's legacy of blessings guarantees His best for you.

The Conclusion

His Legacy Is People

P ioneer of mass miracle evangelism, missionary statesman, and evangelist to the world... a pacesetter, a general, a legend of our time–the weaving of this uniquely fine tapestry of one man's life did not begin with what appeared to be the choicest of threads.

Ordinary, Young, and Poor

T. L. Osborn was an ordinary young man. He came from nothing–the tail end of a huge family of thirteen children. He was poor, poor, poor. But he loved the Lord. He was preaching at sixteen, married at eighteen, a father and a pastor at nineteen, and a missionary to India at twenty-one–where he seemingly failed in his assignment and returned to the U. S. in disgrace.

Yet, less than four years later–while still in his mid-twenties–he was back on the mission field, this time in Jamaica. He saw over 9,000 people accept Jesus Christ as Savior, over 90 totally blind people receive their sight instantly and hundreds of others gradually, and over 125 deaf mutes instantly receive their hearing and talk. There were also numerous miracles and healings of other kinds, the number of which, only the Lord knows.

His is a story that shows others that they can be ordinary, poor, young…and even fail; yet God can turn them into mighty movers and shakers for His will and purpose in the earth. He can even do it amidst criticism, condemnation, and lack of support from those around. God had chosen T.L. and Daisy to re-announce the gospel to the world in demonstration of the Spirit and of power, (1 Corinthians2:4.) They also pioneered the concept of mass miracle evangelism. As we come closer and closer as the body of Christ to the unity of the faith and of the knowledge of the Son of God, to a perfect man, to the measure of the stature of the fullness of Christ (Ephesians 4:13), what has been manifested through one man or one woman, or a few men and a few women on a small scale, will now be manifested on a larger scale through a people. The distance between the pulpit and the pew, the clergy and the laity, is becoming less and less prominent. What has been relegated so strongly to leadership, what they have been unduly pressured to solely perform, is becoming the ministry of the entire body of Christ…as in healings and miracles.

This has been God's plan from the beginning. He will have a people that will reveal Him to this world. The exaltation of man, worship of man, and carnal competition in spiritual ranks, will diminish, as it becomes all about exalting the one and only, true and living God. This is what   T. L. Osborn "saw" and fought for all along, even years before this revelation hit mainstream Christianity. Decades ago he understood it, embraced it, taught it, and modeled it—calling it The Greatest Revelation.

T.L. and Daisy have laid a foundation through mass evangelism and instruction to establish people in Christ and help them understand how much God loves and values them. *God's Love Plan, You Are God's Best, The Good Life,* and *The Best of Life* are some of T.L.'s books along this line. *The Power of Positive Desire, Why? Tragedy, Trauma, Triumph,* and *Soulwinning* are also three of his books that also relate to these topics. This foundation of people in Christ and Christ in people does not need to be re-laid. God sent men, such as T. L. Osborn, to get this job done so that today's generation can go on to lead God's people into their inheritance.

True Wealth, True Greatness

Throughout his ministry, T.L. has impressed upon everyone that God has made us all members of Divine Royalty. He has modeled and taught that God made no one for failure, poverty, sickness, or shame and that everybody is a real somebody in God's eyes. T. L. proclaimed: "We are royalty. We are rich. Our wealth is inside us; and nothing on this earth can take away the lifestyle of dignity, divine royalty, and self-esteem from us."

He has also modeled and taught true greatness. In Jesus' words, *"Whoever desires to become great among you, let him be your servant"* (Matthew 20:26). Dr. Osborn has demonstrated coming in the spirit of a servant-leader, one who undergirds and does not lord over the body of Christ, one who is touchable, and who does not exalt himself above others.

Along the same line, Dr. Osborn emphasized that what has taken place in his ministry is not because of some special faith or anointing on his life. He emphasized that miracles are not occasional wonders performed by specially gifted intermediaries or mysterious phenomena, bestowed upon a select few.

A Legacy in Flesh and Blood

We all leave our legacy of influence after our earthly life has ended. We leave our mark on those who follow us. Our thoughts, words, and actions become the seeds of our lives that are sown. While passing on a legacy of salvation, miracles, and hope, T. L. Osborn's greatest legacy is in flesh and blood –his legacy is people. The seed procreates itself. And that seed is continuing to produce in nations around the world as his legacy is manifested through the lives of those who have embraced Christ, and have been recipients of Jesus' healing and miracle power. Now they are the carriers of the seeds–running with them, planting them, and reaping a greater harvest of souls for the Kingdom of God.

Although he is now in his advancing years, T.L.'s world ministry continues unabated in the twenty-first century. Following Daisy's demise, T. L. has persevered in his global evangelism crusades. His daughter, LaDonna, now carries the torch of the gospel to this century's new frontiers, focusing on gospel-neglected areas of the world such as China, Russia, French-speaking Africa, and the ex-communist nations of Eurasia. She has also expanded the Osborn ministries of soulwinning, preaching, teaching, and church leadership training to every continent.

Today in his phase of ministry, T.L. is embracing and enjoying the opportunity to influence a younger generation. For a long time in his life, he would say that he wasn't into that, because he was too busy. The advice he used to give was: "Jesus told me what to do, and He'll tell you. Go ask Him." He had no patience for an explanation other than that. His writing was his style of mentoring, because he was working in the ministry and winning the lost as he presented the message that Jesus is alive and He is the same yesterday, today, and forever.

T. L. never went to Bible school, because he felt that he did not have time for that. However, today he is taking time to reflect and put together golden principles and stories to share with the younger generation. He is focusing on the who, what, why, when, where, and how, that this generation needs to know, when it comes to God and His plan.

T. L. is also continuing to work on his and Daisy's twenty-four-volume Encyclo-Biographical Anthology. It contains more than 23,000 pages, 30,946 photos, 636 Faith Digest magazines, 2,024 pages of personal, hand-written diary notes, 1,011 pages of the Osborns' newsletters, 1,062 pages of unpublished historical data about their world ministry, 2,516 world mission reports, and 6,113 Christian ministry reports. These volumes have already been placed in select Bible schools, institutions of higher learning, and renowned ministries in nations globally, continuing to witness to coming generations the unchanging gospel message they preached.

It is safe to say that a major phase of T. L. Osborn's ministry is yet to unfold, as his legacy becomes a catalyst for another generation to carry out their ministries and accomplish their destinies more fully than they otherwise would have been able to. This literary work is for the Jacobs of today, who will value and embrace their spiritual legacy and birthright, of which the contributions of such spiritual giants, like T. L. Osborn, play a major part.

Epilogue

by LaDonna Osborn

My father is a prolific writer because he understands the power of words and believes that they are seeds that produce change in people's lives. I have observed throughout my own life his wielding of words, like chisels in his hands, to skillfully sculpt sentences and then paragraphs and then entire expositions that would most effectively convey the truths and principles of the Jesus-Life that every person deserves to know.

Because of the words that my father has penned, the power of his legacy will never diminish. His books (and those of others in this ministry family) are translated into languages that communicate to people worldwide, the marvelous truths he has written down–penetrating truths of Jesus that have never changed and that continue every day to transform the hearts, minds, and very existences of human beings far and wide.

You, who hold this book in your hands, have now been seeded with many of these life-changing truths. You have in this volume a resource to be treasured, one that will continue to guide your thoughts and your choices and your behavior as you continue to discover and embrace the miracle-life of Jesus Christ that is heralded within.

I am often asked what it has been like, being the daughter of T. L. and Daisy Osborn. My first thought is how my life has been shaped by the influence of both my father and my mother. Each one of them has passed invaluable gifts on to me. My mother gave to me, firstly, a love of learning (which prepared me to live as a continual learner and disciple of Jesus Christ); secondly, a living example of Jesus in a human person; and, thirdly, instruction in living and choosing based on biblical principles rather than on any other standards. My father gave to me, firstly, an appetite for a continuing revelation of Jesus Christ and His glorious gospel; secondly, an opportunity to witness the power of Christ among the people of the world; and, thirdly, a name (more precious than riches) that opens nations to me today so that I can be a carrier of Christ's marvelous life to people of every tribe. My heritage is a precious gift that I continue to steward for the purposes of Christ and His mission to people.

What was it like growing up as the daughter of T. L. and Daisy Osborn? How does a person answer that question? To me our lifestyle was "normal." We would arise every morning, dress, eat breakfast, and have family devotions. These times of Bible study included reading the Bible through, over and over, with each of us (my father, mother, brother, and me) reading five verses and then making comments. Of course, as children, my brother and I had very few comments. But how we loved listening to our parents pluck out of each Bible story the great principles for living that are to guide believers today. My parents seemed to know just when to end the reading, bringing it to a cliff-hanger, so that we children were eager for the next day's devotion time.

After devotions we would all kneel at our chairs, cots, or simple furnishings, in whatever place we called "home" at that time; and we would pray out loud. I thought that all Christians read the Bible and prayed every day. To me this was normal. Then my brother and I would "go to school," which meant that we would position ourselves at whatever "desks" mother had created for us. She was our teacher for the first eight years of our education. While I know that this was a great burden to her, I thank God for her influence and teaching genius that shaped my attitude toward knowledge and learning.

After school, we all pitched in to do whatever was necessary to prepare for the late afternoon mass evangelism crusade service. As a child it seemed that we conducted a crusade service every day. We would arrive on the crusade grounds, seeing the multitudes of hurting people who had gathered. My mother would open the services and prepare the people to hear the Word of God. Then my father would stand with his interpreter, holding his small New Testament; and he would present the living Jesus to the people.

So many tens of thousands of people would accept Christ. The platform would soon be filled with people testifying of their physical healing. Lepers were cleansed. Demon-possessed people were delivered. Blind and deaf were restored to wholeness. All manner of diseases were cured by the power of the resurrected Christ. There was no question in my and my brother's minds that Jesus was a Healer…and that He is alive today…and that He loves people.

So what was it like being the daughter of T. L. and Daisy Osborn? It was a life of discipline, of learning, of work, of purpose, of serving, and of great joy among the diverse cultures and peoples of the nations.

While normal for me, life for the Osborn family certainly was not like that of an average American family. We didn't go on vacations or celebrate Thanksgiving, Christmas, or birthdays like others did. If we happened to be in the States during one of the traditional holidays, we ate turkey or decorated a Christmas tree like everyone else. But when we were in another country, these events passed unnoticed. We lived with a sense of urgency that people in the next town, region, or country were waiting to hear the healing good news of Jesus' love.

We never learned to have a "favorite" food or to demand other petty preferences. We ate what was served in whatever country we were in. I still love all kinds of food and cultural distinctions. God is creative; and His handiwork is evident within humanity's colors, flavors, scents and shapes.

Of course, there were day to day challenges. We would travel and live in towns or cities for long periods of time. We would always have a place of our own to live, however simple, so that we could do our own cooking. We learned to boil our water, to shop for food at the local market, to wash our clothes on a rock (if necessary), and to enjoy the simple things of life. It's a different world today compared to what I experienced as part of this pioneering ministry family. Yet, something that stands out to me even during that time in my life, is that the daily hardships of battling mosquitoes and patching mosquito nets, or looking for candles when the electrical power would fail, were miniscule amidst my memories of our lives being poured out for those things that have eternal value.

Often I listened as my father and mother discussed the next mission. God would guide them in supernatural ways, sometimes speaking a country name to them, showing them a place on a map, or causing a letter of invitation to arrive at just the right time. The money provision miracles were continual. We sold all of our belongings to purchase our travel tickets to a certain nation. Then we moved to the next country, and then the next, as God guided us and provided the funds.

We lived by faith, understanding that we were doing God's work, not our own. We understood that ministry to people is God's business, not ours. If He sent us to a place, we were convinced of His provision and divine protection. Jesus said to give no thought for tomorrow (Matthew 6:34.) This was a lifestyle of faith for us—this is the way our family lived.

Understandably, as a ministry that has continued for more than six decades, many changes have been required to keep pace with the changing times. We have determined to remain faithful to the unchanging message of Christ and His gospel, knowing that it is this message that hurting people are waiting to hear. Methods can change, but the message remains the same. As the apostle Paul said, *"It [the gospel] is the power of God…"* (Romans 1:16).

Although this ministry began during an epoch when personalities were a pivotal factor, Osborn Ministries International is more than the personal ministry of one man. Its mission is driven forward into the future by the enduring values that have been the guiding principles of this ministry from the beginning:

- *Jesus gave instructions to His followers to go everywhere and to announce the Good News about Him, expecting Him to work with them through signs and wonders and undeniable proofs of His resurrection. We are going and telling, and Jesus is doing His miracles! Miracles are the proof that the message of the gospel is true.*

- *People everywhere are waiting for the love, hope, and healing that only Jesus brings. We are loving people in Christ's name and bringing His miracle hope and healing to broken lives and bodies. People are valuable to God; He loves each one.*

- *Every person who believes in Christ—whether male or female— is empowered by His Spirit to be a carrier of His message and His life. We are training and empowering a new generation of men and women in every country to be Christ's agents of forgiveness and healing and hope to their own people and to regions beyond.*

Today, Osborn Ministries International remains grounded in the fundamental values that were the essence of the character, the faith, the lifestyle, and the ministry of T. L. and Daisy Osborn. The influence and the effectiveness of this ministry are enduring because the values that we embrace and the truths that we live and proclaim are rooted in the timeless and unchanging life of the living Jesus Christ, whose mission was to seek and to save the lost. His love-mission continues through us.

Our mission is about souls—bringing Jesus to people. My mother and father were the first to produce films reproducing our evangelistic events. They are wonderful; they are salvation prompting. And of great significance is the fact that the idea behind them and the purpose for them was just that–to win souls.

Just this last week, Papa was talking to our ministry staff and he was reflecting and telling about some young men who wanted him to view their DVD's about their crusades. He watched one of the DVD's, and then asked them, "Now why did you produce this?"

One young man said, "Well, to promote the ministry."

My father said, "Well, that's nice. Just remember–that's not why we ever produced a miracle film or DVD. We produced them to reproduce the crusades in villages where we could never go. We never thought about promoting the ministry."

This has been my father's ministry philosophy–everything was for the purpose of helping people know Jesus and believe on Him. His priority has never been to promote the ministry itself.

How do I carry on the legacy of the ministry of a remarkable man who, along with his wife, challenged the status quo of global missions? The answer is simple: I too have seen Jesus face to face. He is alive. He loves people. He can do nothing without people. All that He does is for people. So, because my life is committed to Jesus Christ, I will continue allowing Jesus' love and life to be expressed to yet more people through me. This commitment is not mine alone, but is shared by five generations of our family who embody the passion that burns in my father. It is shared, as well, by our ministry teammates and the untold thousands of spiritual sons and daughters in the gospel who are following the example set by my father and mother.

Visit our website to read the miracle testimonies that are post-ed almost daily, to learn the many ways that we are conveying the ministry of Christ to people around the world, and to experience the message that works, as it is proclaimed through the various books, audio and video materials, and Bible courses that are available. Remember, this ministry has never boastfully said, "Look at what we have done." Rather, we have emphasized to men and women, "Look at what you can do! Now is your time!"

Endnotes

[1]Thomas Pakenham, *The Scramble for Africa,* London, Clays Ltd, 1991, pp. 1-39.

[2]ibid

[3]*World Wide Revival,* Vol. 11:12, March 1959

[4]Ibid, pg 6-7.

[5]Mary L. Schneider, "Review: Are All Things Really Possible?," *Reviews in American History Vol. 5, No. 1* (Baltimore: The Johns Hopkins University Press Stable) pp. 118-123. http://www.jstor.org/stable/2701779

[6]Edwin Harrell, Jr., *All Things Are Possible: The Healing and Charismatic Revivals in Modern America,* (Bloomington: Indiana University Press, 1975).

[7]William K. Kay, "Pentecostalism and Religious Broadcasting," *Journal of Beliefs & Values, Vol. 30:3 Dec. 2009,* (London: Routledge Press), pp. 245 – 254.

[8]Harrell, 63.

[9]Paul Gifford, "Ghana's Charismatic Churches," *Journal of Religion in Africa, Vol. 24, Fasc. 3 (Aug. 1994),* pp. 241-265. http://www.jstor.org/stable/1581301

[10]Harrell., 169.

[11]Harrell., 171.

[12]Vinson Synan, *An Eyewitness Remembers the Century of the Holy Spirit,* (Grand Rapids: Baker Publishing Group, 2010).

[13]Harrell., 169.

[14]Ibid., 170.

[15]Ibid., 170.

[16]Ibid., 170.

[17]Synan,. 120.

[18]Ibid., 121.

[19]Ibid., 124.

[20]Ibid., 124.

[21]Ibid., 124.

[22]Harrell., 171.

[23]Ibid., 169.

[24]Ibid., 171.

Additional Resources

Bill Sherman, "T.L. Osborn recalls times with Oral Roberts," *Tulsa World,* December 20, 2009, accessed December 7, 2010, http://www.tulsaworld.com/news/article.aspx?subjectid=18&articleid=20091220_298_0_Whenin269888

Cindy Gunther Brown, "From Tent Meetings and Store-front Healing Rooms to Walmarts and the Internet: Healing Spaces in the United States, the Americas, and the World, 1906–2006" *Church History*, 75: 631-647. Published online by: Cambridge University Press, 28 Jul 2009.

Grant Lea, "T. L. (Tommy Lee) Osborne. Accessed 22 Mar. 2010 <http://www.pastornet.net.au/renewal/revival/osborn.html>.

Paul Gifford, "Christian Fundamentalism and Development," *Review of African Political Economy, Vol. 18:52 Nov. 1991.* (London: Routledge Press, pp. 9 – 20.

Sen. Joseph McCarthy, "Speech Explaining the Communist Threat." Accessed 20 April 2010 <http://teachingamericanhistory.org/library/index.asp?documentprint=858>

About the Author

Dr. T.L. OSBORN, world missionary evangelist, statesman, teacher, author, publisher, linguist, designer, pianist, and administrator is best known for his mass-miracle ministry to millions. With his wife & associate minister, Dr. Daisy Washburn Osborn, they established their headquarters in Tulsa, Oklahoma in 1949. Together they proclaimed the Gospel to millions of unreached people in over 90 nations for well over half a century of world-changing missionary evangelism, preaching daily to multitudes from 20,000 to 300,000 people with God confirming his Word by many astounding miracles.

To proclaim Christ and to pray for miracles as proof that He is alive

Dr. Osborn was the first missionary evangelist to go to open fields or parks, in non-Christian nations, to proclaim Christ and to pray for miracles as proof that He is alive. Today it has become standard procedure. The Osborn DocuMiracle films and videos in 70 languages have been shown in thousands of villages and towns in one hundred and fifteen nations, influencing millions to believe the Gospel. The Osborn National

Missionary Assistance Program has sponsored over 30,000 national men and women as full time Missionaries to unevangelized tribes and villages. Over 150,000 new churches have been established and have become self-supporting through this evangelism program.

Over 30,000 missionaries–over 150,000 churches through this evangelism

As a prolific writer, Dr. T.L. Osborn's books have stimulated today's worldwide miracle-evangelism and soulwinning awakening in the developing nations. His living classic, Healing the Sick, has been a faith-building best seller since 1951, and over one million copies are in print in English alone.

Several of Dr. T.L.'s books such as Soulwinning, God's Love Plan, The Good Life and The Message That Works, are pacesetters in lifting people to positive faith and super living. They have become textbooks in Bible schools around the world and are esteemed as prime reference materials for successful pastors and church leaders.

PRAYER OF SALVATION

God loves you—no matter who you are, no matter what your past. God loves you so much that He gave His one and only begotten Son for you. The Bible tells us that "...whoever believes in him shall not perish but have eternal life" (John 3:16 NIV). Jesus laid down His life and rose again so that we could spend eternity with Him in heaven and experience His absolute best on earth. If you would like to receive Jesus into your life, say the following prayer out loud and mean it from your heart.

Heavenly Father, I come to You admitting that I am a sinner. Right now, I choose to turn away from sin, and I ask You to cleanse me of all unrighteousness. I believe that Your Son, Jesus, died on the cross to take away my sins. I also believe that He rose again from the dead so that I might be forgiven of my sins and made righteous through faith in Him. I call upon the name of Jesus Christ to be the Savior and Lord of my life. Jesus, I choose to follow You and ask that You fill me with the power of the Holy Spirit. I declare that right now I am a child of God. I am free from sin and full of the righteousness of God. I am saved in Jesus' name. Amen.

If you prayed this prayer to receive Jesus Christ as your Savior for the first time, please contact us on the Web at **www.harrisonhouse.com** to receive a free book.

Or you may write to us at

Harrison House • P.O. Box 35035 • Tulsa, Oklahoma 74153

Other Books in the Legacy of Faith Series

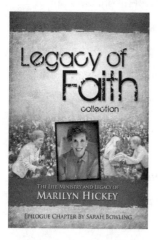

Legacy of Faith Marilyn Hickey
978-160683-028-4
$22.99

The Legacy of Faith Collection is a biographical collection that highlights the founding leaders of the Word of Faith and Charismatic movements. Each volume includes a summary of the most notable teachings and signature messages from each of these ministers and underscores the contribution of each to the modern day movement. This volume includes the ongoing legacy, teachings and impact that Marilyn Hickey has had on the body of Christ. Known for her insightful teaching and worldwide missions emphasis, Marilyn Hickey has reached millions of people through radio, print, television and through her travels internationally.

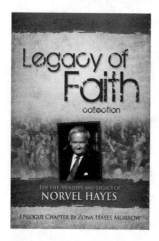

Legacy of Faith Norvel Hayes
978-160683-016-1
$22.99

This volume highlights the continuing legacy, teachings and impact that Norvel Hayes has had on the body of Christ throughout the last several decades. Known for his teaching on miracle healing, gifts of the Holy Spirit and worship, Norvel Hayes has written several landmark books such as How to Live and Not Die and Stand in the Gap. Through his writing and life of ministry, thousands have come into a deeper walk with God.

The Harrison House Vision

Proclaiming the truth and the power

Of the Gospel of Jesus Christ

With excellence;

Challenging Christians to

Live victoriously,

Grow spiritually,

Know God intimately.

Fast. Easy.
Convenient.

For the latest Harrison House product information and
author news, look no further than your computer. All
the details on our powerful, life-changing products are
just a click away. New releases, E-mail subscriptions,
testimonies, monthly specials—find it all in one place.
Visit harrisonhouse.com today!

harrisonhouse